Computer Programming

6 Books in 1: The Ultimate Guide to Python and Sql Programming with Step-by-Step Exercises from Beginners to Advanced, A Crash Course to Start Coding in 7 Days

John Russel

Table of Contents

Book 1

Computer Programming..0

Table of Contents...3

Python Programming 14

Introduction... 15

Chapter 1: What is Python 17

The History of Python 18
The Versions of Python 20
Python 2.X 20
Python 3.X 21
What Can I Do with Python? 23

Chapter 2: The Benefits of Using Python..................... 27

Chapter 3: How to Install the Python Program...........32

Chapter 4: The Basics of Working with This Language 38

Keywords 38
Naming Your Identifiers 39
Comments 40
Statements... 41
Flow of Control.. 41
Functions.. 41
Operators..43

Chapter 5: Working with the Conditional Statements .44

What are the If Statements? 45
Moving to the If Else Statements.....................................46
The Elif Statements and How They Work 48

Chapter 6: Working with Your Files.......................... 51

How to Create Our Files 51
The Binary Files in Python 54
How to Open Up Your File 56
Seeking Out a File 57
Chapter 7: Dealing with Local vs. Global in Python..... 58
The Local Variable 59
Looking at a Global Variable 61
Putting It All Together 63
Chapter 8: Handling the Operators in Python 65
Arithmetic Operators 66
The Comparison Operators 67
The Logical Operators 68
The Assignment Operators 68
Chapter 9: What are the Strings 70
Functions That Work with the Strings 72
Chapter 10: How to Debug Your Programs 74
Chapter 11: How Does Python Compare to Other Coding Languages 82
A Look at Python 83
The Java Language 85
The JavaScript Language 87
The Perl Language 88
The TCL Language 90
The Smalltalk Language 91
C++ Language 92
Chapter 12: Practical Exercises to Get Some Practice . 95
Creating a Magic 8 Ball 95
How to Make a Game of Hangman with Python 97
How to Use Python Coding to Send Emails 101
Conclusion 106

Book 2

Python Programming 108

Introduction 109

Day 1: The Basics 113

What is Python 113
Your Choices in Python Versions 115
The Benefits of Python 118
How to Install Python On Your Computer 121

Day 2: The Variables and the Operators 124

Python and Its Keywords 124
The Comments 125
The Statements 126
Strings and Numbers 126
How to Name the Variables 128
The Importance of the Functions 131
The Python Operators 133
The Basics of the Python Class 137

Day 3: Understanding How Functions Work in Python 138

How to Define and Call Functions 138
Returning a Value of the Function 140
The Arguments in Our Functions 143
Some Tips to Get Started 144

Day 4: The Data Types 146

What are the Python Variables? 146
The Different Types of Data in Python 148

Day 5: Files in Python 157

Creating a New Python File 158
The Binary Files 160
How to Open Up Your Files 160
Seeking Out Your File 162

Day 6: Data Structures 164

The Dictionary 164
Lists 170
How to Create a Class 171
The Class Objects 176
Inheritances 177
Encapsulation 180
Polymorphism..182
Day 7: Getting Started; Python Tips and Tricks..........184
Web Scraping...184
Debugging 192
Conclusion 203

Book 3

Python Programming... 205
Introduction 206
Chapter 1: What is the Python Language 208
What is the Python Language?..208
The Benefits of Working with Python? 211
Chapter 2: Installing Python On Your Computer 215
How to Install Python on a Mac Computer...........................215
Installing Python On a Windows Computer 217
How to Install Python On a Linux System 220
Chapter 3: How to Install Homebrew 222
Downloading and Configuring This Browser....................... 222
Chapter 4: The Importance of Data Types and Variables 228
The Python Data Types...228
The Python Variables..230
Chapter 5: How to Create a Class............................. 234
Creating Our Own Classes 234
Class Definition.. 236

Special Attributes 237
How to Access Members of the Class 237
Chapter 6: Working with an Inheritance and Why These are Important 241
Override the Base Class 243
Chapter 7: Raising Your Own Exceptions 246
Raising an Exception 248
How to Define Your Own Exceptions 251
Chapter 8: Creating Loops in Python 254
The While Loop 255
Working on the For Loop 257
The Nested Loop 257
Chapter 9: What is Machine Learning 260
Why Is Machine Learning So Important? 262
How Does Machine Learning Work? 263
Supervised Machine Learning 266
Unsupervised Machine Learning 268
Reinforcement Machine Learning 271
Chapter 10: How Can Python Work with Machine Learning 274
Chapter 11: Adding in Some Data Analysis to the Mix 278
The Steps of Your Data Analysis 280
The Benefits of a Data Analysis 284
Chapter 12: The Best Machine Learning and Data Analysis Libraries with Python 287
The NumPy and SciPy Library 288
The Pandas Library 288
The Matplotlib Library 290
The Scikit-Learn Library 291
The TensorFlow Library 293
The Keras Library 294
The Theano Library 295
Conclusion 297

Book 4

Introduction 300

Chapter 1: What Is Data Science? 302

Why Is Data Science So Important?................................... 303

Chapter 2: How Can I Use Data Science? 308

Chapter 3: The Best Python Libraries for Data Science 316

Core Libraries and Statistics...317
Visualization 319
Machine Learning Libraries 320
Deep Learning... 320

Chapter 4: Setting Up Your Virtual Environments for Data Science 323

Chapter 5: The Importance of the NumPy Arrays 329

Chapter 6: Gathering and Collecting Your Data........ 336

Where to Get Our Data 336
Getting High-Quality Data 342
When Do I Have Enough Data? 344

Chapter 7: Loading and Preparing Your Dataset....... 346

Chapter 8: Data Mining...353

How Does Data Mining Work?... 354

Chapter 9: Completing the Data Analysis 359

Why Does the Analysis of Data Matter?.............................. 363
Choices in Data Analysis... 364
What Are the Benefits of a Data Analysis?.......................... 366

Chapter 10: How Machine Learning Can Help 369

The Different Types of Machine Learning 372

Chapter 11: How to Work with Data Visualization 378

What Makes for a Good Data Visual?...................................380

Why Is Data Visualization Important? 382
Conclusion 385

Book 5

Preface 388
What is SQL? 388
SQL to Work with Databases? 388
Client and Server Technology 389
Chapter 1: A Look At The Basics of SQL 395
A Look at SQL 396
Working with the Database 398
Relational Database 399
Client and Server Technology 400
Internet-Based Database Systems 401
The Benefits of Using SQL 404
Chapter 2: Some of the Basic Commands We Need to Know 408
Data Definition Language 409
Data Manipulation Language 410
Data Query Language 410
Data Control Language 411
Data Administration Commands 412
Transactional Control Commands 413
Chapter 3: Creating Your SQL Tables 415
Chapter 4: Learning Phase One - The Basics 423
Extract Data - SELECT Statement 423
SELECT; 424
Elimination of Duplicates - DISTINCT Clause 425
The ORDER BY Command 426
Sample - WHERE Clause 427
Boolean Operators AND, OR, NOT and Three-Valued Logic - Predicates 427

Comparison Queries 429
Chapter 5: A Look at Queries................................... 430
Working with the Queries...431
Working with the SELECT Command 432
A Look at Case Sensitivity... 435
Chapter 5: A Bit About Subqueries 440
More About Subqueries.. 440
Type Conversion 443
CAST (AS)... 445
SELECT AVG(launched) FROM ships; 445
SELECT CAST(AVG(launched) AS NUMERIC(6,2)) FROM ships; 446
SELECT AVG(CAST(launched AS NUMERIC(6,2))) FROM ships; 447
SELECT CAST(AVG(CAST(launched AS NUMERIC(6,2))) AS NUMERIC(6,2)) FROM ships;.................................. 447
SELECT CAST(AVG(launched*1.0) AS NUMERIC(6,2)) FROM ships; 447
SELECT CONVERT(NUMERIC(6,2),AVG(launched*1.0)) FROM ships; 448
CONVERT ([()], [,]) 448
CASE Statement.. 449
.... 449
Chapter 6: Transact-SQL Functions for Date / Time Processing 453
DATEADD (datepart, number, date)............................... 454
DATEDIFF Function.. 454
Datename Function... 458
Chapter 7: Data Modification Operators.................. 460
INSERT Statement 461
Operator Syntax..461
Insert Rows into a Table Containing an Auto-Increment Field 466
UPDATE Statement 470

DELETE Statement 475
DELETE FROM [WHERE]; 475
TRUNCATE TABLE 476
Chapter 8: Some More Learning Phases to Work With 478
Tasks Solved by PL / SQL 480
Use Case for PL / SQL Programs 481
Advantages and Disadvantages of Stored Programs 484
Advantages of Stored Programs 485
Disadvantages of Stored Programs 487
Portability of PL / SQL Programs 488
Evaluating PL / SQL 490
First PL / SQL Program 494
PL / SQL Data Types 497
Types of Data Types 498
Scalar PL / SQL Data Types 499
PL / SQL Records 501
Purpose of PL / SQL Records 501
Bind Variable Declarations 504
Benefits of Declaring Bind Variables 506
Chapter 9: PL / SQL Program Structure 509
Block Structure 509
PL / SQL Block Sections 510
Types of PL / SQL Blocks 511
Chapter 10: Other Things We Can Work On In SQL .. 514
Geometry Functions 515
Property Limitations 516
Views Limitations 516
Chapter 11: Data Security - What Could Go Wrong? .. 522
Why do SQL Injections Happen? 525
How to Prevent an SQL Injection 526
Conclusion 530
SQL Commands 530

Book 6

SQL **532**

Introduction **533**

Day 1: Introducing SQL **536**

A Look at SQL 537
What are Relational Databases 539
New Databases vs. Old Databases 543
The Benefits of a Relational Database 545
SQL and the Relational Model 546
The Major Components of SQL 548

Day 2: Database Development **551**

The Components of a Database 551
The Lifecycle of System Development 553
How to Build a Database 557
How to Create a Table 560
How to Delete Tables 561
Checking the Integrity of a Database 562

Day 3: Database Administration **564**

How to Set Up Your SQL Server Maintenance Plan 564
Backup and Recovery for Best Results 569
The Transaction Log 570
Database Restores 572
Recovery Models, You Can Use 573

Day 4: Working with Simple Queries in SQL **577**

What is a Query? 577
Bringing in the Functions 578
Using Expressions 580
Some of the Common Commands in SQL 580
The Operators and Predicates 584

Day 5: The SQL Server **586**

How to Install the Oracle Database 586
Installing the SQL Developer 588

Creating a System Connection 590
Running a Statement 591
Inserting Rows 594
How to Store Things in the Database 597
How to Run SQL from a File 599
Deleting the System Connection 602
Day 6: Users and Roles 604
Logins to the Server 604
Assigning Roles in the Database 606
Commands to Help with Users and Roles 608
Day 7: Tables and Data Modification 610
What is a Table in SQL? 610
How to Insert a Data 613
Doing a Bulk Insert 613
Deleting Data 616
What is the process of Truncate? 616
How to Merge Your Data 619
How to Combine and Join Tables 621
Doing an Outer Join 622
Conclusion 624

Python Programming

The Ultimate Beginner's Guide to Python Language Fundamentals, a Crash Course with Step-by-Step Exercises, Tips, and Tricks to Learn Programming In a Short Time

John Russel

Introduction

Congratulations on purchasing *Python Programming* and thank you for doing so.

The following chapters will discuss all of the different parts that you need to know when it is time to work with the Python code for your own needs. There are a lot of different coding languages that are out there that you are able to give a try and see how they work. Some of them may even work better for some of the specific tasks that you want to do with coding. But none will provide you with the ease of use, and the ability to handle so many different aspects of coding at once like you will see with the Python language.

This guidebook is going to spend some time learning more about the Python language, and what this language is going to be able to do for your needs. We will first start out with a good introduction as to what the Python language is all about, including some of the histories that are there on this language, some of the benefits, and even how to install this language so it works on any of the operating systems that you want to use it with. We will also take a look at some of the basics that come with this language so we can start writing some of the codes that we need.

Once we have some of those basics out of the way, it is time for us to explore a bit more about what the Python language is going to offer to us. We are going to look at a few different types of coding processes that we are able to work with including how to handle the conditional statements, working with your own files, the difference between local and global positions in this language, and even how to handle the strings and the operators in Python. All of these are going to be important to some of the coding that you want to do in this language and learning how to make it all possible is so important to the success that you see.

In addition to learning a bit of the different ways that you can code and program with the Python language, we are going to look at a few more technical aspects that come with this language as well. For example, we will spend some time looking at the best steps to help debug some of the systems that you are trying to create with Python, look at how you can compare the Python language with other similar coding languages out there like JavaScript, and C++ and more. We will then end the guidebook with a look at some of the practical ways that you are able to do some coding with this language, and get some practice with the topics that we have learned along the way as well.

There is just so much that we are able to do when it comes to handling the Python language and all of the parts that come with it. It is one of the best languages for a beginner to learn to use because there are so many features, it has a lot of power, and it is still easy to learn how to work with. When you are ready to learn more about the basics of the Python language, make sure to check out this guidebook to help you get started.

There are plenty of books on this subject on the market, thanks again for choosing this one! Every effort was made to ensure it is full of as much useful information as possible, please enjoy it!

Chapter 1: What is Python

Welcome to the world of Python! There is so much that we are able to focus on when it comes to handling some of the different coding aspects of our projects, and we are going to spend some time looking at how to make all of this work for our needs. Keep in mind that there are a lot of other coding languages out there that you can focus on, but when it comes to a language that has all of the features you want, all of the ease of use that you want, all of the power that you want, and more, nothing is going to compare to what we will see with the Python language.

To help us out with seeing why the Python language is such a good one to go with, and to make sure that we really understand how this is going to work for some of our coding needs, we need to get a little background on the Python language and what it is all going to do for us. For example, we need to really learn some of the history that comes with the Python language, some of the different options that come with the Python versions and more. We are going to explore that a bit in this chapter now, before moving on to some of the benefits that we will be able to get from using this coding language.

There is just so much that we are able to do when it is time to work with the Python language, and really any kind of coding language that we want to handle, and being able to learn as much about it before starting with some of your own projects along the way. let's dive into some of the information that we need to know about the Python language and what it is able to do for us.

The History of Python

The history of the Python language can be quite interesting, and it has really helped to change up the landscape of coding that we see today. When we are looking at some of the histories that come with Python, we can't miss out on a brief discussion of the ABC programming language, because this was the influence that later led to the design and then the development of the Python coding language.

Early on in the 1980s, Van Rossum used to work as an implementer of the programming language that is known as ABC. Later on, the company that worked on the ABC language started working with a brand new distributed operating system that was known at the time as AMOEBA. During this kind, Van Rossum, who was the mind behind Python, started to look for a new scripting language that has a syntax like ABC but would have access to the system calls of AMOEBA. Because there wasn't really something out at the time that was able to handle this, van Rossum started to design a new scripting language that could handle some of the flaws that were there with ABC.

Van Rossum started to develop this new script in the latter part of the 1980s and then introduced the first version of this programming language in 1991. This initial release has a module system of Modula-3. Later on, the name was changed and is now the language that we know, and love called Python.

Often people assume that the name that was given to this coding language was based on a snake. Even what we see in the logo for this language depicts the picture of two snakes that are yellow and blue. But the story that comes behind this name is a bit different.

Back in the 1970s, there was a popular comedy tv show from the BBC that was known as Monty Python's Fly Circus, and van Rossum was a huge fan of this show. Because of this, when the new scripting language was developed, Rossum decided to give the name of the project "Python" and that is the name that has stuck ever since.

Since the first-ever version of Python was released, known as Python 1.0, in 1991, many programmers have gotten on board to see what this language is able to do and why it is such a good language for them to learn how to use in the first place. Since that version was released, there are newer versions that are out there that we are able to use as well including all the way up to version 3.

Today, Python is recognized as one of the best coding languages out there for programmers to rely on when it is time for them to get their coding done. We will talk about some of the different benefits that come with this kind of language when it is used in the proper manner, but you will find that it is one of the best options to help out with a wide range of different coding options that you want to handle. Learning how to work with this coding language is going to be a great way for you to either learn a new skill and pick up another coding language to work with, or it is going to be a great way for you to learn your very first coding language from the start.

The Versions of Python

There are actually a few different versions of Python that you are able to work with, depending on your own needs and what you are hoping to get out of the process. All of the versions are going to help you to do some good things with the language and can make coding a breeze. But it is often going to be more of a matter of opinion, and personal preferences, which one you will think is the best for you.

Over the years, there have been a number of versions that come with the Python language, and as time goes on, more of these are released as well. Each one is going to add on some new benefits and features compared to the version that came before it, which can make things easier for you like programming. The two main options that you are able to find when it comes to writing codes in Python will include:

Python 2.X

This version was released in 2000 and has gone through several improvements since then. The 2.7 version was released in 2010 and is the most current version of this branch right now. Even though there aren't any more plans for the future development of this version, there are still some reasons that it is the one you would want to go with.

First, if you have any familiarity with 2.X or it is already installed on your computer, it is an easy version to work with and can save some time and hassle. It can do a lot of the coding that you want, and it has many of the features that you will need, without a lot of extras that could slow down the system.

You may also have a few programming needs in your organization that would do better with older technology, then the 2.X is the best option. For example, if your organization has policies that discourage or ban the installation of unapproved software from outside sources, then this version may be the best one for you to choose from. Many times, this version of Python was already installed on the system so this is the one that you would want to use.

In addition, there are many third-party libraries and packages that are used to help extend what capabilities the 2.X version can handle, and some of them are not present in the newer 3.X version. If you want to work with a specific library for your application, you may find that it is only available in the 2.X version. You would need to download this version to get it to work for you.

If you do decide that this version is the best one, you should still take a look at the 3.X version. There are some differences in the best programming practices of each and you may even be able to make slight modifications to your code on the 2.X version and get it to work on the newer version.

Python 3.X

Then we are able to move on to the Python 3 versions. Many people who are ready to get started with Python in the first place are going to pick one of the Python 3 versions. This was the version of Python that was originally released in 2008 and it has seen some major improvements in that time frame. The most current version as of the release of this book is 3.6.5, but there are always more improvements and developments that are happening with this language.

Like the current version, it is often recommended that beginners download that one and work with it, and focus on using that to help them get their work done. If you have been working with one of the Python 2 versions as well, it may be beneficial to move off those and start focusing more on Python 3 to help make things easier.

Since this version is going to be seen as the most current of the language, the examples that we will do within this guidebook with Python will be done in Python 3. It comes with all of the latest Python libraries and all of the features and developments that we would need with some of our coding. However, you will find that both of these versions are easy to work with, and you can definitely choose the version that you like to get the work done.

What Can I Do with Python?

You are probably wondering right now what people are able to do with Python in the real world. We can spend a lot of time looking at what you individually can do with Python, but first, we are going to spend a moment looking at what some of the big companies throughout the world are able to do with this kind of coding language.

First, start out with Google. This is a huge company that has been working with Python right from the start. And because of this, or at least with the help of this, Google is now one of the biggest companies in the world, and Python is one of the main server-side languages for Google. Instagram also likes working with Python because it brings about a lot of simplicity to the process. The service is actually known for running the world's largest deployment of the Django web framework, one that is written only in Python.

Another example of how Python is used in the world of business is with Spotify. This company is going to put Python to use in its back-end and data analysis services right now. According to the Spotify team, Python's ease of use is going to help them to come up with a lightning-fast development pipeline that they are able to use. Basically, Spotify is able to work with Python in order to perform a lot of analysis and provide some accurate and good recommendations to its users. They like that Python is easy to use while also does the work well.

Of course, these are just some of the different things that you are able to do when it comes to working with the Python language overall. Even individual programmers are going to be able to use this kind of coding language to help them to get some of the more complex, and even some of the boring stuff, take care of for them. What can't Python help us with when it comes to the world of programming.

The better question to focus on here is what you can't do with the Python language. There are so many benefits that come with the Python language, and being able to understand all of the features and more that come with the Python language can be a challenge. There is just so much that we are able to do when we want to focus on the Python language, and many beginners of this language are surprised at the number of doors that this can open to them.

Of course, you are able to handle some of the basics of coding that you want to learn with this language. We will go through a lot of examples of how coding can happen in the Python language, and all of the different techniques that you are able to use. It will not take long before we can see that this is a great coding language to work with and that you can do some wonderful things with it in no time.

We will see that the Python language is a great option to work with when it is time to automate some of the boring stuff. There are a lot of things that we may find boring and tedious in our world, and we can work with Python in order to handle all of them. For example, it is going to work well for renaming files on the computer and even updating your spreadsheets. It is going to be one of the best things that you can do to gain some more practice with this language.

As you learn more about the Python language, you will find that there are plenty of chances for you to gain some practice on what you have learned. When you spend time working with files, creating your own classes and objects, creating your own dictionary and even scraping the web, you will already have some of the basics that you need to get started. it will not take long before you can bring this to the real-world and see some good results.

You can make your own games. Sometimes it is nice to work with a coding language because it allows us to do some things that are fun and entertaining to do. Coding doesn't have to be boring all of the time, and we will take a look at just a few of the games that you are able to create when you work with the Python language overall. There are a ton of options in games that you can choose from with Python, and you will find that even when the codes get a bit longer overall and may seem complicated, once you learn some of the basics of the Python language, you will be able to make these codes in no time.

The best thing about working with these games, outside of being able to show off to your friends and have a fun game to play with at the same time, is that you will be able to add in some challenge to yourself in the mix, and get some practice with some of the basics that we are talking about in this guidebook. The more that you can get some practice and the more that you are able to challenge yourself when learning a new language, the easier it is going to become for you to really get some of the basics down and improve your coding skills.

You can great algorithms that will help out with machine learning and data analysis. Many businesses, whether they are big or small, are starting to rely more on machine learning and the process of data analysis. This allows them a way to work with the data they have been collecting and will help you to figure out the best steps to take in order to handle that data, make some good decisions for your business, meet the needs of your customers, and so much more.

But in order to really go through this data and learn how to analyze it the proper way, you need to first go through and learn how to work with Python. There are a number of options that you are able to make when it is time to handle machine learning. But overall, Python is one of the best. Not only is the language an easy one to learn when you would like to handle machine learning, but Python also comes with a ton of extensions and libraries that are perfect for data science and the analysis that you want to work with, and will ensure that you will be able to get the results and more that you want in no time, without it seeming as complicated as some other coding languages make it.

In addition to all of this, you will find that there are a lot of other things that you are able to do with Python as well. This is a language that comes with a lot of power behind it, even though it looks like a simple and easy to use language. This means that you are able to work with this to help you with machine learning, data science, data analysis, and so much more.

The possibilities of what you are able to do when you add in the Python language are astounding. It is a great general-purpose kind of language that can take your coding to the next level. Make sure to check out some of the different coding options that we are going to talk about in this guidebook, and see just how great this language can be for your needs as well.

Chapter 2: The Benefits of Using Python

There are a lot of different operating systems that you are able to work without there. each of them is set up to handle different situations and help you to get different things done with your work. But you will find that one of the best coding languages out there, the one that will help you to get the most done while still being easy to maintain and work with, is the Python language.

There are a lot of coders and programmers out there who love to work with the Python language. And as we go through this guidebook and learn a bit more about this language and what it is able to help us do, you will not take long before you realize why it is such a popular option to work with, and why so many people love it. Some of the different benefits that you will be able to see when it is time to work with the Python language includes:

Python is an easy coding language to learn how to use. If you have never had a chance to work with any coding language at all, then you are going to really enjoy working with the Python language overall. This is going to make it easier for us to handle some of the coding that we are not used to, and you will be able to catch on to some of the basics that come with coding in Python and more in no time at all.

Python has a lot of power and resources behind it. Sometimes there is worry that working with this language is going to be too easy that you will not be able to handle some of the more complicated codes that you would like to work with. The Python language is often going to be advertised as a beginner's language, and this can keep a few programmers away from it.

The good news here is that the Python language is not just a good coding language for beginners to get started with. It is also a good language that is going to help you to get a lot of the different codes that you want. We will take a look at some of the different options that you can do when it is time to code, and we are going to spend some time on them in this guidebook as well. And you will be able to handle them with plenty of strength that comes in the Python language.

And if there are a few things that you may struggle within this language, or that are not strong enough to handle, then you will be able to combine in another language, while still relying on the Python syntax. You will find that Python works well with a lot of other coding languages, and several of the libraries that work with Python can help you to get this done. This will ensure that the few tasks you need help with will work well, while still choosing the Python language.

Python has a great standard library to work with. For the beginner coder, and someone who is just getting started with some of the work that comes with the Python language, or any coding for that matter, you will find that the regular library of Python is going to have all of the parts that you need. You will be able to use the standard library of Python in order to handle all of the coding that we are going to explore in this guidebook.

Python has a lot of extensions and other libraries that can help to add to the capabilities that come with this language. Even though there is a lot that we are able to do when it comes to working on the Python language, you will find that there are also some good extensions that you can take a look at as well. These are going to be good options to go with because they will extend out what the Python language is able to handle, and will make it easier to handle things like science, math, machine learning, data science, and so much more.

The kinds of extensions that you are going to use will really depend on what your goals are overall with the language. If you want to work with machine learning and this language, then there are a lot of great libraries and extensions that you are able to choose to help with that as well. But there are also some that work with other features and capabilities as well, so you need to make sure that you are choosing the right one for your needs.

Python has a large community that can provide beginners with the support and helps they need. At some point, there will be some part of coding that you are not sure how to do, or you are going to run into something that may not make sense when it is time to work on your coding. This is going to happen with many beginners, so it is nothing to be worried about But since there is a nice community out there of other programmers and coders who like to use Python, you will be able to find the assistance that you need in no time.

This community will be there to help you to get going overall, and they can answer all of your questions, make sure that you understand what is going on, and just provide you with all of the resources that you need to make sure you are doing well. You can visit this community as often as you need to make sure that you are able to handle all of the different coding options that you want to work with too.

Python is considered an OOP language that relies on classes and objects to keep things nice and organized Right now, that may not seem to mean all that much for you. But in the long run, it is going to help us to make sure that we can keep all of the parts of our code organized and easy to work with. The code is set up so that you can create the classes that you need while still ensuring that you can add in the objects of the code and find everything later on.

This was not something that we were able to find with some of the traditional coding languages out there. These could sometimes be harder to work with than Python and other options because they are not going to be that organized and things can move around on you. But in Python, the code is going to rely on those classes and more to ensure that it works the way that you want, and that you are able to find the objects that you need.

Python is a great general-purpose language that is easy to learn, has all of the features that you would want in a coding language, and so much more. If you don't want to get into a language that is too technical, but you do want to make sure that you pick out a language that is able to handle a lot of different programming tasks at the same time, then Python is the right language for your needs.

There are a lot of reasons why someone would want to go through and work with the Python language, especially when you are brand new to the world of coding. For those who have never been able to do any coding in the past, you will find that the Python coding adds in all of the ease of use that you need to see success while still ensuring that you are going to be able to get all of the power that you need to actually complete some of the coding that you would like.

Chapter 3: How to Install the Python Program

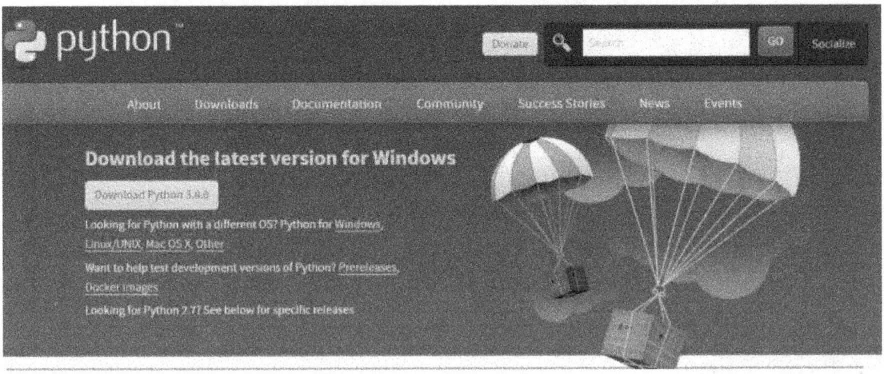

The next thing that we need to spend a moment looking at is the steps that we are able to take in order to install the Python coding language on our own computers. The good news is that this process is a pretty simple one to work with, and you can get it to work on all three of the major operating systems so you will be able to use this coding language, no matter what system you want to work with behind it as well.

Before we dive into some of the steps though, keep in mind that we are going to download Python from the www.python.org website. There are other places where you are able to download Python if you choose. But this website is safe and secure, and we know that it will come with all of the additional files and parts that we need in order to code with Python. Some of the third party options may offer more features, but won't bring in all of the files and folders that you need with Python, so you end up having to download from more than one source. The choice is yours, but we will stick with the website above to get it done efficiently and for free.

The first place we are going to go in order to download and install the Python language is our Windows computers. This is a very popular operating system to work with, and it is likely that many of the programmers reading this book will want to work with Windows as well. The good news is that Python works really well with Windows. The bad news is that Windows has its own coding language so you will have to go through a number of steps to actually get Python on and working with your computer. The steps that you will need to take in order to get the Python coding language, and all of its necessary files, on your system, will include the following:

1. To set this up, you need to visit the official Python download page and grab the Windows installer. You can choose to do the latest version of Python 3, or go with another option. By default, the installer is going to provide you with the 32-bit version of Python, but you can choose to switch this to the 64-bit version if you wish. The 32-bit is often best to make sure that there aren't any compatibility issues with the older packages, but you can experiment if you wish.
2. Now right-click on the installer and select "Run as Administrator". There are going to be two options to choose from. You will want to pick out "Customize Installation"
3. On the following screen, make sure all of the boxes under "Optional Features" are clicked and then click to move on.
4. While under Advanced Options" you should pick out the location where you want Python to be installed. Click on

Install. Give it some time to finish and then close the installer.

5. Next, set the PATH variable for the system so that it includes directories that will include packages and other components that you will need later. To do this use the following instructions:
    a. Open up the Control Panel. Do this by clicking on the taskbar and typing in Control Panel. Click on the icon.
    b. Inside the Control Panel, search for Environment. Then click on Edit the System Environment Variables. From here, you can click on the button for Environment Variables.
    c. Go to the section for User Variables. You can either edit the PATH variable that is there, or you can create one.
    d. If there isn't a variable for PATH on the system, then create one by clicking on New. Make the name for the PATH variable and add it to the directories that you want. Click on close all the control Panel dialogs and move on.
6. Now you can open up your command prompt. Do this by clicking on Start Menu, then Windows System, and then Command Prompt. Type in "python". This is going to load up the Python interpreter for you.

From here, the program should be ready to use on your Windows system. You can choose to open up the interpreter and everything else that you need, and then start writing code when you are ready!

In addition to being able to put the Python coding language on your Windows operating system, it is also possible to add it to a computer that relies on the Linux operating system. This is a great way to help you to work with all sorts of coding, and many programmers are starting to see that there are quite a few benefits when they start working with this system compared to some of the others.

One of the first steps that we are going to need to take when it is time to install Python on the Linux operating system is to double-check whether there is a version of Python 3 on your system or not. This will sometimes be there, and sometimes won't. We can open up the command prompt in Linux and run the code below to check this out:

$ python3 - - version

If you are on Ubuntu 16.10 or newer, then it is a simple process to install Python 3.6. you just need to use the following commands:

```
$ sudo apt-get update
$ sudo apt-get install Python3.6
```

If you are relying on an older version of Ubuntu or another version, then you may want to work with the deadsnakes PPA, or another tool, to help you download the Python 3.6 version. The code that you need to do this includes:

```
$ sudo apt-get install software-properties-common
$ sudo add-apt repository ppa:deadsnakes/ppa
# sudo apt-get update
$ sudo apt-get install python3.6
```

The good news here is that if you are working with other distributions of Linux, it is likely that you already have Python 3 installed on the system. If not, you can use the distribution's package manager. And if the package of Python 3 is not recent enough, or not the right one for you, you can go through and use these same steps to help install a more recent version of Python on your computer as needed.

And finally, we need to take a look at how we can install the Python language on a Mac operating system. If you are working with one of these computers, it is possible that there will be one of the versions of Python 2 already on it. The exact version that we are talking about is going to depend on the operating system that you have, and how old your computer system is at the time. To figure out which version of Python is on your computer, you can open up your computer terminal app and then write out the following command:

python – V

This is going to show you the version you get so a number will come up. You can also choose to install Python 3 on this system if you would like, and it isn't required to uninstall the 2.X version on the computer. To check for the 3.X installation, you just need to open up the terminal app and then type in the following prompt:

Python3 – V

The default on OS X is that Python 3 is not going to be installed at all. If you want to use Python 3, you can install it using some of the installers that are on Python.org. This is a good place to go because it will install everything that you need to write and execute your codes with Python. It will have the Python shell, the IDLE development tools, and the interpreter. Unlike what happens with Python 2.X, these tools are installed as a standard application in the Applications folder.

As we can see from above, working with the Python language is easy and you will be able to install it on all of the major operating systems that you would like to use. Make sure that you go through some of the steps that are listed above for your chosen operating system, and get the files from www.python.org, and you are sure to have it set up the way that you would like in no time at all.

Chapter 4: The Basics of Working with This Language

Before we get into any of the codes that we would like to write in the Python language, we first need to take a look at some of the basics that we are able to find with this language. These basics are going to make up all of the codes that you write, whether they are simple codes like what we will start with or some of the more complicated codes that we will get to as time goes on for us.

Learning some of these basics is one of the best things that you are able to do to ensure that your codes are going to behave in the manner that you would like. We are going to take a look at some of these basics, and why they are so important, below:

Keywords

The first thing that we need to take a look at when it comes to working with the Python language is the keywords. These keywords are going to help us to make sure we provide the proper commands to the compiler, and that we are able to get the compiler to execute the codes that we would like to work with.

You will find that there are a number of different keywords that we are able to work with, and often it is just important to remember what they are so that we can write the codes we want

If we go through and put the keywords into the code at the wrong places, then the code is not going to behave the way that we would like. You will most likely get some kind of error message because the compiler is not certain about what steps it needs to take next in order to execute the code in the manner that you want. But if you put the keywords in the right places, you will get them to behave well and will be able to keep the code running smoothly.

Naming Your Identifiers

One thing that is going to serve you well when you work with some of the codes that are found in the Python language is knowing how to name some of the identifiers that show up in your code. There are a number of different identifiers that you are able to work with the Python language, but even though they handle different parts of your coding, they are all going to be important, and learning how to name them is simple since they all follow the same rules to get the work all done.

The first rule to remember is when you name these identifiers. You have many options when you are naming your identifiers. For example, you can rely on both uppercase and lowercase letters with naming, as well as any number and the underscore symbol. You can also combine any of these together. One thing to remember here is that you can't start the name with a number and there shouldn't be any spaces between the words that you write out. So, you can't write out 3words as a name, but you can write out words3 or threewords. Make sure that you don't use one of the keywords that we discussed above or you will end up with an error.

when you pick out the identifier name, you can follow the rules above, and try to pick out a name that you can remember. Later on, when writing the code, you will need to pull it back up, and if you give it a name that is difficult to remember, you could run into problems or raise errors because things aren't showing up the way that you want. Outside of these rules, you will be fine naming the identifiers anything that you want.

Comments

In all of the coding languages that you would like to learn how to work with, there will be a part that is known as comments. This is going to be helpful when you would like to leave some messages in your code, and you want to make sure that other programmers, and yourself, will be able to recognize those messages, without them messing up with the compiler at all. And the good news is that these are simple and easy to work with, no matter how many you would like to add to your code.

To add in a comment to your code, you simply need to add in the # symbol before any of the comments that you would like to work within this language. You can then add in as many of these as you would like, and the compiler will know that this is not something that it needs to read through in order to get the code to work the way that you want. You can use as many of these comments as you would like, but remember that you want to keep the code as clean and neat as possible, so try to keep these as limited as possible to just the ones that you really need.

Statements

Statements are pretty simple in Python. These are just the strings of code that you write out and that you want the compiler to list out on the string. When you tell the compiler the instructions that you want it to work on, you will find that those are the statements of your code. As long as you write them out properly, the compiler will read them and show up the message that you want on your screen. The statements can be as short or as long as you would like, depending on the code that you are working on.

Flow of Control

Another thing that we need to spend a moment looking at is the control flow that happens in Python. This is important to make sure that we are able to write out the codes that we want in the Python language. There are going to be some types of strings that are going to be inside the code, and you may choose to write these out in a manner so that the compiler is able to read and execute them in the right manner.

But if you do not write out the string in the right manner, then the compiler is going to send out an error in the system. We are going to spend some of our time looking at a variety of codes in this guidebook, and they will help us to learn a bit more about the control flow that Python would like us to follow. This makes it easier for us to know what we need to get done, and how you are able to write out codes.

Functions

We can also take a look at how these functions in Python are going to work for some of our own needs as well. These functions are basically just a set of expressions that you can go through and name. There are a lot of times when these functions are going to show up in your code and be useful, it is a good idea that we are taking a look at them right now. You are able to work with the functions in a manner that is similar to some of the other values that you want to handle in your codes, like with the strings and numbers, and they also have their own attributes that we are able to bring out when needed.

One of the best parts of working with some of these functions is that they are going to be really diverse to work with. This will ensure that you are going to get the most out of these and that they are going to behave in the manner that you would like. Some of the different choices that you are able to make when it is time to work on these functions will include:

- __doc__: This is going to return the docstring of the function that you are requesting.
- Func_default: This one is going to return a tuple of the values of your default argument.
- Func_globals: This one will return a reference that points to the dictionary holding the global variables for that function.
- Func_dict: This one is responsible for returning the namespace that will support the attributes for all your arbitrary functions.
- Func_closure: This will return to you a tuple of all the cells that hold the bindings for the free variables inside of the function.

As you go through the process of writing out codes and using functions, you will discover that there are a lot of things that you can do with your functions. We can pass over arguments to another function if needed. Any function that you are able to use in order to make a new argument is going to be seen as the higher-order function in that code so keep that in mind as well.

Operators

We can also take a look at some of the operators that we are able to work within this language. These operators are meant to help us get a lot of different things done in our codes and will ensure that we are able to see some great results in the process as well. There are also a few operators that you are able to work with, depending on what results you are hoping to get out of the process.

For example, you are able to work with mathematical operators that will help you to handle any addition, subtraction, multiplication, and division that come up in your codes. There are assignment operators that are going to help you to take a value and add it to one of your variables to tell the compiler what belongs there. and there are comparison operators that you can work with as well that help you to compare more than one part of the code together.

These are just a few of the examples of what you are able to do in order to handle the operators. And as we go through some of the coding that shows up in this guidebook, you will be able to see a lot of benefits of these operators, as well as more examples of where these operators are going to show up overall. Getting some experience with them and how they work can make a big difference in how well some of the coding are going to work for you.

There are a lot of basics that come with coding in the Python language, and it often depends on what kinds of codes you would like to write out in the first place. Taking the time to learn a few of these basics can be important. They will ensure that you have a chance to go through and learn the parts that, when they are put together, they are able to work in even the more complex codes that you are looking to write out later on.

Chapter 5: Working with the Conditional Statements

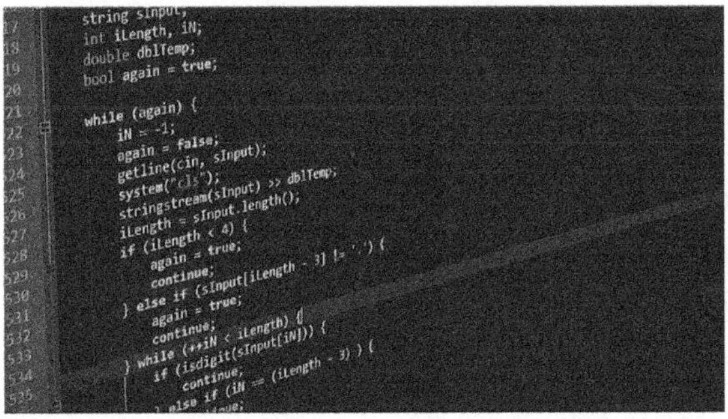

Now that we have spent some time looking at the basics of the Python language, what it is all about, the benefits, and even how to install that language to work with your operating system, it is now time to work with the conditional statements. These statements are important to learn right from the beginning because they will ensure that your system is going to be able to give some kind of response, no matter what input or answer your user is providing to you.

As a programmer, no matter how hard you try, there are times when the user is going to put in an answer that you can't think of ahead of time. With the conditional statements, this is not going to be a big deal because you will be able to use these to handle any of the answers that the user gives to you.

There are a lot of programs where you are able to work with these conditional statements, which makes them a good thing to know how to use. They are also a fairly simple idea to work with, you just need to make sure that you know which of the conditional statements is the right one for your code. We are going to focus on the three main types of conditional statements known as the if statement, if-else statements, and the elif statement. Let's take a look at how each one of these will work for your needs.

What are the If Statements?

First, we need to take a look at the if statement. This is the most basic of the three and can give us something to work off when we start to do the other two statements. The if statement is the most basic of these and will only let the program you write proceed forward if the answer provides it with the right answer. If the user puts in an answer, and the program determines that the answer is false based on the conditions that you set, then nothing will happen. If the answer is deemed true based on your set conditions, then the program will display some message or do another task you assigned to it.

You can probably already guess that this will cause some problems with most codes, but it is still important to know how to use these statements. A simple code that you can work with for these conditional statements include:

```
age = int(input("Enter your age:"))
if (age <=18):
        print("You are not eligible for voting, try next election!")
```

print("Program ends")

When we are working with this, you will find that your code is going to have a few things to show up. If you are working with a user who goes to the program and states that their age is anything under 18, then your program is going to proceed forward and the statement that we added to the code above is going to show up on the screen. The user is going to be able to read this message, and the program will take them further in or execute more of what you wanted.

But, we can see that there are sometimes when this is not going to work the way that we would like. Think about what is going to happen when the user enters in an age that is over 18. The user, of course, is entering in their actual age, but they are not meeting the requirements that come with your chosen code. With the code written out the way that we have it, the message is not going to show up and the screen is going to stay blank.

Moving to the If Else Statements

The if statements are good to practice within the coding, but there aren't many times in your program where that is going to work. You want to have something come up on the screen when the user puts in their age, regardless of what their age is. If you used the if statement in the example above, your user will end up with a blank screen and no idea what is going on if they say their age is above 18. That doesn't look very professional and won't help you to keep people looking at your program.

A better option to use is the if-else statement. These statements will provide an output to the user, no matter what they provide as their input. With the example above, the user may get the previous message if they state their age is 16, but then the code would also have a response if the user says their age is 32. It will respond to any answer that it is given, helping the code to keep moving through the program and ensuring that nothing just stops.

With the voting example that we had above, you can implement the following code to make an if-else statement:

```
age = int(input("Enter your age:"))
if (age <=18):
        print("You are not eligible for voting, try next election!")
else
        print("Congratulations! You are eligible to vote. Check
out your local polling station to find out more information!)
print("Program ends")
```

As we can see already, this option is going to work a lot better with the work that we are handling this program. It is able to cover all of the ages that the user may put in, whether they are under, at, or above 18. If the user lists that their age as 34 or something like that, then the program is still going to have some option that will show up here as well.

This is just one example though. We are able to go through all of this and split it up into as many groups as we would like. This means you could use the code above and split up the ages into five groups, or even have a program that asks the user what their favorite color is. The else is going to handle either the final group of options that you are giving to your user, or it could catch all of the colors, for example, that you would not want to spend so much time listing out all of the time.

These if-else statements are going to come with a lot more power behind them and will ensure that you are able to take on more complex types of codes than what we are going to see with just the if statement. The if statement is pretty simple to work with, and many times as a coder you will not even spend time on it. But it is still a good code to practice with because it gives you a better outlook on how these conditional statements work and why the if-else and the elif statements are often the ones that are chosen.

The Elif Statements and How They Work

You can also look at using the elif statements in your code. The elif statements add on another level, but they are still pretty easy to work with. You can add as many of these into your code as you want, and then we add in an else statement to cover any other decisions that need to be taken care of in your code. Think of the elif statement like the old games where the user could pick from a menu the options that they wanted. This is similar to how the elif statement is going to work.

You can have as few or as many options as you want with the elif statement. You can choose to add in just two or three, or you could expand this out to twenty or more. The fewer options you have though, the easier it is to write out the code that you want to use. A good example of a program that uses the elif statement is the following:

Print("Let's enjoy a Pizza! Ok, let's go inside Pizzahut!")
print("Waiter, Please select Pizza of your choice from the menu")
pizzachoice = int(input("Please enter your choice of Pizza:"))
if pizzachoice == 1:

```
        print('I want to enjoy a pizza napoletana')
elif pizzachoice == 2:
        print('I want to enjoy a pizza rustica')
elif pizzachoice == 3:
        print('I want to enjoy a pizza capricciosa')
else:
        print("Sorry, I do not want any of the listed pizza's, please bring a Coca Cola for me.")
```

When you take a look at the code that is listed above, you can already see that there are some differences between this one and what we found with the other two conditional statements. With this one, we are providing a menu of choices for the user, and they can pick out the pizza that they would like to enjoy. You will be able to use this same kind of syntax on your code, regardless of how you would like the elif statement to show up for your needs.

This is going to be one of the more simple forms of working with the elif statement when you want to provide your user with some choices. In some of the other options, the user could add in a choice that they wanted, but with the elif statement, they are going to pick out from one of the choices that you are providing to them, or they will end up with the default option that comes at the end.

If you are looking to present the user with a type of game or a website where certain choices need to be made, then the elif statement is going to be one of the best options to go with. This can help to limit some of the choices that the user has, and will make it easier for the code to proceed in the manner that you would like.

And that is your introduction to how these if statements are meant to work. You are able to set up the conditions that you are the most interested in working with. You can then make it so that there is only one answer that is seen as the right on, make it so that the user has the option to use any input that they would like, or that the user has to pick from a menu of options along the way. Each of the conditional statements will run in a different manner, and you have to pick out which one is going to suit your needs the most.

Chapter 6: Working with Your Files

Another topic that we need to spend some time on here is the idea of files in Python and how we are able to get them to work. We need to be able to create files, put them together, add things to them, change them into binary files, open the files, and even save them. These are all important parts of ensuring that our work is going to be where we left it and that all of the parts of our code function in the manner that we would like.

The data that you add to the file is going to be saved on a disk or a part of your computer memory, or, you do have the option to work with something known as an inheritance in order to reuse parts or all of the code again and again. In this chapter though, we are going to focus our energy on how to do the different parts of handling these files so that you can write some of the best codes possible.

Now, when we are working with this, there are going to be a few different options that we are able to focus on to ensure that our codes are going to behave in the manner that we would like. In this chapter, we are going to focus on how to write out a new code on a file that we worked on earlier, how to close up a file, how to create a new file, and how to seek or otherwise move one of our files to a new location. Let's dive in and see how these steps can work for us in the Python language.

How to Create Our Files

The first thing that we need to work with when it is time to bring out the idea of these files is how to create a new one that can hold onto some of the codes that we want to write. If you would like to make one of your own files, and then write out the necessary code on it, we first need to get the Python IDLE open and then open up the file inside of it.

During this time, we also need to take some time to choose the best mode that we would like to use for writing out the code. There are three main types of modes that work with the Python language, and these are going to include write, mode, and append.

Any time that you want to make some changes to the current file that is opened, you can use the (w), or write, option because this is often the easiest one to work with. Any time that you are trying to open up a file and then write a new string in that file, you will work with binary files and will need the write() method. This is going to work well because it ensures that you will get the right characters returned at the end.

The write() function is really easy to use and allows you to make as many changes to the file as you would like. You can add some new information to the file or you can make some changes to one that you opened up. If you are interested in doing the writing in the code, you can use this example to make things easier:

```
#file handling operations
#writing to a new file hello.txt
f = open('hello.txt', 'w', encoding = 'utf-8')
f.write("Hello Python Developers!")
f.write("Welcome to Python World")
f.flush()
```

```
f.close()
```

Before we move on here, we need to take a moment to open up our compiler and write out the code above. This code is a good one to work with because it ensures that we are able to create a new file and get all of the information into it. Keep in mind here that the default directory is going to be the current directory that you are in. You can go through and change up the directory that you want to use to store that information, but you need to do that ahead of time, or it is more difficult to find that information later on.

The directory where you are right now, the current one, is the one where you will be able to head back to when you want to search for the file later on. If you would like it to be in a different directory, it is best to move the file over to that directory ahead of time before you try to save. With the option that we are talking about above, you will need to go to the current directory to open up the file. And when you do this, you will get the message of "Hello Python Developers! Welcome to Python World!".

When we reach this point, we will see that the program is written out, but there are still some times when we will need to go back through the file and overwrite the program that we have so that it will get a brand new statement to show up in the file that we have created. This is something that Python will allow, we just need to change up the kind of syntax that we are using to make this happen. An example of how we would be able to do this would include:

```
#file handling operations
#writing to a new file hello.txt
f = open('hello.txt', 'w', encoding = 'utf-8')
```

```
f.write("Hello Python Developers!")
f.write("Welcome to Python World")
mylist = ["Apple", "Orange", "Banana"]
#writelines() is used to write multiple lines into the file
f.write(mylist)
f.flush()
f.close()
```

The example above is a good one to use when you want to make a few changes to a file that you worked on before because you just need to add in one new line. This example wouldn't need to use that third line because it just has some simple words, but you can add in anything that you want to the program, just use the syntax above and change it up for what you need.

The Binary Files in Python

Another thing to work with when doing file sin this language is that you may want to write out the data so that it is a binary file. This is actually pretty simple to do in the Python language because you just take whatever data that you have and change it to an image or sound file rather than writing it as a text file. You can change any of the text that you write in Python into a binary file, no matter if it is a text file, sound, or a picture file in the past. The most important thing to take into consideration is that you need to supply the data inside of the object to make it easier to expose as a bite later on. The syntax that you can use to make this work includes the following:

```
# write binary data to a file
# writing the file hello.dat write binary mode
F = open('hello.dat', 'wb')
# writing as byte strings
```

f.write(b" I am writing data in binary file!/n")
f.write(b" Let's write another list/n")
f.close()

This will help you to get the data changed over to a binary file simply by turning it over to the image or sound file.

How to Open Up Your File

We also need to take a few moments in order to look at the steps that are needed in order to open up a file that you have already created. In the last two examples, we took some time to talk about how we can write out the words that are needed in a file and the way to turn the file into a binary file. Now it is time for us to go through and figure out what steps are needed in order to open up the file.

Once you open up the file one time, you will find that this is a simple process to work with and you will be able to easily open up any of the files that you would like in no time at all. The code that you can use in order to open up a file that we already created, and one that has been saved, will include the syntax below:

```
# read binary data to a file
#writing the file hello.dat write append binary mode

with open("hello.dat", 'rb') as f:
        data = f.read()
        text = data.decode('utf-8'(
print(text)
```

the output that you would get form putting this into the system would be like the following:

Hello, world!
This is a demo using
This file contains three lines
Hello world
This is a demo using

This file contains three lines.

Seeking Out a File

And the final thing that we are going to take a look at here when it comes to working on files will be how to seek a file. This means that we are going to do some steps in order to move our file over to another place, making it easier for us to find it, or ensuring that the file is actually in the place that we want it to be. Sometimes we are not paying attention to where the file is going when we save it, and it is harder to seek it out and find the actual thing that we want to work with. When we are able to seek out the file, we are then able to really find it and then decide whether we would like to move it somewhere else or change up the name if the problem is that we spelled a word wrong.

One thing that Python allows us to do is to go through and change up the position where the file is located so that it goes to the right spot, or even to make it so that you can find that file a bit easier. You just need to tell your code where you would like to find the file, and then make the necessary changes so that this can happen as well.

Working on the various parts of files in Python is going to help you out quite a bit when you are trying to write out your codes and get them to work for your needs. You should take some time to practice some of the codes that we are using in this chapter because they are going to be responsible for helping you to work with these files any time they are needed.

Chapter 7: Dealing with Local vs. Global in Python

Now we need to take a look at some of the different types of variables that you are able to work with when it is time to handle them in Python. The two main types of variables that we are going to work within this language will include the local variable and the global variable.

There are some big differences that are going to show up when we are talking about these variables. To start with is the global variable. This is mainly going to mean that we are looking at a variable that the rest of the program, or any part of the program, is able to declare. It doesn't matter where that part of the program is located, it will be able to use and rely on that global variable when it would like to.

Sometimes this is a good thing and will allow your modules to declare the variables that they want, even when they are not near one another. But other times, this is going to cause some issues.

If the wrong part of the code tries to declare some of the variables that it shouldn't, it can cause the code to not behave the way that you want, and some of the variables are going to get declared at the wrong time. this is never a good thing, and it is going to require you to take some chances if you want to avoid this issue.

The solution to this issue is going to be the local variables. These are the ones that can't be accessed throughout the code. These are the variables are only going to be declared in a specific method or function that you determine ahead of time. This will make sure that the variable is going to only be used in the manner that you would like, and nowhere else.

The Local Variable

The first option that we are going to take some time to look at is the local variable. This is going to be similar to what we will see with a local variable in other languages, and it is going to be the one that is declared at the beginning of the block that the variable is supposed to be local to at that time. It can also show up when we are working with a statement, a switch statement, and more depending on your needs.

The local variable is going to have a declaration with it that can explicitly define the type of the variable that has been declared along with some of the identifiers that will name out the variable at the same time. We will recognize the local variable as a type of variable that we are able to use where the scope and the extent of the variable are within the method or the statement block in which it is declared.

We are able to use these local variables more like an iteration variable in the foreach statement, the exception variable in the specific catch clause, and the resource variable when we are doing the using statement. It can also be used as a type of constant whose value can't be modified within the method or the statement block in which we declare it.

A local variable that is implicitly typed whose type is going to be inferred by the computer from the expression on its right is going to be useful when you would like to deal with the language-integrated queries. These are going to be the types of queries that will return to us some anonymous types in creating a custom type for each of the sets of results that you have.

The memory allocation that you are going to find with this kind of a variable is often going to be based on the type of variable that you are working with. If you are working with something like an integer or a structure, then the entirety of the contents will be stored in a stack. But if you are using a reference type of variable, it is going to be placed in the reference portion of the stack and the contents will be in the heap that goes with it.

A local variable is one that needs to not be referred to in the code in any kind of textual position that will proceed with the declaration statement of your local variable. In addition, we have to remember that when we are in one single block, there can never be more than one variable that has the same name. Doing this is going to be a bad thing because it is going to cause an error to show up and will basically just confuse the code that you are working with. However, multiple local variables of the same type can be declared, and it can be initialized, in one single statement.

Within the method of a class that you find one of these local variables and it is named in a manner that is similar to its field, you will find that the local variable is going to hide the field while still being able to access it within the method. It is often more efficient for us to work with a local variable rather than a field.

Looking at a Global Variable

The other thing that we need to take a look at here is what a global variable is all about. This is going to be a type of variable that we will declare outside of any of our functions, which means that it is easy to access by all of the functions that are found in the program that you are writing. A group of these variables is called a global environment or a global state, because when they are combined, and they are going to define various aspects of a program or an environment when the program is going to run.

A global variable is going to be the one that is declared on top of all the other functions, and it is usually best if we can keep this to a minimum. This is because all of the functions will be able to manipulate these variables during the run time of the program. For most of the programs that you want to handle in this language, this can be dangerous because there is the possibility that they can be changed on accident, and that causes bugs in the system.

Global variables, as we can guess by the name, will be some variables that we can access globally, or everywhere throughout the program. Once we go through the process of declaring them, these are going to stay in the memory throughout the runtime of the program. This means that we are able to get them changed with any function that we want, at any time when the program is running, and this can definitely cause some issues with the program as a whole.

During some of the earlier years when computers can be used but they had a limited amount of memory, these global variables were seen as bad practice because they would take up a lot of valuable information and memory, and it was easier for the programmer to start losing track of the values they worked with, especially in longer programs. And basically, it brought in a lot of bugs to the program that was hard to locate and fix.

Source code is always going to be easier to use and to understand when the scope of its elements is limited. This is something that is hard to do when we are working with the global variables because they are not local, and it becomes really hard to figure out and see where these variables have been changed or even the reason why they were changed in the first place.

Even with this kind of stigma, these global variables are going to be pretty valuable when we are working in functions that do not chare a relation that is known as caller and called. This means that the function is not going to have signal handlers or any kind of concurrent threads. With the exception of those global variables that are declared as read-only values in the protected memory, the codes need to make sure they are able to deploy some of the proper encapsulation in order to be seen as thread-safe in the process.

As we can see here, there are some benefits, and even some negatives, that come with working on this kind of variable. There are still some uses of working with this, which is why we spent some time taking a look at them and figuring out why they are important, but for the most part, the local variables are better and will keep some more control in the codes that you are writing.

Putting It All Together

This may seem a bit confusing in the beginning, but the good news is that there are a number of things that we are able to do when it is time to work with these two variables. And to help us gain a better understanding of the differences between global and local variables with the program that we used below:

1. The variable "f" is going to be one that has a global scope and it is going to be assigned value 101 which is printed in the output.
2. The variable f is also going to be declared in a function and assumes local scope. It is going to be assigned to a value, and in this case, it is going to be assigned to a value "I am learning Python." Which is going to then be printed out as an output. This variable is different from that global variable f that we tried to define in the previous step.
3. Once we have been able to call the function over, the local variable f is going to be destroyed. At line 12, when we again go through and print off the value off, it is going to show us the global variable that is f = 101.

We can then go through and use the keyword of global, and this will make sure that we are then able to reference the variable that is global inside of the function. Some of the things that we are going to be able to follow with this one will include:

1. The variable "f" is going to be global with its scope, and then it is going to be given a value of 101, which is going to be printed as the output.
2. This same variable is going to be declared when we use the global keyword. This is not going to be the local variable here, but the same global variable that we were able to declare earlier. This means that when we go through and

print out the value, the output that we get is going to be 101.

3. We then went and changed the value of 'f' inside of the function. Once we are done with the function call, the changed value of the variable "f" will persist. At line 12, when we again go through and print off the value of "f", the value that we are going to get here is "changing a global variable."

There are a lot of times when you will be able to use the idea of the global and local variables that you would like to handle. Knowing how each of these is going to work, and when each one is going to be the most important part of working with these when you would like them.

Chapter 8: Handling the Operators in Python

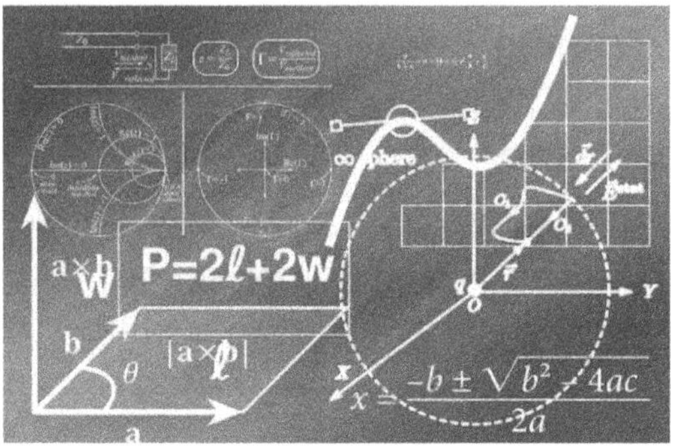

We mentioned working with the operators a bit earlier in this guidebook and how there are a variety of different options with these to ensure that we are able to write out our codes in the manner that we would like. There can be a lot of power that will come with these operators, and knowing how to make them work for your needs, and the proper steps to ensure that you are putting them in the right parts of your code can be imperative.

There are many operators that we are able to focus on, and some of the codes that we have already gone through and written out in this guidebook are going to have these operators in them. These operators are going to be responsible for helping you to get things done, such as comparing parts of the code to one another, assigning the right value to your chosen variable, and even completing some mathematical equations as well. Even with all of this diversity though, it is true that the operators are going to vary quite a bit from one another. Some of the different types of operators that you are able to focus your attention on will include:

Arithmetic Operators

The first type of operator that we should look at when it comes to working in Python is known as the arithmetic operator. If you think back to some of the math classes that you took in the past, you will have a good idea of how these operators are going to behave. You will notice that these are the ones that are responsible for you to finish up some of the mathematical equations that are there. these could be something that is simple like adding together two or more operands in the code, or something else similar. Some of the different operators that fit under this category that may show up in your code will include:

- (+): this is the addition operator and it is responsible for adding together both of your values.
- (-): this is the subtraction operator and it is going to be responsible for taking the right operand and subtracting it from the left.
- (*): this is the multiplication operator and it is used to multiply two or more values in the equation.
- (/): this is the division operator and it is going to divide the value of the left operand from that on the right and gives you the answer.

You will get the freedom with this one to use as many of the arithmetic operators as you would like, and you can even have it so that one statement is going to have more than one of these as well. For example, your code may need to add up ten or more numbers to get it to work.

You can even go through and add in a few different arithmetic operators to make the code work. Maybe you want to multiply a few numbers and then divide or add some others in the same statement. This is possible, we just need to follow the rules of multiplying first, then dividing, then adding, and then subtracting to make sure that the code is set up in the proper manner.

The Comparison Operators

Now that we have had a moment to look at the arithmetic operators, it is time to take a look at the comparison operators as well. When you are creating some of your codes, you may find that there are sometimes when you will need to work with a comparison operator. This is going to be a helpful one to keep your focus on because it will allow us to take two or more values and compare them with one another in the code.

Many times, you will need to bring these out to help with some of your Boolean expressions because the answer that you will receive is either true or false. So, your statements are either going to be the same as one another, or they are not. The good news here is that there are several different comparison operators that are found in the Python language, and these include:

- (>=): this one means to check if the left-hand operand is greater than or equal to the value of the one on the right.
- (<=): this one means to check if the value of the left-hand operand is less than or equal to the one on the right.
- (>): this one means to check whether the values of the left side are greater than the value on the right side of the code.
- (<): this one means to check whether the values of the left side are less than the values that are on the right side.
- (!=): this is not equal to the operator.

- (==): this one is equal to the operator.

The Logical Operators

The next type of operator that is on our list that we need to spend some time learning more about is the logical operators. These may not be a type of operator that will be used as some of the others that we will talk about, but it is still an important one that we need to learn about and focus on. These operators are the ones that programmers can use in order to evaluate the input that a user provides you and then will take those inputs and compare them to some of the conditions that you already went through and set on the code. There are three main logical operators that we are able to use in our codes, and these will include the following options:

- Or: with this one, the compiler is going to evaluate x and if it is false, it will then go over and evaluate y. If x ends up being true, the compiler is going to return the evaluation of x.
- And: if x ends up being the one that is false, the compiler is going to evaluate it. If x ends up being true, it will move on and evaluate y.
- Not: it ends up being false, the compiler is going to return True. But if x ends up being true, the program will return false.

The Assignment Operators

To finish this off, we need to take a look at the final kind of operators that are important to our codes, and these are the assignment operators. These operators are going to be ones that you use quite a bit, and many of the codes that we have already had a chance to work with will show us these assignment operators as well. The reason for this is because the assignment operator is simply an equal sign that is going to take one or more values and assign them over to the chosen variable that you have.

Any time that you are using a variable to save some space on your computer, and you want to then assign a value over to that variable, you just need to work with the assignment operator. And the only assignment operator that is available is going to be the equal sign. Any time that the compiler sees this equal sign, it is going to know that we are assigning a value over to the variable, and it will do the rest of the work for us.

One thing that you are also able to do when you work with the assignment operator is to take more than one value and then use the assignment operator in order to assign all of these to the same variable. As long as the equal sign is in place and being used properly you are able to add in as many values to the same variable as possible.

As we can see with this chapter, working with these operators is actually something that is pretty simple to do. Even with some of this simplicity though, you will find that they are able to add in some good power to the codes that you are writing. No matter which operator you choose to go with, each of these has its own place and can help you to get some good work done in the process.

Chapter 9: What are the Strings

While we are on the topic of the different parts that come with the Python language, it is important for us to stop for a bit and take a look at the idea of the strings. In some of the work that we spent our time on earlier, we went through and looked at the string as a type of data. This was all that we really needed to do with the strings at the time, but now we need to explore these strings in more detail. We will also take a look at some of the operators that come with these strings to see how we are able to make them work in your code.

To start with, we need to take a look at what the string is all about. A string is basically going to be a series of text characters that are going to show up in your code. There are a few operators that you can choose from when it is time to work with these strings. An operator, in this case, is just a type of symbol that is able to perform a specific operation inside of the code. In this case, the operation is just going to be something that you can perform on the strings. Some of the best operators that can help you get things done with strings well will include:

1. The Concatenation Operator: This is going to be the kind of operator that we want to use when it is time to do a process known as concatenating on the strings.
2. The Repetition Operator: This is another operator choice that you can make that is going to help us to create as many copies of one string as we would like. We get the freedom of choosing how many times we would like the string to repeat, as long as we work with this kind of operator.
3. The slice operator: This is going to be the kind of operator that we will want to use anytime that we are looking through a particular string and then we want to retrieve a specific character that is inside of that string. To do this, remember that the start of the string is going to be at 0, and then counts up from there.
4. The range slice operator: The next kind of operator that we are able to use when it comes to working with these operators in strings is the range, slice operator. This is the one that is able to retrieve a range of characters out of the index, rather than just trying to get the one character. If you would like to just have one word or one part of the string show up, this is the operator you would choose.
5. In operator: This is going to be the operator that you can use in order to search for a specific character in your string you are working on, then you will get the answer of True returned back to you. If the character is not inside the string, then you are going to end up with an answer of False returned to you.
6. No in operator: The final operator that we need to work with is the no in the operator. This is going to be the

opposite of what we saw above. It is going to be one that is going to search for whether or not a specified character is in the string. If the character is not found in the string, then the answer of True is going to show up here. But if it is able to find the character in there, then you will get an answer to False.

Functions That Work with the Strings

As we mentioned a bit before, there are going to be some different types of functions that we are able to utilize when it comes to handling these Python strings. Some of the most common of these options that you get to choose from will include:

- Capitalize(): This one is going to take the first letter of the string and capitalize it for you.
- Center(width, char): This is going to return to you a string that is at least the specified width and then it will be created by padding the string with the character.
- Count(str): This is going to return the number of times that a particular string is contained in another string.
- Find(str): This is going to return the index number of the substring in the string.
- Isalpha(): This is going to check if all the characters of a string are alphabetic characters.
- Isdigit(): This part is going to check whether the string contains just numbers or digits or if there is a mixture.
- Islower): This function is going to take a look to see if the string you are checking has all lower case characters.
- Len(): This is going to let you know the length of the string
- Isupper(): This one is going to check to see if all the characters in the string are upper case.

- Lower(): This will give you a return that has all the string in lower case letters.
- Replace(): This is going to take the string that you have and replace it with a new string
- Upper(): This is going to return the string in upper case.
- Split(): This is going to split up the string based on the split character.

There are a lot of different things that we are able to do when it comes to handling strings and all that they are able to do for us in our codes. Make sure to look at some of the methods, and some of the different functions, that come with these strings in order to gain a better perspective on how we are able to use these for our own needs in coding as well.

Chapter 10: How to Debug Your Programs

As you are working through some of the coding that you want to do to make your own program, there are going to be some situations where you will need to debug the program. This is done to make sure that all of the errors are gone, and that the program is going to work the way that you want. But as a beginner, learning how to debug the program and getting it to behave the way that you would like can be a challenge. And just the thought of it may bring about a cold sweat and make you not want to work with the language at all.

The good news here is that everyone has to spend some time working to get rid of the bugs that are in their programs even advanced programmers have to handle this a bit, and while it is no fun, you will find that it is going to get easier with more practice. And there are also a few different methods of debugging your system that you are able to use based on what you think is wrong, and what you feel like using the most.

When it is time to go through and working on debugging your system, the best thing to do is go in with an open mind. If you already are upset about how this is going to work, and you feel that it is going to fail right away, then you are going to have more trouble. If you are tired of working on the code already, then take a step back and consider breaking off from it for a few days before you go back in and try to do the debugging process.

With this in mind, we are going to take a look at some of the steps that you can use in order to work with the PyCharm IDE. This is going to help us have a new experience when it is time to work with debugging the system and we will look through some of the different features that are available with this PyCharm IDE so that it will work in the manner that you would like. Let's get started!

The first thing that we are going to look at with this is the breakpoints. These may not be necessary when we are facing a bug that occurs in a certain condition that we have. and when there are a lot of these breakpoints, we are going to end up with a big mess that we then need to go through and try to fix. The good news with this one is that when we work with the PyCharm IDE< it is going to give us the ability to handle these breakpoints in a more efficient manner. Some of the steps that we are able to use for this one include:

1. First, we can press on Ctrl + Shift + F8. If you would like to go through and make this a little bit easier, you can click on Run and then View Breakpoints in the command prompt.
2. When you do the coding above, you will be able to see all of the breakpoints that are seen in the project listed out for you. This helps you to know how many there are, and

where they are located, and you can make some decisions based on that.

3. For each of the breakpoints that you have, you will then be able to go through and set up a condition that will be able to trigger the breakpoint that we have.
4. In addition, we are able to take this a bit further and set up a very special and individualized condition that is able to control whether the breakpoint is going to be triggered when an exception occurs in two different states. These two different states are going to include:
    a. On termination of the program, or when the script is done and ends.
    b. On the raise: This is going to be before the script ends at some point.

That is just one way that we can go through the process and work on the debugging process. Another method that we will see with the PyCharm IDE is going to include attaching it to a local process. This is a god one that you can use if you have ever wondered to yourself whether it is actually possible to go through the process of debugging with a remote process. It is possible, and it is actually a lot easier to work with than it may seem in the beginning.

Whether you are trying to execute this with a few other processes showing up in the background, or you would like to create these so that they become a part of the flow, the PyCharm IDE is going to provide us with a very efficient and fast method to help debug these remote processes in no time. In order to make this happen we need to use the following steps;

1. We can get into the PyCharm IDE and then open Run and then Attach to Local Process.

2. From this part, we need to go through and choose which of the processes of Python that we would like to debug.
3. There are a number of processes that you are able to choose along the way and it is going to depend on what you are hoping to accomplish with some of the work. Once you choose them, you will find that those processes are going to be debugged with the help of PyCharm.

We also need to take a look at the Python interpreter and how it is going to work with the loaded environment. You will find that going through and making some calculations, and then using that to manipulate the variables of the current debugged code is going to save us some time. It is also a good way for us to make some changes while using the sandbox environment that we are working with. This is a great way for us to save some time and figure out what is going to work with our processes or not.

The neat thing about PyCharm when it comes to this is that it is an interpreter of Python that is considered a loaded environment. This is going to ensure that we are able to handle some of the work that we want along the way. some of the steps that we will need to do with this while in the PyCharm environment to make it work for our needs will include the following:

1. Get onto PyCharm and when you are on the regular console tab, you can then press on the marked button.
2. When you do this, and everything is set up in the manner that you need, you will notice that the interpreter is going to be able to recognize the variables that you are working with.

PyCharm is just one of the methods that we are able to work in order to handle the debugging process that comes with any

Python codes that you would like to use. But it is often considered one of the best and the easiest that we are able to work with and will ensure that we are able to find some of the results that we want, and will make sure that the codes that we write in this language are going to work well without any problems.

You will find that PyCharm, and any of the other libraries that you want to work within Python for debugging, will have a lot of tools. But when you are choosing out the interpreter or the IDE that you would like to use, picking out one that has a nice and strong debugger with it is a good idea. Debugging on your own is going to be hard but with the right tools in place, it can be easy to handle, and it is going to even be fun in some cases.

Now that we have taken some time to look at how you can use something like PyCharm to help you go through and debug the program that you would like to work with, we are going to take a few moments to look at a few tips that you can use when it is time to handle some of the troubleshooting that is needed to keep your programs working the way that you want.

Troubleshooting is such an important part of the process when it is time to handle some of the work that needs to happen with your coding. There will always be a few different things that bring up errors and do not work in the manner that you would like, and this can be frustrating. But when you have the right tips in place ahead of time, you will find that this is going to be an easier process to work with as well. Some of the tips that you are able to use in order to help make it easier to debug your program and handle some of the troubleshooting that comes in will include:

1. Only do a little bit of coding at a time. As a beginner, and even as someone who is more advanced with some of the work that happens with coding in any language, you have to make sure that you do not go through and do coding for five hours without stopping or testing out the code at all. It may seem like a good idea, but often this is going to cause you more problems than it is worth. You will finally run the code and have a bunch of errors that show up and then you have to spend twice as much time looking up the information and figuring out how to fix those errors.
    a. If you just do a small amount of the code at a time and run it after a few minutes or so, you will be able to fix any of the potential errors that show up in a few minutes. You will know exactly where the error is, and you can go through and get it fixed in no time.
2. Read through the error codes: When something is going wrong with the code you are writing, often the compiler is going to send up an error message that you can look through. This is an important part that you can view because it often will tell you what is wrong with the code, and can give you some information on where the error is going to occur in the first place. It is normal to start panicking when one of these errors does show up, but since all of the information is right there in the code, you may as well read through it and find out what you can do.
3. Look online at some of the error codes: If reading through the error code doesn't seem to be enough to help you figure out what is wrong with the code, then it is time to go online and do a search. Just copy and paste the error code into a search engine and see what comes up. It is likely that someone else has had the same kind of issue along the

way as well, and you can then use this to provide you with help and advice on what to do next.

4. Take a break when things get tough: Sometimes the best thing that you can do to make sure that your code is going to get fixed is to take a break. This is hard to handle sometimes because you get so stuck on the work that you are doing that you don't want to give up. But the best way for you to make sure that you are going to fix the problem, and not make it worse, is to take a break and do something else for a little bit.
    a. If you find that you are going through the code and things just seem to be getting worse, rather than anything getting fixed and working better, then this is a sign that you need to take a break. It can be hard to walk away and take a break, but sometimes that is the best thing that you can do. When you come back, you will have an open mind, and have thrown out some of the negative thoughts and frustrations. And you can fix the issue on your code in no time.
5. Ask someone else for help: Sometimes, you may go through and work with some of the coding that we talked about, and you have tried all of the different things that you can think about when it is time to work with troubleshooting the program. But still, the code is not going to work the way that you would like. With this, you may need to talk to another programmer to see if they are able to help out with the work that you have, and the problem that you would like to solve.
    a. There are a few things that you are able to do to make sure that the other programmer is able to help us out. Make sure you explain the problem and list out the different things that you tried out on

this problem as well. This will ensure that the programmer knows where to start, and they are not wasting their time going through and trying to work on things that you already did.

Debugging your program is something that you have to do when it is time to handle some of the work that comes with programming in Python. It is not always as easy as we may think in the beginning, but the good news is that with some practice, you are going to be able to learn some of the steps that are needed in order to handle this process, and you will see how much better it makes your codes work overall.

Chapter 11: How Does Python Compare to Other Coding Languages

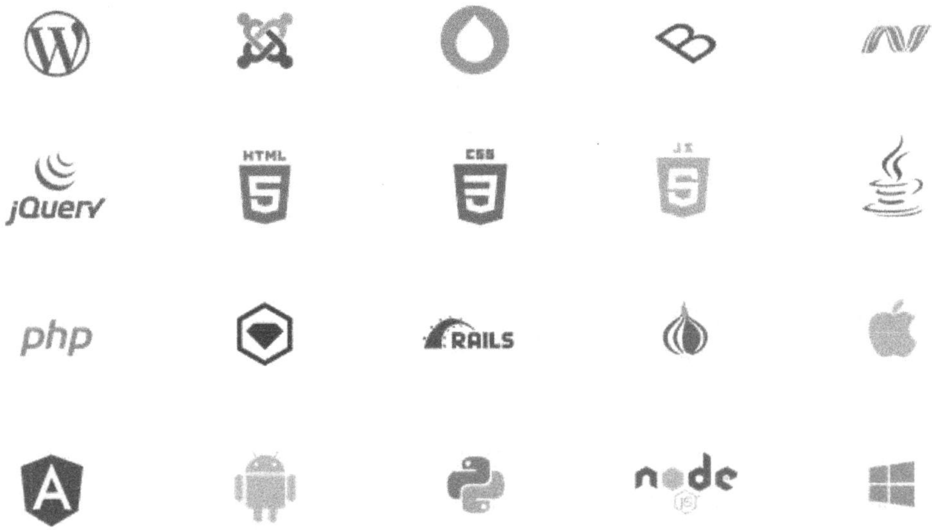

This guidebook has spent some time taking a look at the Python language and some of the different coding parts that you are able to add in with the help of this language. This is a great way to learn how to work with the coding language, and how to handle some of the programs that you would like to create on your own later on.

But we have to remember that there are a ton of other coding languages out there. Ever since computers were invented, programmers were making coding languages to help handle some of these issues and to take care of the different ways that you can work with the computer. This resulted in a ton of different coding languages that we are able to explore, and it is natural for us to take a look at some of the comparisons that are there between the Python language and some of the other options for languages that are out there.

Since there are so many coding languages out there that we are able to work with, it is time for us to look through some of the biggest and most well-known coding languages that are out there. we won't have time to look at all of the coding languages out there since there are hundreds, but we are going to put the Python up to some of the more popular options so we can see where it shines, where it may lack a little bit compared to some of those languages, and more.

A Look at Python

The first language that we need to take a look at here to get a good comparison with the others is the Python language. We have spent some time in this guidebook looking at what the Python language is all about and how we can use it, but you will find that there are a lot of other good coding languages out there that you are able to use as well. At this point, you may be curious as to why this is the best language to go with and how it is going to compare to some of the other popular and well-known coding languages that are out there. So, with that in mind, let's start with a look at the Python language and what we are able to do with this amazing language.

There are a lot of things that you will enjoy when it comes to working with the Python coding language. This is one of the best languages out there to handle a lot of different types of programs that you would like to work with. There may be other languages out there that you are able to work with, but none of them will be able to handle as many different things, with a nice simple syntax that you are able to work with as well.

If you would like to work with something online or create a website, then Python is going to be able to handle it with you. If you would like to create your own game, then the Python language will be able to help you take care of it. If you would like to learn to code, work with machine learning, handle data science, mathematics, or some other project, then the Python language is going to be able to help you get this done as well. There are so many different ways that you are able to work with this language, and it is not going to be stuck on just one or two methods or choices in programs to make.

Python is a great option to help you to handle a lot of the different types of programming that you would like to handle. And when you compare it to some of the other coding languages that we will talk about through this chapter, you will quickly see that this is one of the best ones to choose from. There are just so many benefits, and while the other languages may slightly beat Python in a few small things, the Python language can beat them in general and in many of the more complex parts that you want to do with coding as well.

Add in that the Python language is really easy to learn how to work with, and that it has all of the power and the features that you need found in just its standard library, and you will see why this is one of the best choices that any programmer can make, whether they are beginners, or they have been coding with other languages for some time.

The Java Language

In addition to being able to work with the Python language, we also need to take a look at the Java language. This is one of the most commonly compared languages to Python because there are some key similarities and differences that can make both of them good choices based on what you would like to do with some of your coding. Let's explore how both of these work and how we would be able to choose each one for some of our own coding needs.

The first thing to look at is that the programs that are run on Python are generally going to be seen to run at a slower rate than what we see with Java programs, but they are also going to be faster to develop. The speed is often going to be really hard to tell, so if you are not as worried about the speed, and want to focus on getting the development time of a project down, then the Python language is going to be easier and better to work with.

In addition, these Python programs are usually going to be much shorter than what we see with an equivalent Java program. In fact, these programs can be three to five times shorter, which is why it is so much quicker to just write them in Python instead of using another language. This difference is often going to be attributed back to Python's built-in high-level data types and what is known as its dynamic typing along the way as well.

For example, a programmer in Python is not going to have to waste any of their time declaring the types of variables and arguments that they want to use, and the powerful polymorphic list and dictionary types, for which there is a lot of syntactic support in Python, will already be right in the language, rather than needing you to go through and declare them.

Because of the run-time typing, Python needs to have a run time in a place that is able to work harder than what we see with Java. For example, when we are evaluating the expression of a + b, it must first inspect the objects a and b to figure out what type they are, which is not something that it is going to know when compile time happens. It is then going to invoke the appropriate addition operation at this time, which can then be overloaded in a user-defined method.

But then we have Java that is going to work with a different approach to make all of this happen. For example, Java is able to perform an efficient floating-point or integer addition, but it is going to need to declare a variable for a and b, and it is not going to allow for the overloading process of the + operator for instances of any classes that are defined by the user.

This is the reason that the Python language is going to be better suited as a "glue" language, while Java is going to be a good one when you need a low-level implementation language. In fact, the two together, when you decide to combine them, can do some amazing things in coding. Components can be developed with the help of Java and then combined in order to form some of the applications that you need in Python. And Python can be used to help prototype some of the components here until the designed can be hardened up with an implementation of Java.

To help us work on supporting this kind of development, a Python implementation that is written out in Java is going to be underdeveloped, which is going to allow calling the Python code from Java, and going the other way when needed as well. The Python source code is then going to be translated into the Java bytecode when needed, as long as we are using the run-time library to help support the dynamic semantics that is needed.

As we can see here, there are a lot of benefits that come with both languages, and if you are able to combine both of these together into one, you can definitely write out some strong languages. The Java language is going to be designed to execute a bit faster, so if speed is the thing that you need, then this is the language that you need to focus on. But if you are looking for a language that has some more of the features that are needed in coding, and can take up less work and fewer lines of code, then the Python language may be the better one to work with.

The JavaScript Language

JavaScript is a great language to bring out when it is time to work on a comparison with how the Python language works. This is a very popular kind of language that we are able to focus our time and attention on when it is time to do some work online. JavaScript is behind a lot of the websites and online work that we are used to seeing, which makes it a very powerful kind of language to put our attention on as well.

This doesn't mean that it is going to replace Python though. While JavaScript is the language that we will traditionally see as an online and website kind of language, Python is able to handle some of these same tasks along the way as well. You need to pick out which option is the best based on what you would like to do online at the time.

The object-based subset that you are going to see in Python is going to be considered roughly equivalent to what we are able to see with JavaScript. Like with JavaScript, and unlike what we will see with Java, Python is going to support a style of programming that is able to use simple functions and variables, without having to take the work of engaging the class definition all of the time. this can save us some time and hassle when we are writing out some of the codes that we want to use in this language.

However, when we are talking about JavaScript, that is all there is to the language. With Python though, we are going to support writing that can handle a lot of larger programs, while using better code reuse thanks to a programming style that really does rely on object-oriented ideas. This means that in the coding that we are trying to do, the inheritances and classes are definitely going to play a big and important role.

If you are just doing a little bit of work online and with a website, then you will find that the JavaScript language will have all of the features and more that you are looking for to get the work done. But if you would like to write a more in-depth kind of program and really make sure that it is strong and able to handle a lot of the work that you are trying to do online, then it is better to go with the Python language to get it all done.

The Perl Language

One thing that you will quickly notice when you are working with programming is that Perl and Python are going to come from some similar backgrounds. Both of them started out with some Unix scripting, even though both have long outgrown this and don't work on this kind of idea any longer. And both of these languages are going to support many similar features as one another. The big difference that you are going to see with both of these is that they have different philosophies that come with each one.

For example, Perl is going to put a big emphasis on support for some of the common application-oriented tasks. This would include things like having built-in regular expressions, file scanning and report generating features, things that are not seen as important, at least not quite as highly important, as we are going to see with what Python would like us to focus our time and attention on.

With Python, we are going to see a bigger emphasis on the support for more common methodologies of programming such as the object-oriented programming and the design of the data structure, while encouraging the programmer of this language to write out codes that are readable, as well as maintainable, by providing an elegant, but not a cryptic, kind of notation along the way.

Because of this, Python is going to come close to what Perl is able to do, but it rarely is going to beat it as an original application domain. But even though it is going to fall short on helping out with that right now, you will find that Python is going to be applicable to more programming situations than what we will find with Perl, and for this reason, Python is usually the language that programmers are going to find themselves gravitating towards.

For the most part, Python is going to be the language that programmers are going to pick when it is time to do a lot of coding. Python is able to take on more work than we will see with Perl and is going to be a bit easier to work with. The two languages do have a lot of similarities to one another though and can provide us with the different features and more that are needed to do some good coding along the way if we would like.

The TCL Language

Another language that we can spend some time on is the TCL language. This is going to be an application extension kind of language, but it can also be used in some cases as a programming language on its own. It is traditionally going to store all of the data that it has as strings, but it is going to be weaker when it comes to some of the data structure that you want and executes the codes at a much slower pace than what we see with Python.

There are also a few other issues that are going to show up with the TCL language. For example, it is not going to have all of the features that you need in order to write out some longer programs, such as a modular namespace. Because of this, while a typical large application that has the TCL language is going to contain some extensions of TCL written in C++ or C, that are going to be specific to the application, an equivalent Python application can be written out in pure Python and is often a lot easier to work with and execute.

As you can imagine already, pure Python development is definitely going to be a lot faster to write out and is much better than having to write out or debug a C or C++ component that you would have to do with a longer program written in TCL. One of the biggest redeeming qualities that come with TCL though is that it comes with the Tk toolkit. Python has adopted an interface though to have this toolkit as part of the standard GUI component library so you can work over this problem and still get some results.

Overall, there are not a lot of times when you would use the TCL language over the Python language. Maybe on a few of the smaller programs that you would like to write or for a few applications where you need C or C++ anyway. But many times, the Python language is going to have more of the features that you are looking for and can provide you with a ton of different options when it is time to write long or short programs along the way.

The Smalltalk Language

The next language that we will want to take a look at here is known as Smalltalk. This one definitely doesn't have the benefit of being as well-known as the Python language, but there are still some benefits of using it out there, and this can really make it one of the best languages for you to consider for some of your coding needs as well.

One of the biggest differences that we are going to see between the Smalltalk language and Python is that Python is going to have a syntax that is considered more mainstream when it comes to coding languages. This is going to give it a big leg up on programmer training. Like what we can see with Smalltalk, Python is going to come with some binding and dynamic typing, and everything that shows up in the Python language is going to be an object.

However, this is about where the similarities are going to stop. Python is going to really use us that there is a difference between the user-defined classes and built-in defined objects, and it does not allow us to work with inheritances, at least right now when we are handling the types that are built-in. ON the other hand, the standard library of Smalltalk is going to have a more refined list of data types, while the library that comes with Python is going to have more facilities to handle the realities of WWW, such as FTP, HTML, and email, and it works better for some of the things that you want to get done online.

Another thing that you will notice is that Python is going to come with a different philosophy when it comes to the development environment as well as the distribution of the code that it uses. Where Smalltalk is going to have a more monolithic kind of system image that is going to have both the user's program and the environment for coding, Python is going to store both the user module and the standard module on their own individual files.

This is going to be useful because it allows us to rearrange and distribute these two modules, even when we are not on the system that was used to create it. One consequence with this one though is that there is more than one option for attaching the GUI or the Graphical User Interface program since this is not something that was going to see built into the system.

There are some benefits that come with working on the Smalltalk language, but you will also notice that there are a few times when it is not going to be the best option for you to work with. Learning when these times are, and when the Python language can really take a step up and help you to see some amazing results will help you to make sure that you are getting things done.

C++ Language

One language that the Python language is going to be compared to on a regular basis is the C++ language. C++ is also going to be a general-purpose kind of coding language that we are able to work with and it is going to be developed out of the original C programming language, so we are going to see a bunch of similarities on there that we need to worry about as well. You will see though that there are going to be some differences in the two though, and that is why programmers usually pick one or another.

To start, the C++ language is going to be a general-purpose language for programming that was developed out from the original C programming language by Bjarne Strutstup. In the beginning, this was a language that was just called C with Classes, but in 1983 it was changed to be called C++.

When compared to some of the other coding languages that are out there, the C++ language is going to be seen as a more intermediate-level language to use, and it is going to be made up of both features that are seen in low-level and high-level features, which is going to make it pretty unique. When we are able to compare it to the C language, the C++ language is going to have a lot of the features of classes and objects, just like what we see with the Python language as well.

Because of the use of classes and some of the other features that are there, the C++ language has taken over some of the popularity that used to be there for the C language. In many situations, we will see that C++ is being used in a ton of hardware that is there on computers, and it is the power that comes on many platforms for operating systems. It is also seen as an efficient compiler to some of the native codes. It is able to incorporate a lot of different things like systems software, application software, embedded software, device drivers, and even high-performance client and server applications as part of the application domains. It also works to help out with video games as well.

For a language that started out just as an enhancement and some of the improvements that were needed with the C language, it is going to be a really nice one to work with on a regular basis. There are so many things that we are able to do when we focus on the C++ language, and how this is one of the best languages that has gone through and increased in popularity compared to the language that it is based on.

This makes it a big competition that comes with the Python language. This is going to ensure that we are going to hear a lot of competition out there between the two. It is often going to depend on what you would like to do with the coding language, and how much power you would like with it. While there are a lot of similarities that happen with these two languages, you will also find that many times when you want a more powerful language, then the C++ language is going to be the one that is the best for your needs.

There are a ton of benefits that come with using the python language, but there are also other coding languages out there that you are able to work with. This is not meant to distract you from all of the neat things that the Python language is able to focus on for you, but instead, it is meant to show you just how this language compares to some of the others, and why you would want to choose to go with the Python language instead of some of the others that are offered above.

Chapter 12: Practical Exercises to Get Some Practice

Now that we have had some time to look at some of the different parts that come with the Python language, it is time for us to go further and actually create a few of our own programs using the parts that we have just learned. These are going to be mostly games that you are able to work with, but they still show us some of the practical options of what we can do with Python and how we can actually use the options that we are talking about. Let's take a look at some of the practical exercises that we are able to use in order to gain some practice with the Python language.

Creating a Magic 8 Ball

The first exercise that we will work on creating for ourselves is the Magic 8 Ball. This one is going to work like the toy of the Magic 8 Ball that we used when we were younger. We would ask the question to the ball, and then shake it to get an answer. You could ask any kind of question that you wanted, and then after you asked the question you would shake the ball and get an answer from one of the predetermined answers that are inside of the ball.

In this project, we are going to take a look at how we can create this kind of project but on our computers. We are going to look at how we can make this project, using the conditional statements that we talked about before, and more. We are also going to work with eight different answers to help us get what we are looking for in this process.

The code that you will be able to use to make the Magic 8 Ball work for you is below. Write this into your code, watching the equal signs to make sure that you get them in the right way. Watch for the semicolons as well so that you don't confuse the compiler.

```
# Import the modules
import sys
import random

ans = True

while ans:
        question = raw_input("Ask the magic 8 ball a question:
(press enter to quit)")

answers = random.randint(1,8)

if question == ""
        sys.exit()
```

```
elif answers ==1:
        print("It is certain")

elif answers == 2:
        print("Outlook good")

elif answers == 3:
print("You may rely on it")

elif answers == 4:
        print("Ask again later")

elif answers == 5:
        print("Concentrate and ask again")

elif answers == 6:
        print("Reply hazy, try again.")

elif answers == 7:
        print("My reply is no")

elif answers == 8:
        print("My sources say no")
```

For this one, we specifically worked with eight options because we are working with our own Magic 8 Ball. You are able to change up how many options are going to show up for answers here based on what you would like to see the program work. You will just need to add in some more elif statements to add in the number that you want.

How to Make a Game of Hangman with Python

The second kind of code that we are going to take some time to look at a bit more is how to make our own Hangman game. This one is going to help us take a look at a lot of new topics that we discussed before, and a lot of things that you as a beginner should know as well. For example, you will see how the comments will work inside of the code, and even how some of these loops are going to work for your code as well. These all come together to help make it so that the user is not going to end up stuck in the game, and that they will be able to go through it the right number of times.

Just like with the other one, you will also spend some time working with the conditional statements. These statements are going to help us determine whether the user came up with the right letter or answer for handling the word that we set the computer up to pick out randomly. For this example, we are not responsible for picking out the secret words for it because we will set up the code to do all of the work.

If the user guesses a letter that is right, then the conditional statement is going to let them know they are right, and they will add this letter to the right spot. If the user puts in a letter that is seen as wrong, then the code is going to let them know that they chose the wrong answer.

This may seem like it is a more complicated thing to work with, but considering all of the parts that go with it, and how many guesses you want to allow the user to go with, it is actually going to be easier to work with. It is going to bring out a ton of beginner options like loops, conditional statements, comments, and variables so we can learn how these work in our code. When you are ready to create this game, you can open up your compiler and then write out the code below to get started:

```
# importing the time module
importing time

#welcoming the user
Name = raw_input("What is your name?")

print("Hello, + name, "Time to play hangman!")

print("
"


#wait for 1 second
time.sleep(1)

print("Start guessing...")
time.sleep(.05)

#here we set the secret
word = "secret"

#creates a variable with an empty value
guesses = ' '

#determine the number of turns
turns = 10

#create a while loop

#check if the turns are more than zero
while turns > 0:

#make a counter that starts with zero
```

```
failed = 0

#for every character in secret_word
for car in word:
#see if the character is in the players guess
if char in guesses:

#print then out the character
print char,

else

# if not found, print a dash
print "_",

# and increase the failed counter with one
failed += 1

#if failed is equal to zero

#print You Won
if failed == 0:
print("You Won")

#exit the script
Break

print

# ask the user go guess a character
guess = raw_input("guess a character:")

#set the players guess to guesses
```

```
guesses += guess

# if the guess is not found in the secret word
if guess not in word:

#turns counter decreases with 1 (now 9)
turns -= 1

#print wrong
print("Wrong")

# how many turns are left
Print("You have," + turns, 'more guesses')
#if the turns are equal to zero
        if turns == 0

#print "You Loose"
```

This code may take some time to write in, but it is meant to help us to really work on some of the codes that we want in order to write some of our own games. But with this length of code, you can work with a nice program that can play a game either on your own or with some friends.

How to Use Python Coding to Send Emails

Another thing that we are able to do with the right codes of Python uses it to send out emails to others. There are actually a number of modules that you are able to find in the standard Python library that is going to work with your email and email servers. The first one we are going to look at is the smtplib module.

This kind of module is going to help define the SMTP client session object that you can then use in order to send mail to any internet machine that has an SMTP or ESMTP listener with it. To recap a bit to help make sure that we are all on the same page, the SMTP is going to stand for the Simple Mail Transfer Protocol. This module is going to be useful when we are working with communication that happens with mail servers when it is time to send out the mail. The actual usage is going to change up based on the complexity of the email and the settings that you want to have with the email server.

The first step that we want to do is create our SMTP object. Each of the objects is going to be used for a connection over to one server. The code that you will want to use to make this happen includes:

```
import smtplib
server = smtplib.SMTP('smtp.gmail.com', 587)

#Next, log in to the server
Server.login("youremailusername", "password")

#Send the mail
msg = "
Hello!" #The /n separates the message from the headers
server.sendmail(you@gmail.com, target@example.com, msg)
```

If you want to include subject headers, To, and From, you would need to use the email package to do this because smtplib will not be able to modify the headers or the content for you at all.

We also need to take some time to work with the email package. The one that we are able to find in Python is going to come with a lot of classes and functions that can help us to compose and parse together our email messages before sending them out. We are going to start out with this by importing just the classes that are necessary right now. This is going to save us some time and can make it easier overall since we are not going to need to work with the full name of the module. Some of the coding that we will need to use to make all of this happen includes:

from email.MIMEMultipart import MIMEMultipart
from email.MIMEText import MIMEText

Then you can move on and compose some of the headers. The code that you need for this includes:

fromaddr – you@gmail.com
toaddr = target@example.com
msg = MIMEMultipart()
msg['From'] = fromaddr
msg['To'] = toaddr
msg['Subject'] = "Python email"

After this code is done, you will want to take the time to attach the body, or the message, of the email to the code that we have been doing. To do this, use the following code:

body = "Python test mail"
msg.attach(MIMEText(body, 'plain'))

When you want to send out the mail, it is important to convert your object to make it into a string. From there, you are able to use the same procedure that we talked about above in order to send this message with the help of your SMTP server. The code you need to make this happen includes:

Import smtplib
Server = smtplib.SMTP('smtp.gmail.com', 587)
Server.ehlo()
Server.startts()
server.ehlo()
Server.login("youremailusername", "password")
text = msg.as_string()
server.sendmail(fromaddr, toaddr, text)

Now we have spent some time taking a look at some of the different parts that come together to work with the email server that you would like. We can take this further as well. Say that there is a time when you are going toned to verify one of the addresses of the email that you would like. The protocol that we are using of SMTP is going to include a command that can actually check through the server to see if the email address is valid or not.

The reason that this is done and why the VRFY is disabled is because it is going to help them prevent spammers from finding out who is there. But if you do decide to enable this for a bit, you will be able to get the server to ask about an address, and then a code will be sent back to you, giving you an idea whether the email is valid and letting you see the full name of the person who is using it.

This may seem like a lot of things that you have to put together in order to make sure things work the way that we want. But some of the coding that we need to use in order to get this feature enabled and ready to work will include:

```
import smtplib

server – smtplib.SMTP('mail')
server.set_debuglevel(True) #show communication with the
server
try:
        dhellman_result = server.verify('dhellmann')
        notthere_rseult = server.verify('notthere')
finally:
        server.quit)_

print 'dhellmann', dhellmann_result
print 'notthere', notthere_result
```

When you use these codes together, you will find that it works much better for sending out your email. You won't have to go through and use your traditional email and can just use your own coding with the help of the Python compiler. You can even check out an email address to make sure that it is a legitimate one and that your message is going to the place that you would like. Go through the steps of this project and see how easy it can be to use Python to send all of your emails from now on.

There are a lot of different things that you are able to do when it comes to working with the Python code, and getting some experience with this and how you are able to work with Python for all of your needs can be important to really get some of the parts down that you would like. Make sure to try out a few of the codes above to ensure that you are able to get it all down and ready to work with before you move on to something that is more complicated.

Conclusion

Thank you for making it through to the end of *Python Programming*, let's hope it was informative and able to provide you with all of the tools you need to achieve your goals whatever they may be.

The next step is to get started with some of your own programming and coding today. We spent a lot of time taking a look at all of the neat things that you are able to do when it comes to working with the Python code, and all of the ways that you can make this code do the work that you want. Now it is time to take some of that beginner's knowledge and learn the best ways to write out some of your own codes in no time.

This guidebook took some time to explore why so many programmers like to use the Python language, and then we took the time to follow all of the necessary steps to start writing your own codes in Python. We looked at the benefits of working with this language, how to install this language on your computer, and even some of the history of this language and why it is such an important aspect of your coding world.

We then moved on to some of the basics that you need to know in order to handle some of the different types of programs that you would like to work with inside of the Python code. We looked at handling conditional statements, strings, operators, functions and so much more. All of these are going to be so important to some of the codes that you want to write in this language, and learning how to make them work for your own needs is going to be so important to some of the success that you would like to see overall.

When you are ready to learn a little bit more about the Python language and how you would be able to benefit from learning how to make this language your own and what all you are able to do with it, then this is the guidebook that is the best for you. Make sure to read through this guidebook today to learn more about the Python language and how easy it is to learn to work with this language, even as a beginner.

Finally, if you found this book useful in any way, a review on Amazon is always appreciated!

Python Programming

A 7-Day Crash Course to Learn Python Language for the Absolute Beginner, Including Practical Exercises, Tips & Tricks to Quickly Getting Started with Computer Programming

John Russel

Introduction

Congratulations on purchasing *Python Programming* and thank you for doing so.

The following chapters will discuss everything that you need to know in order to get started with Python programming. If you have never spent time working on coding at all, you will find that this is the best option for you to choose, because Python is easy, with lots of power, and you can catch on pretty quickly. And with this guidebook, we are going to provide you with all of the basics that you are looking for, and teach you how to code in just seven days!

- For our first day, we are going to start out nice and easy and learn a bit about the Python language. We are going to learn what some of the benefits are, a bit about the different versions that come with this language, and why you would want to choose to work with this language compared to some of the other options out there. We will also take a brief time to look at some of the steps that you need to take in order to download this language onto any operating system that you want, ensuring that you can jump right into coding when you are ready.

- On the second day, we are going to look at some of the basics that you need to know when it is time to start coding. We will spend time looking at strings, numbers, how to handle variables, statements, classes, comments and more. And then on day 3, we will move on to looking a bit at the Python functions and how we are able to make these work for our needs. These functions are important to many of the codes that you want to write, and we will spend our time looking at how to define them, and how to make some of our own as well.

- On day 4 we are going to move into some of the information about data in Python. Data is going to be so important when you are working in Python, and we will definitely explore this one a bit later on. But for this chapter, we are going to take a look at some of the different types of data, what types of numbers are recognized, and more all inside.

- On Day 5, we will move on to looking at the files in Python and what these are all about. These files are important because they are where we are going to write out some of our codes in this language, and being able to start a new one, find your file, overwrite parts, and save them properly can all be important to some of the coding that we will spend our time on in this chapter and on this day.

- When we are done with all of the neat things that we are able to do with the files in Python, it is time to move on to some more about data, and in specific, we are going to focus on data structures in Python. This chapter is going to dive into more of the different data structures that we are able to focus on including the dictionary, how to create a class and access members of the class, what objects are about along with the ideas of inheritances, encapsulation, and polymorphism all wrapped up in one.

- Then on day seven or last and final day, we are going to take a look at some of the tips and tricks to make all of the information that we have used in the other days and put it to use. We will look at things like web scraping and how to do it, how to debug your program, and some of the other steps that you can take in order to get the most out of some of the coding that you will do in Python.

And that is all that it takes! Even if you have never worked with a coding language in the past, and this is the very first time that you have even worked with it at all, you will find that this guidebook has some of the tips and tricks that you need to get this done. It only takes seven days for you to get started with a new coding language, especially one as simple as Python, and soon you will be able to write out some of your own codes and see some great results in the process.

You don't have to be scared or worried that coding is going to be too hard to learn. This is often the biggest issue that will prevent new programmers from getting into the game and learning how to do some of their own coding for their own projects or applications. It only takes seven days to work wit and learn how the Python language works, and in that time, you can master one of the most popular and widely used coding languages out there.

Learning a new coding language can be a great thing for many different reasons, and figuring out how to get all of the different parts to line up and do the work that you want is sometimes a challenge. When you are ready to learn how to work with the Python coding language, no matter what project or application you plan to use it with, and you want to learn how to use this language quickly and efficiently, then make sure to take the time to read through this guidebook and learn how to master the basics of the Python language in just one week.

There are plenty of books on this subject on the market, thanks again for choosing this one! Every effort was made to ensure it is full of as much useful information as possible, please enjoy it!

Day 1: The Basics

There are many things that you are going to love about working with the Python language. Many people may be wary of starting on a new coding language because they may think it is too hard for them to focus on or learn. They may not think they have the time to learn. Or they may worry that each time they want to create a new project, they will have to go through and start from scratch.

In addition to the benefits that you get simply because the Python code is an OOP language, you will also enjoy that Python is open-sourced. This means that there are a ton of codes that you are able to use with Python that is free and available for you. You could even choose a few and just tweak them to fit your needs.

This open-source of Python is great because it allows you to get ahold of codes and encourages more advanced programmers to get into the game and make the needed changes and adjustments to the program as time goes on. Some people can have their own copyrights on specific third-party libraries or IDLE's or more, but the basics of the Python code are open-sourced to make it easier for you to use as needed.

There are a lot of good coding languages out there that we are able to work with, and learning how to make this work can be a challenge, as can choosing which one is the best for our needs. This is why we are going to spend some of our time exploring the Python language and all that this kind of language is able to do for our needs. When you are ready to get started, let's dive right in!

What is Python

Python is going to be a programming language that is known as interpreted, general-purpose, high-level, and multiparadigm. Python is going to allow the programmers who use it some different styles of programming in order to create simple or even some complex programs, get quicker results than before, and write out code almost as if they are speaking in a human language, rather than like they are talking to a computer.

This language is so popular that you will find a lot of major companies that are already using it for their systems, including Google App Engine, Google Search, YouTube, iRobot machines and more. And as the knowledge about this language continues to increase, it is likely that we are going to see even more of the applications and sites that we rely on each day working with this language as well.

The initial development of Python was started by Guido van Rossum in the late 1980s. Today, it is going to be developed and run by the Python Software Foundation. Because of the features behind this language, programmers of Python can accomplish their tasks with many different styles of programming. Python can be used for a variety of things as well including serial port access, game development, numeric programming, and web development to name a few.

There are going to be a few different attributes that we can look at that show us why the development time that we see in Python is going to be faster and more efficient than what we are seeing with some of the other programming languages out there. These will include:

1. Python is an interpreted language. This means that there is no need for us to compile the code before we try to

execute the program because Python will not need this compilation in the background. It is also going to be a more high-level language that will abstract many sophisticated details from the programming code. Much of this abstraction is going to be focused so that the code could be understood even by those who are just getting started with coding.

2. Python codes are often going to be shorter than similar codes in other languages. Although it does offer some fast times for development, keep in mind that the execution time is going to lag a little bit. Compared to some of the other languages, such as fully compiling options like C and C++< Python is going to execute at a slower rate. Of course, with the processing speeds that we see in most computers today, the differences in the speed are not really going to be noticed by the people who are using the system.

There are a lot of different things that we are able to do when it comes to the Python language, and we are going to spend some time looking at how we can do some of the different parts as well. From some of the basics that we are able to do with the help of Python all the way to some of the more complex things that we are able to do with data science and machine learning that we can talk about a little later.

And all of this can be done with the ease of the Python language. You will find that when we spend some time focusing on this language and some of the basics that we are able to do will help to prepare us for some of the more complicated things that we are able to do with this code as well.

Your Choices in Python Versions

As a type of interpreted language, Python does have a lot of advantages over the other programming languages. One of these advantages is that it has the ability to grow and make changes as your computing needs change. Like your desktop applications, the fact that Python is continually developed will allow for new features to be added to the language, and you will see a lot of refinements added to Python to make it easier to use.

Throughout the years, there have been various versions of the Python language released, each one providing different features and benefits compared to the one before. Some of the different options you can choose when it comes to working with Python include:

The first version of Python that we need to take a look at here is going to be Python 2. This was the version of Python that was released in 2000, but there have been a few versions of this that were released over time. The latest version of this one, Python 2.7 was released in 2010 and is likely to be the last of the Python 2 family that developers are going to work on since focus has moved over to working with Python 3.

While most programmers are going to work with Python 3 because it is the newer version out of the two, you will find that if this version is already on your computer, you will be able to complete a lot of the coding that you want. And it is an easy version to work with, providing us with many of the features that we need to complete Python coding, without all of the extras that seem neat, but tend to slow down the system

There are also times when the programming requirements for your company, such as ones that maybe have a little bit older technology, will benefit more from the Python 2 version that is available. For example, if you are working on a company that has some policies in place that discourage or ban the installation of unapproved software from other sources, then you may find that Python 2 will fit the bill a bit better. This is because the Python 2 version is pre-installed on many computers ahead of time, so you won't have to worry about doing this yourself.

In addition, there are many third-party libraries and packages that are used to help extend what capabilities the 2.X version can handle, and some of them are not present in the newer 3.X version. If you want to work with a specific library for your application, you may find that it is only available in the 2.X version. You would need to download this version to get it to work for you.

If you do decide that this version is the best one, you should still take a look at the 3.X version. There are some differences in the best programming practices of each and you may even be able to make slight modifications to your code on the 2.X version and get it to work on the newer version.

Then you have the option of working with the Python 3 library. Many people who decide to work with Python are going to take some time to look at how they can work with Python 3 because it is the newest and the one that the Python developers are working on right now. This is the version that was originally released in 2008. There are several versions that have come out since that time so you are able to pick the one that works the best for you.

Since Python 3 is the most current version of this language, most of the examples and the codes that we are going to talk about in this guidebook will be based on this version. You will find that there are many benefits that work with Python 3 because it has a lot of add-ons that we need, has the latest libraries, and since it is the version that developers are working on right now, it will get the latest in features, developments, and updates as time goes on.

The Benefits of Python

It will not take long for you to work with the Python language before you are able to see some of the benefits that are available when it comes to working with this kind of language. In fact, you may already know some of the benefits that are present, and you may already have a list of your own reasons as to why you would like to choose this language as the one that you choose to work with. Some of the different benefits that come with working on the Python language will include:

Python is one of the best languages for beginners to learn about. If you have ever wanted to get into coding and learning how to write some of your own programs then the Python language is one of the best to help you get this done. You will quickly find that this is a language that is simple to learn how to use, even though it does come with a lot of power along the way. For those who might have been afraid in the past to try something new, it won't take long to see the benefits that come with Python, and why it is such a good coding language to get you started.

You are able to use and make modifications to the Python program for free because it is open-sourced. This is great news because it means that you will be able to go to the Python website and download the version of Python that you want, for whatever operating system you would like as well, without having to pay anything. Python is open-sourced so you will be able to write some of the codes that you want, and get it all taken care of, without a lot of hassle along the way either.

There are a lot of resources out there that will help you to take charge of your programs. This is due to the fact that there is a large community of programmers out there who are willing to answer your questions, show you new ways to do some of the codings, and so much more. Because Python has so many benefits and is such a good coding language to work with, there are a ton of developers out there who know how to use this language, and they are found all throughout the world.

As a beginner, it is likely that you are going to run into some trouble with the coding on occasion, or have some questions. And the fact that there are so many other programmers and coders who know how to use Python and who are active online is going to be good news for you. These individuals will be able to help you with any of the programming problems that you have, making it easier for you to get the results in no time.

It is easy to read this language and it is likely that without even starting, you will have a good idea of what is found in some of the codes in this guidebook already. Take a look at some of the codes that are further down in this guidebook and see if you are able to read through and understand some of them for your own needs. Python was designed to be easy not only to use but also to read as well. This makes it possible for us to really work on some of the codes that we would like and will ensure that we are going to see some of the best results with this in no time.

Python is also going to work well with some of the other coding languages that are out there. This can be good news when you want to work with some of the more complicated parts of coding along the way. when you are able to work with this language and combine it with some of the other options that are out there, especially during machine learning and data analysis, you are going to get some amazing results in the process as well.

There is a lot of power that is available with the Python language. We have spent some time talking about the Python language and how it is designed to help out with some of the different parts that you would like as a beginner. But this doesn't mean that you are going to have to sacrifice the power and the functionality of this language, just because it works well for those who are just starting out with the coding.

There is actually some good power behind this language, which is going to make it the perfect option to use for those who are just beginning on this process. You will find that this language is able to handle a lot of the more complex parts of coding that you would like to focus on, and it works well no matter what kind of coding you would like to focus your attention on at the time. Don't be fooled by hearing that this is a language for beginners. The Python language works well whether you are a beginner or you are more advanced in coding, and it can definitely help you to get your work done in no time.

The standard library that comes with Python will help you to get a ton of things done no matter what your level of coding may be. When you download the Python language like we will talk about later, you will find that it has a lot of the capabilities that you need to get some coding done. We will take a look at some of the different coding things that we are able to do when it comes to working with Python, but there is so much more than the Python language is able to do to help us see results.

There are also a lot of extensions and other libraries that come with the Python language that can increase the capabilities of what you are able to do with this language. This is a great option for you to work with when it is time to handle a few different parts of things like machine learning, data analysis, and more. These are hot topics when it comes to working with the Python language, and many businesses want to be able to use these for their own needs as well. The Python language allows you to work with some of these ideas without having to worry about how complicated they are, or whether or not the coding is going to be too difficult overall.

As we can see here, there are a ton of benefits that are going to be yours when it is time to work with the Python language. Knowing how to work with this language, and some of the different parts that come with it are critical to making sure that you get what you want out of coding. Whether you would like to add in another language to your skills after already knowing some coding in other languages, or you are starting out with this one as your very first language, the Python coding is the best one to use.

How to Install Python On Your Computer

The good news here is that the Python language is going to work no matter what operating system you plan to use. This makes it really easy for you to go through and use it on your system no matter which one you have, and you will not have to go through and change up a lot of things along the way. This can be a great thing for programmers who are just getting started and who do not want to work with a new coding language and a new operating system at the same time.

Downloading Python is going to be a simple process to use. We are going to keep it basic, but you can just visit the www.python.org website and look for the version that you would like to work with. This website is going to come with a lot of the options that you will want to use when it comes to Python, and you can choose from which operating system you would like to use, and which version of Python as well.

You simply need to go through and click on the version, and the operating system, that you would like to focus your attention on, and then follow the instructions that come with it. Be aware that working with the Windows system is going to take a bit longer than working with the Mac or Linux systems. This is because Windows already has its own operating system found on it, so we will have to go through and add this on, and there are a few more steps.

Another thing to note while we are here is that the Python language is going to be available on many different platforms and third-party options. The reason that we get it off of www.python.org for our purposes is that this is the original website that will offer Python for free. And it will make sure that all of the files and shell and other parts that you need with Python are going to be present in the download that you do.

When you download from other sites, you may be able to get some really cool features and more that come with it, but sometimes they only download the IDE, and only download the shell and not some of the other features you need. And sometimes they even charge for the use of that product. Getting it off the website above will ensure that the program is going to work for your needs.

As we can see here, there are a lot of parts that come with the Python language and being able to use this properly and getting them to work the way that we want, and there is just so much that we are able to do with this language. Now that we have some of the basics down of what works with Python, let's explore a little bit more about some of the different things that we are able to do with this language to make it work the best for us.

Day 2: The Variables and the Operators

The next topic that we need to spend time on is some of the basics that come with the Python language. Knowing these basics will ensure that you are able to write not just simple codes that come with Python, but also some of the more complex codes that you will reach when it comes to data science, machine learning, math, and science as well.

Of course, for right now those are in the future, and we are going to spend our time looking at some of the basics that come with coding. Still, some of the topics that we are going to spend our time on in this chapter will be things that you can see in all sorts of programs that you work with and can be reused over and over again. These include things like the Python keywords, the comments, functions, operators, and more. Let's dive into some of these topics and see what they are all about so we can learn how to make them work for some of our needs as well.

Python and Its Keywords

The first thing that we are going to take a look at when it comes to doing some of the codings that we want to complete in Python is to take a look at some of the keywords that come with this language. These keywords are so important because they are going to help us to really give the right commands to the compiler. When these keywords are used in the proper manner, you will find that they are going to provide you with the right execution when it is all said and done.

You have to make sure that you are using the keywords in the right spots of your code. If you use them outside of the prescribed areas, you will end up confusing the compiler that you are using because it will not know what you would like to have done. Make sure that you are learning what some of these keywords are all about, and where to put them properly in your code, to ensure that they are going to do the right work for you.

The Comments

Another part of the code that is pretty simple to work with, but can make a world of difference in some of the parts of coding that you do here will be the comments. Sometimes, you may go through the code and need to leave a little note or an explanation about what is going on inside of the code. But you don't want to have the compiler read these at all and ruin the program. This is where you will need to bring in the comments.

Writing these comments in Python is going to be pretty easy to work with. You simply need to add in the # sign before the comment that you want to write out, and then the compiler will know that you would like to have that part of the code skipped over for now. You can add in a lot of these comments to your code, as long as you have that symbol showing up before it.

If you forget the comment symbol before one of the comments that you want to write, this will end up confusing the compiler you are working with and can cause some problems along the way. it is likely that the compiler is going to send up an error message with this, and that could cause a lot of issues and the code will not keep working. Make sure that the # symbol is before the comment that you want to make, and then keep the comments down to just the ones that you really need in the code, and you will find that the code will work the way that you want in no time.

The Statements

We can also take a look at the statements in Python. These are pretty basic. If you would like to have the compiler put a sentence, or even a paragraph, on the screen at some point of the code, then you will be working with a statement. These are going to show up quite a bit in the code that we have written, and you will find that they can be as short or as long as you would like them to be overall. You get to be in control of this one, and you will find that they are pretty prevalent in some of the work that you do with this one.

Strings and Numbers

In this section, we need to take a look at a few of the different parts that are going to come with the strings and numbers. First, we will take a look at how the strings are going to work in this kind of programming language. The string, to keep things simple for now, is going to be just a series of text characters that are going to show up in the code that you are trying to write.

There are going to be a few different operators that you are able to use when it is time to focus on these Python strings. An operator for this case (we will discuss more of them in a moment), is going to just be a symbol that is meant to work with a specific operation inside the code that you are writing. In this scenario, the operation that we are working with is any of those that can be performed on the string that you have.

The good news with this one is that there are quite a few operators that we are able to work with that relate directly to the strings that we are focusing on. Some of these string specific operators that we can work with will include:

- *Concatenation operator:* This is the operator that you would want to use when it is time to concatenate strings.

- *Repetition operator:* This is the operator that you will use in order to create many copies of a string. You can choose how many times you would like to repeat the string.

- *Slice operator:* This is the operator that is going to look through your string and then retrieve the specific character that you want from there. Any time that you use this one, you would need to remember that zero is going to be the first character of the string.

- *Range slice operator:* This is the operator that is going to retrieve a range of characters from your index, rather than just one character. If you just want to showcase one word or one part of your string, you would use this kind of operator.

- *In operator:* This operator is going to search for a specified character in a target string. If the character is present somewhere in the string, then you will get an answer of True returned to you. If that character is not inside the string, then you will get an answer of False returned to you.

- *No in operator:* This is the operator that will work in the opposite manner as the in operator. It is going to search for a specified character in your string. But if the operator is not able to find that character in the string, then you will get the True answer returned. If that character is found in the string, then it is going to return False.

We can also work with some of the numbers that show up in Python. We are able to work with a number in a similar manner as what we would od with some of the other applications. You can have integers and floating numbers in your code, and often they are going to be used in some of the mathematical methods that you will want to focus on. This again is going to bring up the use of the operators as well and can help us to do a variety of mathematical equations in Python as well when we would like.

How to Name the Variables

While we are here, we need to spend some time looking at the importance of the variables in Python, and how we are able to handle these, as well as name them. There are a lot of times when we will need to focus on these variables, and they are going to show up in a lot of the different codes that we are working with as well because the variables are there to help us bring out the values that we would like to use.

To start with, we need to know that these variables are basically going to be anything that is able to hold onto a value, and that can also change in the process A variable is just going to be a box that reserves some space on the memory of your computer and that can hold onto things for the code. These are going to be important for us to learn about because they will ensure that the value you need can be attached to a variable and then pulled out at the time that we want.

As a programmer who is learning more about Python, you will find that these variables are going to be really good for us to learn because they are the parts that store information in the memory of our computer for the code. Then the compiler is able to pull out these values when it is time to execute them. The variables that you will create will be found in a certain location, based on where the computer would like to store it, and then we can find them later during the execution of the code. Depending on the kind of data that you are using, the variable is going to be there to tell the compiler where it should save this information to use later.

One of the most important things that we are able to do with these variables is to assign one or more values over to it. If we do not complete this step, then we are going to end up with an empty space in the memory of our computer, and it is hard to pull this out later when it is needed. If the variable has a value that is assigned to it, and sometimes we may see that it has two or more values assigned to it then it is set up in a manner that it will react how you want inside of the code.

As you write some programs and start to work with these variables, you will find that the Python code is going to provide us with three good options that we are able to pick from. It is often going to depend on what you would like to do with your code, and what values you are assigning to the variables to help you figure out how to handle things here. The variables that we are able to pick from for this will include:

- *Float:* this would include numbers like 3.14 and so on.

- *String:* this is going to be like a statement where you could write out something like "Thank you for visiting my page!" or another similar phrase.

- *Whole number:* this would be any of the other numbers that you would use that do not have a decimal point.

When you are working with variables in your code, you need to remember that you don't need to take the time to make a declaration to save up this spot in the memory. This is automatically going to happen once you assign a value over to the variable using the equal sign. If you want to check that this is going to happen, just look to see that you added that equal sign in, and everything is going to work.

Assigning a value over to your variable is pretty easy. Some examples of how you can do this in your code would include the following:

x = 12 #this is an example of an integer assignment
pi = 3.14 #this is an example of a floating-point assignment
customer name = John Doe #this is an example of a string assignment

Another option that you can do here, and that we have mentioned a little bit in this chapter already, has a variable assigned to two or more values. There are some instances when you are writing code and you will need to take two values and place them with the same variable.

To do this, you simply need to use the same procedure that we talked about above. Just make sure that you add in an equal sign to each part to help the compiler know that these are all associated with the same variable. So, you would want to write out something like a = b = c = 1 to show the compiler that each of these variables equals one. Or you could have 1 = b = 2 to show that there are two values to a variable.

As you work with these variables, you will need to always remember that the best way to get these to work the way that you want is to assign a value over to the variable in the code. These variables on their own are not able to do much except reserve a bit of space in the memory of your computer that can be pulled out later on. But when we combine them together with a value, and sometimes more than one value, then you will find that the variable will be able to bring out this value when the variable is called.

The Importance of the Functions

The next basic on our lists that we need to spend some time on here is the importance of functions and how we can use these to our advantage as well. These functions are basically just going to be sets of expressions, which we can also call statements in some cases. They are going to fall as some of the first-class objects that show up in the code, which helps to take off some of the restrictions and other issues that can come upon how you will work with these.

The nice thing here is that you are able to use these functions in a manner that is similar to some of the other values out there, including strings or numbers. Plus, they are going to have some nice attributes that we are able to bring out, simply with the use of the dir function.

It will not take long for us to work with these functions before we notice that they are really diverse. Plus they come with a lot of attributes that the programmer is able to use when they would like to create these functions. Some of the different attributes and types of functions that we are able to work with here will include:

- __doc__: This is going to return the docstring of the function that you are requesting.
- Func_default: This one is going to return a tuple of the values of your default argument.
- Func_globals: This one will return a reference that points to the dictionary holding the global variables for that function.
- Func_dict: This one is responsible for returning the namespace that will support the attributes for all your arbitrary functions.
- Func_closure: This will return to you a tuple of all the cells that hold the bindings for the free variables inside of the function.

There are different things that you can do with your functions, such as passing it as an argument over to one of your other functions if you need it. Any function that is able to take on a new one as the argument will be considered the higher-order function in the code. These are good to learn because they are important to your code as you move.

The Python Operators

While we are here, we want to look at the topic of the Python operators and what these are able to do for some of our codings. As we go through some of the codings that need to be done as a beginner throughout this guidebook, you will find that these operators are pretty common and we are going to use them on a regular basis. There are actually a number of operators, but we are able to split them up into a few different types based on our needs. Some of the different operators that we are able to work with will include:

1. *The arithmetic operators.* These are the ones that will allow you to complete some mathematical equations inside of your code, such as addition or subtraction. You can simply add together two operands in the code, or two parts of the code together, subtract them, multiply them, and divide them and work from there. These can be used in many of the different codes that you would want to write along the way. Some of the options that you will be able to use when it comes to the arithmetic operators will include:

    a. (+): this is the addition operator and it is responsible for adding together both of your values.

    b. (-): this is the subtraction operator and it is going to be responsible for taking the right operand and subtracting it from the left.

    c. (*): this is the multiplication operator and it is used to multiply two or more values in the equation.

    d. (/): this is the division operator and it is going to divide the value of the left operand from that on the right and gives you the answer.

2. *Comparison operators:* We are also able to work with the comparison operators. These are going to be a good option when we would like to take two or more parts of the code, such as the statements or the values, and then compare them with one another. This one is going to rely on the Boolean expressions to help us get things done because it will allow us to look at true or false answers along the way. so, the statements that you are comparing will either be true or they will be false based on how they compare.

    a. (>=): this one means to check if the left-hand operand is greater than or equal to the value of the one on the right.

    b. (<=): this one means to check if the value of the left-hand operand is less than or equal to the one on the right.

    c. (>): this one means to check whether the values of the left side are greater than the value on the right side of the code.

    d. (<): this one means to check whether the values of the left side are less than the values that are on the right side.

    e. (!=): this is not equal to operator.

f. (==): this one is equal to operator.

3. *The logical operators:* The next option is going to be the logical operators. These ones are often not used until we get to some of the more advanced codes that you may write later. These types of operators are going to be the ones that we will need to use to evaluate the input that a user is able to give to you with any of the conditions that you decide to set in the code, and there are three of them that can be used to help us with this goal.

    a. Or: with this one, the compiler is going to evaluate x and if it is false, it will then go over and evaluate y. If x ends up being true, the compiler is going to return the evaluation of x.

    b. And: if x ends up being the one that is false, the compiler is going to evaluate it. If x ends up being true, it will move on and evaluate y.

    c. Not: it ends up being false, the compiler is going to return True. But if x ends up being true, the program will return false.

4. *Assignment operators:* And finally, we are going to take a look at the assignment operators. These are going to be ones that are used all of the time, and we have actually already seen them in some coding in this chapter. The assignment operator is simply going to be an equal sign because it takes a value and assigns it over to one of your variables. You can use any variable or value that you want here, and do the assigning s much as you would like, just make sure that the equal sign is in the right place.

These operators are going to be important to the codes that you write for many reasons, and it often depends on what you are hoping to accomplish out of some of the codes that you are writing along the way. Take some time to look these over and learn a bit more about these operators and how you are able to use them in some of your own codings along the way for the best results.

The Basics of the Python Class

While we will dive into the classes with Python a bit more as we progress through this guidebook, we are going to do a little glance at these right now to see what they are all about. The Python class is going to be a unique feature that comes with OOP languages like Python, and it helps to keep everything organized and easy to find at execution, especially when it is compared to some of the older programming languages.

Python classes are basically just little boxes in the program that are able to hold onto the objects that you work with. These objects are going to be based on real-world items, so we can really understand what they are and how we are using them within the code. But if we did not organize these objects and put them in the right place it is likely they would just bounce around and get lost and your code would not work the way that you want.

On the other hand, we can work with the classes to help keep all of these objects organized and easy to work with along the way. You can easily create a class in Python and then add in any of the objects that you choose. As long as the objects that are in the same class make sense to go with one another, your code is going to work the way that you would like.

As we can see here, there are a lot of different parts that come together when we are working with the Python language and all of the different parts that come with it.

Learning some of these basics and what we are able to do with this language is a great start to ensuring that we are going to get some of the results that we want in no time. And once we get some of the basics down, we will find that it is much easier to work with some of the more complex and hard codings later on.

Day 3: Understanding How Functions Work in Python

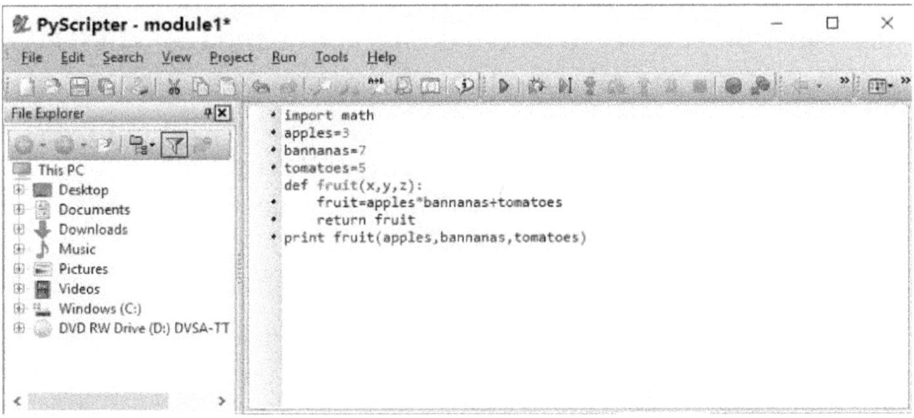

We spent a bit of time earlier in this guidebook looking at the functions and what these are all about, and now it is time for us to take a look at how these functions are supposed to work in more depth. There are many times when we will want to focus on these functions, and being able to use them in the proper manner will ensure that we are going to get the results that we want in no time. With this in mind, let's dive into what these functions are and what they mean to some of the codes that we are writing.

The function is going to be used in the Python language in order to utilize the code in more than one place in our program, and sometimes it is going to be known as the procedure or the method. Python is going to be a nice language to work with because it will come with many inbuilt functions that we have. But it also provides us with some of the freedom that we need in order to create our own functions in the process.

How to Define and Call Functions

To start, we need to take a look at how we are able to define our own functions in this language. The function in Python is going to be defined when we use the statement of "def" and then follow it with a function name and some parentheses in place as well. This lets the compiler know that you are defining a function, and which function you would like to define at this time as well. There are going to be a few rules in place when it comes to defining one of these functions though, and it is important to do these in the proper manner to ensure your code acts in the way that you would like. Some of the Python rules that we need to follow for defining these functions will include:

1. Any of the arguments or input parameters that you would like to use have to be placed within the parentheses so that the compiler knows what is going on.

2. The function first statement is something that can be an optional statement something like a documentation string that goes with your function if needed.

3. The code that is found within all of the functions that we are working with needs to start out with a colon, and then we need to indent it as well.

4. The statement return that we get, or the expression, will need to exit a function at this time. We can then have the option of passing back a value to the caller. A return statement that doesn't have an argument with it is going to give us the same return as None.

Before we get too familiar with some of the work that can be done with these Python functions, we need to take some time to understand the rules of indentation when we are declaring these functions in Python. The same kinds of rules are going to be applicable to some of the other elements of Python as well, such as declaring conditions, variables, and loops, so learning how this work can be important here.

You will find that Python is going to follow a particular style when it comes to indentation to help define the code because the functions in this language are not going to have any explicit begin or end like the curly braces in order languages to help indicate the start and the stop for that function. This is why we are going to rely on the indentation instead. When we work with the proper kind of indentation here, we are able to really see some good results and ensures that the compiler is going to know when the function is being used.

Returning a Value of the Function

The next thing that we need to take a look at here is how to return a command in Python. This is important because it is going to specify what value we are able to give back to the caller of our function. We are going to take some time to look at an example to see how we can return the value of our function and get it to perform in the manner that we want.

The first step is that we are going to see when a function is going to not be "return". In this example, we are going to get the square of 4, which is going to give us an answer, if it is working properly, of 16, when we execute the code. This is what we are going to get when we simply use the code of "print x*x" in the code, but when you call the function, "print square" you may find that the output that you are getting is going to be "None".

The reason that this is happening is that when you call up the function, the recursion is not happening right now, and it is going to end up falling off at the end of the function that we are working with. Because of this falling off at the end of our function that is going on here, the Python compiler is going to return to us the answer of "none" for right now.

To make sure that this is a little bit clearer, we need to go through and replace the print command that we had above with a command for an assignment. When we runt the command of "print square (4)" it is going to actually return to us a value of that object that we inserted. This is because we don't end up having any specific function to run over here that caused the original issue in the first place.

Then we can take this a little bit further as well. Here we are going to see how we are able to retrieve the output with the use of the "return" command. When you work with this function, and then execute out the code that we are going to have, and we used the command of "print square (4) " from above, our output is going to be 16.

And finally, the functions in Python are going to be objects on their own. And all of the objects need to have some kind of value. This is where we are going to really see how we are supposed to treat an object in the Python language. When you go through and run the command of the print square, it is going to help us out because it returns the value of the object. At this point, we have not passed any argument over yet, which means that we are not going to end up with a specific function to run over here and it is going to return to us a default value, which is going to reveal to us the location of the object.

One thing to note here is that while we are explaining what all of this means and why it is important, in most of the programming that you are going to do with Python, you will not need to work with this so it is not a big deal.

The Arguments in Our Functions

We mentioned the importance of those arguments earlier when it comes to our functions, so now it is time for us to take a look at them again. The argument is going to be a value that we can pass to the function when we call it up. In other words, when we find ourselves on the calling side, it is going to be an argument and when we are on the function side instead, it is going to be our parameter. Let's take a look at how these arguments are going to work when it comes to these functions.

First, the arguments are going to be declared in the function definition. While calling the function, you are able to pass the values for that argument as you would like. Then it is time to declare our default value of an argument while also assigning a value to it. We can work with the following code to help us get an idea of how this is going to work:

```
def multiply(z, y=0):
```

When we look at the example above, we will find that the x we are working with is not going to have any kind of default value to work with. Then the default that we will see with y is going to be 0. When we supply only one of the arguments when we call up the multiply function, Python is going to assign the supplied value to x while keeping the value of y = 0 This is why we are going to end up with the multiply of *y=0.

This time we are going to change things around and we want to find out what is going to happen when we have the value of y be 2 instead of the default of 0 that we had before. In this one, we are going to get the output of (4 X 2) = 8.

You are also able to go through and change up the order that you are using when it is time to pass the argument over in Python. Here, we are working with the order of the value x and y to x = 4 and y = 2. Multiple arguments are also something that is possible in this kind of coding, and we are able to pass them as long as we work with an array. Here, we can work with the multiple arguments of (1, 2, 3, 4, 5) by calling out the (*args) function that we have. for example, we went through and declared the multiple arguments as number (1, 2, 3, 4, 5), when we call the (*args) function. When this is called up, we are going to get an output that says (1, 2, 3, 4, 5).

Some Tips to Get Started

Before we end this chapter, we need to look at a few of the important things that you have to remember when working with this kind of code. In some of the previous versions of Python, including Python 2.7, the function overloading is not going to be supported with Python. Function overloading is when the code has the ability to create more than one method that has the same name but gives them different implementations. This process may not be possible in some of the older versions of Python, but it is possible and supported in Python 3.

In addition, there can sometimes be confusion between functions and methods. These are similar, but there are some important differences that we need to know. For example, methods are going to be associated with instances of objects like functions that are not. When Python has called up a method, it is going to bind the first parameter of that call to the right object reference. To keep this simple, a standalone function in Python is going to be known as a function while the function that goes with classes or instances will be a method.

To summarize this chapter, we will find that a function is going to be a piece of code that we can reuse and can help us to perform a single related action. We took some time to look at how to define these functions in your code, and how to handle some of the different parts of the functions to make things easier overall. Learning how to work with these functions and how you can explore using them in your own codes can be an important part of the whole process and helping you to see some good results in the process as well.

Day 4: The Data Types

Right now Python is one of the most sought after languages for programming today. Many developers want to make sure that they are focusing on the implementation part rather than spending time writing complex programs. This is a place where we are going to see Python be able to deliver, with the ease of access and readability that we are. The fundamental concepts that come with this are going to be the foundation of Python, as well as some of the programming language and hence we are going to spend some time on this day looking at the concepts of data types and variables and how they work with Python. Let's dive in and see what we are able to do with these data types.

What are the Python Variables?

The first thing that we need to take a look at is the variables in Python. Variables and data types in Python are going to be the values that are able to vary. In a programming language, a variable is going to be a location on the memory of your computer where you store a value with it. The value that you have been able to store with this variable can change in the future based on what your specifications are all about.

A variable in this language is going to be created once you have assigned a value over to it. It does not need you to go through and add in additional commands in order to declare this variable. There are going to be certain kinds of regulations and rules that we need to follow when we are writing these variables. But to help us get started with this is to look at how to define and declare the variable so that we can really see how these work in our language.

To start, Python is not going to provide us with any additional commands to use to declare these variables. As soon as you have gone through and assigned a value to the variable, it has been declared. There are a few rules though that we should remember when we go through this process of declaring a variable. These rules are going to include:

1. The variable name is not able to start out with a number. It can only start out with either an underscore or a character.

2. Variables that show up in Python are going to be case sensitive.

3. These names can only have characters that are alphanumeric and underscores.

4. You are not allowed to work with any special characters when you are doing these names.

With this in mind, we can remember that there are several types of data that show up in Python. We need to spend some time looking at these to figure out how to use them, and how we are able to work with the variables to work with this. Data types are basically going to be the classes, and then the variables are going to be the instances of these classes

The Different Types of Data in Python

There are actually a few different types of data that we are able to work with when it comes to assigning these values over to your variables. According to the kind of properties that these are going to possess, we are able to see six types of data that show up in this language. Although there is going to be one more data type range that is also used when it is time to make loops in Python, we are going to focus mainly on these six. We will find that we have numbers, strings, lists, tuples, sets dictionary, and range.

We can go into these in a little more depth to figure out what is going on with them. We will start out with the numerical types of data. These are the types of data that are going to hold onto a numerical value. In this kind of data, we are going to find four subtypes that we need to focus on including complex numbers, float, integers, and Boolean. Let's explore what all of these are going to be all about:

1. *Integers:* These are the types of data that we are able to work with that can represent whole number values. If you would like to check out the type of any of these, we are able to work with the function of type(). This is then going to return to us the type of the mentioned variable data type that we need to focus on.

2. *Float:* This is going to be a type of data that is used in order to represent decimal point values.

3. *Complex:* These are going to be the numbers that we are able to use in order to represent imaginary values. These values are going to be the ones that are denoted with a "j" at the end of the number to help us know that we are working with these or not.

4. *Boolean:* This is going to be the type that we can use for some output that is categorical because it will show us whether the output is true or false.

We can then move on to working with the type of data that is known as strings. These strings are going to be helpful in Python because they are going to help us to represent the Unicode character values. Python is not going to have a data type that is just a character, so you can find that even one single character is going to be considered as a strong here. We are going to denote or declare the string values inside of either a double quote or a single quote based on what we would like to accomplish. To help us access the values that are in the string, we would just need to work with square brackets and indexes.

Another thing that we need to remember with this one is that these strings are going to be immutable. This means that when you make one of the strings that you want to use in your coding, you will not be able to change it at all. If you would like to replace one, you would need to work with the list to help make this happen.

Then we are able to work with the list. The list is going to be one of the four collection data types that we have in Python. When we are working with a collection type and picking out which one we want to work with, it is important for us to understand the limitations as well as the functionality of the collection. Dictionaries, sets, and tuples are going to be some of the other collection data types that come with Python. A list is ordered and changeable, unlike the string. We are then going to be able to add some duplicate values to this as well. And we can do the declaration of these with some square brackets as well.

The nice thing about these lists is that you are able to work with this process and then make some changes to the items that are on the list. Some of the different methods that we need to know about when it comes to working with these lists include:

1. Clear(): This is going to be the one that can help us to remove all of the elements that are on the list.

2. Copy(): This is going to help return a copy of our list to us.

3. Extend(): This is going to help add on some elements to your list but will make sure that these are added to the very end of our current list.

4. Count(): This is going to help return the number of elements that meet with a specified value.

5. Index(): This is going to return the index of our element .

6. Pop(): This is the one that we are going to use when we would like to take an element that is in one specific space in the list and then remove it.

7. Remove(): This is going to be the one that is able to remove the item that has a specified value.

8. Sort(): This one is going to help us to sort our list.

9. Reverse(): This is the one that is going to provide us with a reversed list in the process.

The list that we are working with is going to be helpful because it will store any type of data as an item. This is true whether you are working with strings, numbers, or some other kind of data in the process.

Once we have a good understanding of what these lists are able to do, it is time to work with the tuples. The tuple is going to be a collection that is not changeable, and also immutable in the process it is going to be ordered, and we are able to access the values when we are using the index values. In addition, you will find that we are able to have some duplicate values out there as well. To help us declare these tuples, we need to use the round brackets.

Since we will find that the tuple is unchangeable once we have had a chance to declare it, there are not going to be a ton of operations or actions that we are able to perform on these. But the good news is that there are some benefits that come with using a tuple. This bright side is that you are able to store the values in a tuple when you do not wish for these values to be changed during the project. Although you can still have the access that you need to these values, you will not be able to go through and make any changes to them at all.

Next on the list is going to be a set. This is going to be another example of a collection that we are able to work with, but this collection is not going to be ordered. It is also not going to come with any indexes attached to it either. To help us to declare one of these sets in Python, we are going to work with the curly brackets.

A set is not going to come with any duplicate values even though it is not going to show us the errors when we declare the set. Instead, the output that you get is only going to have distinct values instead to access some of the values that come with a set, we have a few options. We can either loop our way through this set. Or we can work with a membership operator to help us find the value that we need. With this in mind, some of the codings that we need to work with to access the parts and the values of a class will include:

```
for x in myset:
print(x)
#this will get all the values.
20 in myset
#this will return true if the value is in the set.
#to add value in a set
myset.add('edureka')
#to add multiple values in a list
myset.update([ 10, 20, 30, 40, 50])
#to remove an item from a set
myset.remove('edureka')
#we can use the discard or pop method to remove an item from
a set as well.
myset = {10, 20, 30}
myset1 = {10,30,50}
myset.issubset(myset1)
```

#this will return false
myset.union(myset1)
#this will return a set with the union of the two sets.

The methods that we talked about earlier will be the same for what we see with the sets, but there are a few differences that we are able to focus on as well. Some of the other method names that we are able to explore in this part about sets will include:

1. Clear(): This one is going to help you clear out some of the items from a set.

2. Copy(): This one is going to help us to return a copy of the set that we are working with.

3. Difference(): This one is going to return to us a set with the difference between the two sets that you want to work with.

4. Isdisjoint(): This is going to help us see whether or not the set we see have an intersection somewhere.

5. Issubset(): This one is going to return our set if it is considered a subset of some sort.

6. Symmetricdifference(): This one is going to return to us a set with the symmetric difference that is found.

7. Update(): This is going to be helpful because it helps update the sets that we have with the union that we get out of that set.

Now we need to move on to some of the information that we will need to know about a dictionary. We will explore this in a bit more detail later on, but we can still add it in here. A dictionary is going to be similar to any of the other collection arrays that we find in Python. But the big difference that we are going to see that this one is going to come with a key value pair that you need to use to get the values to show up.

A dictionary is going to be unordered and you can change it up. This is why we are going to work with the keys to access the items out of the dictionary. And any time that you are working on a code where you need to declare a dictionary, we are going to declare one of these dictionaries, we are going to need to use the curly braces as well.

Since we are working with the keys to help access the items that are there, we have to remember that we can't duplicate them at all. If we do, then the compiler is going to get confused about the key value pairs that you want to use, and it just makes a mess. The values can have duplicate items though. Some of the other operations that are needed when we are working with this dictionary is going to include some of the following:

1. Copy(): This is going to return to us a copy of the dictionary.

2. Clear(): This one is going to help us to clear off the dictionary.

3. Items(): This one is going to help us return a list that contains a tuple of key-value pairs that you would like to work with.

4. Keys(): this one is going to help us out because it returns a list that contains all of the keys.

5. Update(): This one is going to update the dictionary with the help of all the pairs of key values that you want to work with.

6. Values(): This one is going to return to us a list of all the values that we are able to find inside of a dictionary.

7. Setdefault(): This one is going to help us to return the value of a specified key.

The range is important when we are on this topic as well. The range is going to be a type of data that is going to be used when it is time to handle a loop. These can really help us to go through the code in the manner that we would like and will ensure that we are going to get the loop to work the way that we want. It is not used as often as some of the others that we have, but when we come to working on loops, it is more likely that we are going to see these ranges.

Now that we have had some time to look at the variety of data types that are found in Python, there is another topic that is pretty important to our code, and this is going to be known as typecasting. This is going to be a helpful process when we would like to change from one type of data over to another. This may sound confusing, but we need to take a look at it a bit closer to figure out what is going on with this to see how to work through some of our codings.

Typecasting is going to be the simple idea of changing one type of data that we have into another type of data. We will be able to work with some constructors for each of these in Python and switching them over is easier to handle than it may seem. We are able to do some of this typecasting with the help of data types including lists, sets tuples, dictionaries, strings, integers, and floating.

We are able to just use these kinds of constructors on a specified type of data, or we are able to change a type of data over to another with the help of these constructors. Using these can really help us to use the various types of data with the functionality of the other. Suppose that we declare the list as a tuple in our program. What this does is turn that list into something that is immutable for that part of the code at least. We can always work with other kinds of constructors as well.

There are a lot of different types of functions that we are able to use based on what we are hoping to get out of the program we are working with. This takes some time to handle, and learning all of the different types is not always as easy as it may seem. But when we are able to put it all together, and we know how to work with the different data types in this language, it can add in so much power to some of the work that we are doing.

Day 5: Files in Python

Now it is time for us to take a look at how to handle some of the files that show up in the Python language. There are many times when we will want to open up a new file in Python and start writing our codes, but we may also want to go through and make changes on the file, delete a file, open up an older file, and more. We are able to do so much with these files, similar to what we would think of when opening a Word document but instead we are going to need to type in codes to make this happen in Python.

In this chapter, we are going to spend some time looking at how to create some of these files in Python, and even how to create a new file, work on writing some code into a file that was already created, how to close up a file, and how to move or seek one of our files so that it ends up in the location that we want, such as when we saved it to the wrong directory. Let's get started on seeing how all of this will work.

Creating a New Python File

The first thing that we are going to take a look at here when we get started with files in Python is how to create a brand new one to work for our needs. Any time that you would like to make a few changes to the file that is already opened on your computer though, we would work with the function of write(w) to help get this done because it is the easiest and can allow us time to start writing right away.

Any time that you would like to open up a new file though and then write out a brand new string inside of there, we will work with a binary file, which we will discuss a bit more in a moment, and then work with the write() method again. This is going to work out well for us because it will make it easier to get all of the characters that you want to be returned to you right away.

The write() function is really easy to use and allows you to make as many changes to the file as you would like. You can add some new information to the file or you can make some changes to one that you opened up. If you are interested in doing the writing in the code, you can use this example to make things easier:

```
#file handling operations
#writing to a new file hello.txt
f = open('hello.txt', 'w', encoding = 'utf-8')
f.write("Hello Python Developers!")
f.write("Welcome to Python World")
f.flush()
f.close()
```

before we move on, make sure to open up your compiler and write out this code. This code is basically helping you to create a file and get all the information into the right directory. The default directory is known as the current directory. It is possible to switch out which directory where you want to store the information, but make sure that you go through and change that ahead of time or you may have trouble finding it later on.

One thing that we need to be able to keep in mind when we are working here is that whichever directory you find yourself in when you get started, this is going to be the one you will need to move back to when you want to search or that file. If you want to put the file into a different directory, that can happen, but you need to move over to that one before you start saving. With the option that we have above, you will need to go to the directory that was your current one at the time, and then you can open up the code and get it to execute in the proper manner.

When we reach this part of the process, we have been able to write out a program. But maybe something isn't working right or you would like to make some changes and overwrite what is there. Maybe you simply want to change up the statement that is on a file that was created in the past. This is possible to do, we just need to work with the syntax below to make it happen:

```
#file handling operations
#writing to a new file hello.txt
f = open('hello.txt', 'w', encoding = 'utf-8')
f.write("Hello Python Developers!")
f.write("Welcome to Python World")
mylist = ["Apple", "Orange", "Banana"]
#writelines() is used to write multiple lines into the file
f.write(mylist)
f.flush()
f.close()
```

The example above is a good one to use when you want to make a few changes to a file that you worked on before because you just need to add in one new line. This example wouldn't need to use that third line because it just has some simple words, but you can add in anything that you want to the program, just use the syntax above and change it up for what you need.

The Binary Files

While we are on this topic, we need to spend some time taking a look at what is known as binary files in this language. This is a simple process to work with because to accomplish it, we just have to take whatever data that we have ahold of and then change it so that it saves as a sound or image file rather than the text file. This is going to make it easier to save and will ensure that the code is going to execute the way that you would like.

Before you jump on this one, the number one thing that we need to consider here is that we have to be able to supply the data inside of our object. This will make it easier for us to expose the byte that is there when we execute the code. The syntax that we are able to use to make this happen will include:

```
# write binary data to a file
# writing the file hello.dat write binary mode
F = open('hello.dat', 'wb')
# writing as byte strings
f.write(b" I am writing data in binary file!/n")
f.write(b" Let's write another list/n")
f.close()
```

This will help you to get the data changed over to a binary file simply by turning it over to the image or sound file.

How to Open Up Your Files

Now that we know how to create and save one of our files, it is time to move on and take a look at the steps that you would need to take in order to open up one of your files. Once you open up that file, you are then able to overwrite what is on it, or just write things on it for the first time. the good news with this one is that opening up the files that you would like to use through Python is going to be relatively easy to accomplish. Some of the codes that we are able to use to make this happen to include the following:

```
# read binary data to a file
#writing the file hello.dat write append binary mode

with open("hello.dat", 'rb') as f:
        data = f.read()
        text = data.decode('utf-8'(
print(text)
```

the output that you would get from putting this into the system would be like the following:

Hello, world!
This is a demo using
This file contains three lines
Hello world
This is a demo using

This file contains three lines.

Seeking Out Your File

You will find that when it comes to some of the Python codes that you want to write, working with these files will be a great option to choose from. We already took some time to look at how to write out a new file, how to overwrite some of the data that we were able to write into the file, and we even looked at how to open up the files. Now we are going to take a look at how to move your file from one directory to a new directory.

Maybe you are working on a file and you then find out that things are not matching up in the manner that you would like, such as misspelling the name of your identifier the wrong way, or you ended up placing it into the wrong directory. When this happens, you would like to use the seek option in order to help you find that file, move it where you want or change the name of the file you are working with.

You will be able to go through on this and change up where the file is located, ensuring that it is going to be in the right spot, or even move it so that this becomes a lot easier for it to find. You can then just tell the code where it should move things, and work from there.

These files may seem like a simple thing to work within Python, but you will find that they are going to be there to help you out a lot when it is time to order and organize things inside of your code.

It can help you to write out the code, make some changes to what you wrote in the first place, and more. Try out some of the different codes that we talked about above and you will find that you can do anything you would like with some of your Python codes.

Day 6: Data Structures

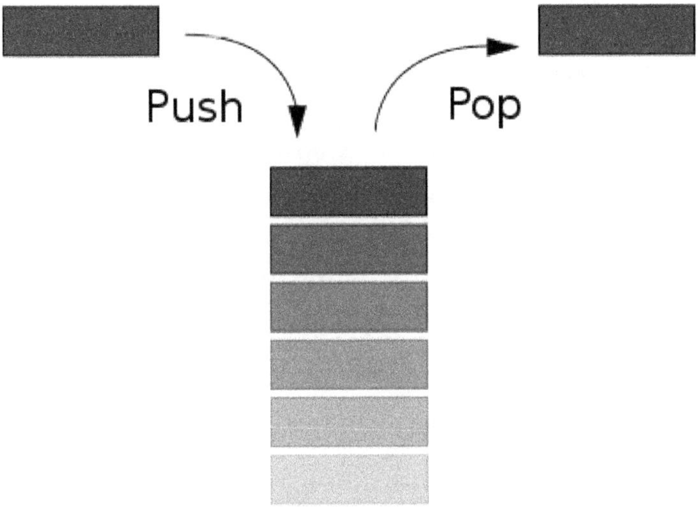

There is so much that we are able to do when it comes to some of the options of coding in Python, and in this chapter, we are going to explore some of the most important parts. Data is a critical component when it comes to writing out many of the Python codes that you want to handle, and we are going to explore how to handle these, the codes that you can use to make this happen, and so much more. Let's dive in and learn about the different structures of data, how to create our own classes, and so much more today!

The Dictionary

There are many times when we are going to work with the Python dictionary. The dictionary that comes in Python is going to basically be an unordered collection of value of our data, that is going to be used to store values of data like a map. Unlike some of the other types of data that are able to just hold onto one single value as their element, the dictionary is going to be able to hold onto a key value pair. This key value pair is going to be something that the dictionary is able to provide to us to make sure that it is optimized.

When we are looking at each key value pair in the dictionary, we will notice that they are going to be separated out with a colon. But then each of the keys is going to be separated out with a comma. The dictionary in Python is going to be pretty similar to how we see a dictionary in the real world. Keys of the dictionary have to be unique and their own, while being an immutable type of data including tuples, integers, and strings. However, you will find that the key values are repeatable and can be of any type that you want.

One thing to note here is that the keys in your dictionary can't have any polymorphism in them. This is something that we are going to explore in a little more detail as we move through this guidebook, but it is still not something that we are able to work with for these keys in the dictionary.

We will also find that in the Python language, a dictionary can be created when we place a sequence of elements inside of curly braces, and it will be separated out by a comma. The dictionary is going to hold onto a value pair for us, with one of these being the key and the other corresponding being the key value here. Values in the dictionary can really be any type of data and you can duplicate it, while the keys are things that we are not able to repeat and we have to set them up to be immutable along the way.

We are able to create a dictionary with the function that is already built into this library called dict(). An empty dictionary is something that we are able to create though, we just need to make sure that we place it inside of the curly braces. Another thing to remember here is that the keys that come with these dictionaries are going to be sensitive. This means that you will be able to use the same name, but if you put it into a different case the key is going to be treated in a different manner.

With this in mind, we need to take a look at some of the code that we are able to do with this dictionary. A good way to create our own dictionary in the Python language will be below:

```
# Creating an empty Dictionary
Dict = {}
print("Empty Dictionary: ")
print(Dict)

# Creating a Dictionary
# with Integer Keys
Dict = {1: 'Geeks', 2: 'For', 3: 'Geeks'}
print("\nDictionary with the use of Integer Keys: ")
print(Dict)

# Creating a Dictionary
# with Mixed keys
Dict = {'Name': 'Geeks', 1: [1, 2, 3, 4]}
print("\nDictionary with the use of Mixed Keys: ")
print(Dict)

# Creating a Dictionary
# with dict() method
Dict = dict({1: 'Geeks', 2: 'For', 3:'Geeks'})
print("\nDictionary with the use of dict(): ")
print(Dict)
```

```
# Creating a Dictionary
# with each item as a Pair
Dict = dict([(1, 'Geeks'), (2, 'For')])
print("\nDictionary with each item as a pair: ")
print(Dict)
```

We are also able to go through this process and add some elements to our dictionary to make it work the way that we would like. There are a few methods that we are able to use for this one though. One value at a time can be added to the dictionary by defining the value along with the key that we want to work with. For example, if you would like to go through and update one of the existing values inside of the dictionary can be done by using the method of update() that is already built into the Python library. The nested key values can be added to the dictionary that is already out there.

Note, while we are working on adding one of these values if there is already a key value in existence that we want to create, the value is just going to be updated. Otherwise, you are going to end up creating and adding in a new key with the corresponding value with it. The code that you would be able to use to make this happen for your needs will include:

```
# Creating an empty Dictionary
Dict = {}
print("Empty Dictionary: ")
print(Dict)

# Creating a Dictionary
# with Integer Keys
Dict = {1: 'Geeks', 2: 'For', 3: 'Geeks'}
```

```
print("\nDictionary with the use of Integer Keys: ")
print(Dict)

# Creating a Dictionary
# with Mixed keys
Dict = {'Name': 'Geeks', 1: [1, 2, 3, 4]}
print("\nDictionary with the use of Mixed Keys: ")
print(Dict)

# Creating a Dictionary
# with dict() method
Dict = dict({1: 'Geeks', 2: 'For', 3:'Geeks'})
print("\nDictionary with the use of dict(): ")
print(Dict)

# Creating a Dictionary
# with each item as a Pair
Dict = dict([(1, 'Geeks'), (2, 'For')])
print("\nDictionary with each item as a pair: ")
print(Dict)
```

While there are other things that we are able to do when it is time to work with the dictionaries in Python, we are going to take a look at one more thing, which is the process of removing some elements out of your dictionary. The Python library allows us to delete some of the keys if we would like, we just need to work with the keyword of "del".

Using this keyword, along with some of the specific values from the dictionary as well as the whole dictionary can be deleted as well. There are also other options that are there that will help us to get this done, such as the functions of popitem() and pop() in order to help delete wither the arbitrary or specific values that are found in our whole set.

You are also able to take this a bit further and delete all of the items that are in your dictionary at once. You just need to use the clear() function. Items that show up in a nested dictionary can also be deleted using that del keyword that we had before, as long as we make sure to provide the specific nested key and a particular key to be deleted from that nested dictionary.

One thing that we need to remember with this one is that if we type in the command of "del Dict" we are going to end up the entire dictionary. If you do this and then try to print off the dictionary, you are going to end up with an error message, so be careful when we are working with this one. Some of the codes that we need to work with here in order to remove the items from the dictionary that we no longer want, or even to delete the whole dictionary, will include some of the following:

```
# Initial Dictionary
Dict = { 5 : 'Welcome', 6 : 'To', 7 : 'Geeks',
     'A' : {1 : 'Geeks', 2 : 'For', 3 : 'Geeks'},
     'B' : {1 : 'Geeks', 2 : 'Life'}}
print("Initial Dictionary: ")
print(Dict)

# Deleting a Key value
del Dict[6]
print("\nDeleting a specific key: ")
print(Dict)

# Deleting a Key from
# Nested Dictionary
```

```
del Dict['A'][2]
print("\nDeleting a key from Nested Dictionary: ")
print(Dict)

# Deleting a Key
# using pop()
Dict.pop(5)
print("\nPopping specific element: ")
print(Dict)

# Deleting an arbitrary Key-value pair
# using popitem()
Dict.popitem()
print("\nPops an arbitrary key-value pair: ")
print(Dict)

# Deleting entire Dictionary
Dict.clear()
print("\nDeleting Entire Dictionary: ")
print(Dict)
```

Lists

We can also take some time to look at what the Python lists are all about. There are going to be four types of collection data in the Python language. We already talked about one of them with dictionaries. But let's spend some time looking at all four of them below:

1. *List:* This is going to be a collection that will be ordered and changeable. This will ensure that you are able to move the information in the list any time that you would like.

And it is going to allow for some duplicate members as well.

2. *Tuple:* This is another option that is going to seem similar to the list, but there are some differences. For example, while the tuple is also ordered, it is not something that we can change. This one will allow for some duplicate numbers though as well.

3. *Set:* This is going to be a collection like the other options, but the collection is not going to be ordered, and it is not going to be indexed. You are also not able to add in duplicate members as well.

4. *Dictionary:* this is going to be a collection that is not ordered, it is changeable, and it can be indexed. You are not able to add in duplicate members to this one either.

When you are choosing which type of collection you would like to work with, it is going to be important that we are able to spend some time understanding the properties of that type. Making sure that you choose the right type of data for your goals could mean retention of meaning, and it could help to increase efficiency and security.

So to keep it simple, you will find that the list is going to be a collection that is ordered and can be changed. Some of the other options are going to look very similar, but they are not going to let you change up the items that are there, and some of them are not going to be ordered. You will be able to write out the lists in Python with the help of the square brackets.

How to Create a Class

One thing that you will quickly find is really important when it comes to working on your Python code is that the classes are going to have a big place. In fact, this is one of the things that is going to make your codes so strong and easy to use in Python. These classes are meant to help you get the most out of what you are doing in this process, and will ensure that you are able to really organize things and get them to show up at the right times for you.

Classes and objects will prove themselves to be really important when you are writing out codes in Python because they will ensure that all of the parts that you write in your codes are going to stay in the right spot, and they won't be able to move at all while the code is going through execution. The objects are important because they are there to help define some of the parts of the code so that it is easier to understand. But the classes are there to help store some of the objects and keep things in place.

Now that we have some of that out of the way, we need to take a few minutes to look at some of the steps that we can take in order to create one of our own classes. To make one of these classes though, we have to start out with the right keywords ahead of naming the class. You can name one of these classes anything that you would like, but we have to make sure that we are working with the right keywords to tell the compiler what to do, and we need to pick out a name that is easy for us to remember at a later time.

After naming the class, it is time to name a subclass, which will be placed inside parenthesis to stick with proper programming rules. Make sure that at the end of that first line, whenever you create a class, that you add in a semicolon. While this isn't technically needed with most newer versions of Python and the code is going to work even if you forget this part, it is still considered part of coding etiquette to do this so make sure that you put it in.

Writing a class sounds more complicated than it really is, so let's stop here and look at an example of how you would write this out in Python. Then we can discuss what the parts mean and why they are important. A good example of creating a class with Python includes the following:

```
class Vehicle(object):
#constructor
def_init_(self, steering, wheels, clutch, breaks, gears):
self._steering = steering
self._wheels = wheels
self._clutch = clutch
self._breaks =breaks
self._gears  = gears
#destructor
def_del_(self):
    print("This is destructor....")

#member functions or methods
def Display_Vehicle(self):
   print('Steering:' , self._steering)
   print('Wheels:', self._wheels)
   print('Clutch:', self._clutch)
   print('Breaks:', self._breaks)
   print('Gears:', self._gears)
#instantiate a vehicle option
myGenericVehicle = Vehicle('Power Steering', 4, 'Super Clutch',
'Disk Breaks', 5)
```

myGenericVehicle.Display_Vehicle()

Keeping track of all of this is hard, and figuring out whether it actually works or not is going to be a challenge as well. This means that we need to get some practice with our code writing skills and open our text editors so we can type in the code above. As you work on typing this option out, you may notice that there are already a few of the basics, and a few of the other topics, that we talked about earlier in this guidebook showing up in this code, which can really help to boost some of our confidence while coding.

There is so much that we are able to discuss when it comes to these classes and objects, but we are going to keep it to the basics for now. This means that it is time for us to move on to how we can access the members of our class when it is time. During this step, we want to make sure that we have a text editor and a compiler that are able to recognize all of the classes that we are trying to create. This is going to help them to execute the code in the proper manner.

To make all of this happen, we, of course, have to ensure that the code is set up in the proper manner. The good news here is that there are a few methods that we are able to use to make all of this work, and all of them are going to be able to provide us with some good results. However, our choice here is to work with the accessor method because it is simple to use, it is the one that most coders are going to rely on, and it has a lot of efficiency behind it as well.

To understand the process of accessing members of your created class better, first take a look at the following code:

```
class Cat(object)
        itsAge = None
        itsWeight = None
        itsName = None
        #set accessor function use to assign values to the fields or
member vars
        def setItsAge(self, itsAge):
        self.itsAge = itsAge

        def setItsWeight(self, itsWeight):
        self.itsWeight = itsWeight

        def setItsName(self, itsName):
        self.itsName =itsName

        #get accessor function use to return the values from a
field
        def getItsAge(self):
        return self.itsAge
        def getItsWeight(self):
        return self.itsWeight

        def getItsName(self):
        return self.itsName

objFrisky = Cat()
objFrisky.setItsAge(5)
objFrisky.setItsWeight(10)
objFrisky.setItsName(“Frisky”)
print(“Cats Name is:”, objFrisky.getItsname())
print(“Its age is:”, objFrisky.getItsAge())
print(“Its weight is:”, objFrisky.getItsName())
```

Before we move on, type this into your compiler. If you have your compiler run this, you are going to get some results that show up on the screen right away. This will include that the cat's name is Frisky (or you can change the name to something else if you want), that the age is 5 and that the weight is 10. This is the information that was put into the code, so the compiler is going to pull them up to give you the results that you want. You can take some time to add different options into the code and see how it changes over time.

Working with these classes can be a great way to see some of the different things that the Python language is able to do overall, and it is likely that with any code you would like to write, you will need to create a few of these to get the best results. With that said, we need to see that these classes are not really all that difficult to work with and they can be just the thing that you need to organize your code and keep everything in place. Take some time to explore the codes that we have above to ensure that you are able to create some of your own Python classes in no time.

The Class Objects

Now that we have explored a bit about the classes above, we also need to take some time to look at the objects of these classes. A good way to think about this is that the class is going to be like a container that is able to hold onto the objects. The objects will be real-life items that we add to the code, and they need to be stored somewhere so that the code is able to find them at the right time. This is where they will fit into the classes that you plan to create.

With this in mind, there are a few rules that we need to use to make sure that the objects work with the classes that we create along the way. You are able to place as many objects as you would like into a class, and you can have any type of class that you would like. But when you or another person takes a look into one of the classes that you created and you look at some of the objects, it needs to make sense why those objects are together in the same class.

This doesn't mean that the objects have to be identical to one another. It simply means that we can't just throw random objects into the same class and hope it works out for us. You could have a class that is about vehicles or fruits for example, but putting things like a horse, the color blue, peas, and pepper into the same class would not make sense and should not be done.

Inheritances

Another cool option that we are able to work with when it comes to the Python language is the idea of inheritances. This is something that is pretty unique when it comes to OOP languages like Python and when you learn how to use them properly, you will find that it is a great way to save time by reusing parts of your code, and can make the codes look nicer and cleaner in the long run. These are going to help us to reuse parts of code that we have used in the past on our program, without having to go through the process of rewriting all of that same code again and again.

Basically, when we are working with one of these inheritances, we are going to take what is considered the parental or base code, and then change up some of the parts, either taking some away or adding to it, before we reuse as the derived code. You can do this in order to save yourself some time or to make the code you are writing even stronger than before. Even as someone who is a beginner in all of this, you will be able to work with these inheritances, bringing the same parts back many times, without having to do so much rewriting of the code in the process.

During this process of the inheritances, you will take the original parent code and then work to copy it over to some other part of the program. This new part is going to be known as the child code because you are able to make any changes to it without any effect happening to the original part of the code in your program. And you can definitely go through and create multiple inheritances in the code that you are writing, following the same steps more than once if you would like.

To help make more sense out of these inheritances, how they work, and how they can help to keep your code clean and tidy and save you time, let's take a look at an example of how they look in your code:

```
#Example of inheritance
#base class
class Student(object):
        def__init__(self, name, rollno):
        self.name = name
        self.rollno = rollno
#Graduate class inherits or derived from Student class
class GraduateStudent(Student):
        def__init__(self, name, rollno, graduate):
        Student__init__(self, name, rollno)
        self.graduate = graduate

def DisplayGraduateStudent(self):
        print"Student Name:", self.name)
        print("Student Rollno:", self.rollno)
        print("Study Group:", self.graduate)
```

```
#Post Graduate class inherits from Student class
class PostGraduate(Student):
        def__init__(self, name, rollno, postgrad):
        Student__init__(self, name, rollno)
        self.postgrad = postgrad

        def DisplayPostGraduateStudent(self):
        print("Student Name:", self.name)
        print("Student Rollno:", self.rollno)
        print("Study Group:", self.postgrad)

#instantiate from Graduate and PostGraduate classes
        objGradStudent = GraduateStudent("Mainu", 1, "MS-
Mathematics")
        objPostGradStudent = PostGraduate("Shainu", 2, "MS-
CS")
        objPostGradStudent.DisplayPostGraduateStudent()
```

When you type this into your interpreter, you are going to get the results:

```
('Student Name:', 'Mainu')
('Student Rollno:', 1)
('Student Group:', 'MSC-Mathematics')
('Student Name:', 'Shainu')
('Student Rollno:', 2)
('Student Group:', 'MSC-CS')
```

As we can see here, writing out some of these inheritances does require a bit of code in order to get it done, but that doesn't mean that things have to be impossible to work with, and you are actually able to get quite a bit done in this process. Taking the time to write this into your compiler and then testing it out can show us just how much we are able to get done in a short amount of coding with this, and can really help us to see how powerful these inheritances can be for our needs.

Encapsulation

Encapsulation is going to be one of the fundamental concepts that come with Object-Oriented programming. When there is going to be a requirement in part of the coding to group the data in one place, while hiding some of the complex details that we see from the user, we are going to work with the process of encapsulation to get it all done.

Encapsulation can help us out here because it will make sure that we are restricting the access methods and variables in the right manner along the way. Depending on the kind of code that we are trying to write, this can help us out because it prevents any accidental modification of the data. And it is achieved when we work with the non-public variable and variable methods.

There are going to be a few advantages that we are able to enjoy when it comes to using this process in Python. First, encapsulation is going to help us establish a better flow of data, and it can help us to protect the data that we have in the code already from some outside forces. The concept and the use of this encapsulation are going to ensure that the code is self-sufficient on its own as well.

Another benefit is that when we use it, the process will provide us a great deal of help at the implementation level as it is going to primarily focus on the questions of "how" in our code while leaving some of the complexities of the when and where questions behind. Hiding the data into a unit can help to make the encapsulation process easier while also securing some of the data that we have.

This brings us to the point of why we would need this encapsulation in the first place in the Python code. Below we are going to take a look at some of the reasons why developers are going to find encapsulation to be a good thing and why they would decide to use it in some of their own programs:

1. There is already a need for interaction that is well-defined in every application and the process of encapsulation is going to make sure that we are able to get this done.

2. The concept of OOP languages in Python has a focus on making codes that can be reusable, and the encapsulation can help.

3. The application maintenance is going to be easier and here is security ensured.

4. Clarity on the procedures of coding as developers are going to be concerned at the objective of the class, and we can take care of complex issues in a more systematic manner.

5. When you have the right organization of your codes, it is going to help with some of the flexibility of the code and can make some of the Unit Testing easier.

6. Users are going to find that it is easier to use the system in this kind of process because it will help them to stay hidden away from the complex design that is involved at the back end of this.

7. Having all of your data that are similar in one place, and having it encapsulated, is going to increase the cohesion inside of the module.

8. This can help to improve how readable the codes are, and can ensure that changes that happen in one part of the code will not end up causing harm to the other parts.

9. Encapsulation is great because it is going to prevent the part of the code that you want to protect from being accessed on accident.

Polymorphism

And finally, while we are on this topic, we need to spend a few minutes looking at the idea of polymorphism. In an OOP language, this is going to be the characteristic of being able to assign a different usage or meaning to something based on the context that it is using. In specific, we will find that this allows an entity, such as an object, function, or variable to have more than one form at a time. In Python there are going to be a few types of polymorphism that we are able to work with including:

A variable that has a given name can sometimes have different forms and the program can then determine which variable form it would like to use when it is time to execute the code.

For example, you could name a variable as USERID, and it could be capable of being a whole number or a string of characters based on what kind of user ID that input is. By giving the program the way to distinguish which form it is handling in each case, this will not be a big issue for the program to handle.

In addition, a named function can also vary based on the kinds of parameters that you decide to give to it. For example, if given a variable that is an integer, the function chosen would then be able to seek a match against lit of numbers fr the employees. But if the variable was a string, then it is going to seek out a match with a list of names instead. In either of these cases, both of the functions will have the same name for the program to work with. Sometimes we are going to call this process overloading instead.

Another version of polymorphism is going to mean something else when we are working with machine learning. It could be a type of data of "any" such that when specified for a list, a list containing any type of data can be processed by the function that you are working with. In this one, if you have a function that can simply determine how long the list is, it won't really matter what types of data show up in that list at all.

And finally, we can look at a polymorphism in PHP. With this one, we will see that B is going to be a descendant of A, and then a function is able to accept A as the parameter that it needs to follow. But this function is also able to accept B for this job as well.

Day 7: Getting Started; Python Tips and Tricks

We have spent the last few days of this guidebook looking at some of the different parts of the Python language that we are able to work with. These are meant to help us get going with some of our own coding in Python and will ensure that we are able to write some of your codes in no time. With some of this information in mind, we are able to work on some of the final skills that we need to focus on before we are done. We are going to look at some of the tips and tricks that will help you to get started with Python, along with how we can work with web scraping and debugging some of our programs as well. Let's get started with this one in order to help us get started and finalize how good our codes can be.

Web Scraping

Imagine for a moment that we are going to pull up a large amount of data from many websites, and we want to be able to do this at a very fast rate. How would we be able to go through this without having to manually go through each of the websites that we have and gathering the data in this manner? This is where the process of web scraping is going to come into play.

Web scraping is going to be used by companies in order to collect a large amount of information form websites. But why does someone want to go through and collect all of this data, in such large amounts, from these websites in the first place? There are a lot of reasons for this, and some of them are going to include the following:

1. *Price comparison:* Some of the different services that are out there, such as ParseHub, will work with this process in order to collect data from websites for online shopping and then can use this in order to compare prices of similar products.

2. *Email address gathering:* We can use the process of web scraping in order to help with marketing. This can help us to collect the email IDs that come with customers and then send out bulk emails to these individuals as well.

3. *Social media scraping:* Web scraping is going to be used to collect data from social media sites and then figure out what is trending.

4. *Research and development:* Web scraping is going to be used to help a company collect a lot of data from websites. We can then analyze this and use it to finish our surveys and to help out with research and development.

5. *Job listing:* Details regarding openings of jobs, interviews, and more can be collected from a variety of websites and

then we can list them in one place in order to make them easier for the user to access

Web scraping is going to be more of an automated method that we can use in order to get a huge amount of data from any website that we choose. The data that we are able to get out of these websites will be unstructured. And this web scraping helps a company to collect all of this data and then will ensure that they are able to store it in a structured for. There are a variety of methods that we are able to use in order to scrape these websites that we want, including online Services, writing out some of your own codes, and APIs.

Talking about whether or not scraping of this kind if seen as legal or not, it can depend on what the website says. Some websites are fine with this and some are not. You can check with each website to figure out whether they are fine with it, and if they are, you are able to continue on with your web scraping tools and gather up the information that you need.

Since we are talking about Python here, we are going to take some time to see how we are able to use Python to help out with web scraping. But this brings up the reasons why we would want to work with Python to help out with this process rather than working with some of the other coding languages that are out there. some of the features that come with Python and can make it more suitable for web scraping will include:

1. *It is easy to use:* The code that you are able to use along with Python is going to be simple. This ensures that any of the codes that you want to use for web scraping will not be as messy to work with and can be easy to use.

2. *A large library collection:* There are a lot of libraries that work with data science and web scraping that are also compatible with what the Python language is able to do. These include options like Pandas, Matplotlib, and NumPy. This is why you will find that the Python language is going to be suitable for web scraping and even for some of the other manipulations that you want to do with the extracted data.

3. *Dynamically typed:* This is something in Python where you will not need to go through and define all of the types of data that you are using with our variables. Instead, you are able to just use these variables wherever you would like. This is going to save a lot of time when it comes to working on the codes and can make your job faster than ever.

4. The syntax of Python is going to be easy to understand the syntax that we are able to see with Python is easy to understand, mainly because the statements that come with this are going to be written in English. It is going to be expressive and easy to read, and the indentations will make it easier for us to figure out between the different parts of the code.

5. A small code is able to handle some large tasks. Web scraping is a process that we are going to use in order to save some time. And with Python, you are able to write out a small amount of code in order to get some of the big tasks that you would like to accomplish done. This is going to save you time not only when it comes to figuring out the important data that comes in that website, but can also

help you to save time when you would like to write out the codes.

6. *Community:* At times, when you are a beginner, you are going to find that there are parts of the code that are hard to work with and are not going to go as smoothly as you had hoped in the process. This is where you will find the Python language to be healthy. If you get stuck while writing out some of your code, you will like that the Python community is going to help you to answer your questions and get things done on the code in no time.

Now that we know some of the benefits that come with Python, especially the ones that are going to help us to handle some of the web scrapings that we want to do, it is time for us to take things to the next step and look at how the process of web scraping is going to work. When you run out the code that you want to work within web scraping, you will find that there is a request that is sent out to the URL that you mentioned. Then there is going to be a response sent back from that request, and then the server is able to send the data and allows you a chance to read the page, whether it is XML or HTML at the time.

The code is then able to go through and parse the XML or HTML page, find the data, and takes it out. The location where you are going to find this data when it is extracted will depend on what you told the code to do. Often it is going to be moved over to a database so that you are able to search through it later and learn more from it as well.

To help us go through the process of extracting the data with the help of web scraping in Python, there are going to be a few simple steps that you are able to take to make this happen. The steps that will help you to use Python to help with web scraping ill include:

1. Find the URL that you would like to scrape in the first place.

2. Inspect the page that you are planning on using.

3. Find the data that is on the page that you would like to extract.

4. Write out the code that you would like to use with the help of Python in order to complete this process.

5. Run the code that you just wrote and then extract out the data that you would like to use.

6. Store the data in the format that would be the most helpful for you in the process.

There are also a few options that you are able to use when it is time to work on the process of web scraping. As we know, Python is already able to be used for a lot of different types of applications, and there are going to be a ton of libraries with Python that is going to be used for different purposes. There are a few libraries that work the best when it comes to working with the process of data web scraping will include:

1. *Selenium:* This is going to be a web testing library. It is going to be used to help automate some of the activities that are found on your browser.

2. *BeautifulSoup:* This is going to be one of those packages that you are able to use with Python to help us to parse HTML and XML documents. It is also able to create parse trees that can help us to extract the data in an easy manner.

3. *Pandas:* This is one of the best libraries to rely on when it is time to handle any kind of work that you would like in data analysis and data science. Pandas are often going to be used to help out with any of the data analysis and the data manipulation that you would like. When it comes to web scraping, you will find that Pandas is going to be used in order to extract the data and then get it stored in the right format in the way that you would like along the way.

There are many times when a company is going to try and gather up data from other websites and from many other sources. This is one of the first steps that is going to be found when we are working with data analysis and using that information to improve a business through their customers, the industry, or from the other competition out there.

But going through and gathering all of that data in a manual manner is going to take too long, and can be really hard to work with as well. And with the large amounts of data that are being used and generated on a daily basis, it is no wonder that so many companies are working with processes like web scraping to handle all of the work in a timely manner as well.

When we work with web scraping and do some of the codings that are necessary with the help of Python, we will find that we are able to get through the information in a fast manner and get it stored in the right place for our needs, without having to do all of the work manually. This can make the process of data analysis much easier overall and will ensure that we are able to see some of the results that we want with this as well. And with some of the right Python algorithms and codes, we can get data scraping done in no time.

Debugging

The next thing that we need to work on here when it comes to the Python program is how to debug some of the programs that you are working on. This is something that you may spend quite a bit of your time working with, simply because you are a beginner and learning how to handle all of this work. As you get more practice with the Python code and you learn how to work with it a bit more, you will find that you may not need to debug much anymore.

No matter how much experience you have with any coding language though, we need to spend some time looking at some of the basics that are there with debugging our code. This ensures that we learn about the coding a little bit more and that we are able to change things up and get them fixed when something doesn't seem to be going the way that we would like.

When we are talking about the process of software development, we will find that debugging is going to be the process of looking for, and then resolving, any issues that are going to prevent the software from running in the proper manner. We all hope that the codes that we are going to write will work the way that we want, but this is not always something that happens. Being prepared, and knowing how to fix these problems, will be a big bonus when we work on the debugging process.

The Python debugger is a great option to go with because it is going to provide us with a good environment for debugging that works for all of our Python programs. It is going to be there to support some of our conditional breakpoints hat we want to set, stepping through the source code one line at a time, stack inspection, and so much more.

The first thing that we need to take a look at here though is how to work interactively with the Python debugger to learn how to work with it. This kind of debugger is going to come as part of the Python distribution that is standard, and the module that we are talking about here is going to be the pdb. The debugger is also going to be extensible, and we are able to define it as the class of pdb. You are able to go and read through some of the official documentation of this if that helps out as well.

We are going to begin this with a short program that will come in with two global variables, a function that is going to create for us a nested loop, and then the if __name__ == '__main__': construction that is something we will need to call up to give us the function for the nested_loop(). An example of how to work with all of this and the code that we are able to use here will include the following:

```
num_list = [500, 600, 700]
alpha_list = ['x', 'y', 'z']


def nested_loop():
  for number in num_list:
     print(number)
     for letter in alpha_list:
        print(letter)

if __name__ == '__main__':
  nested_loop()
```

we are then able to go through and run the program through the debugger that we are working with using the following command:

$ python -m pdb looping.py.

The -m command flag is going to help us out here because it is responsible for importing any of the modules of Python for us that we need and then running it as a script. In this case, for what we want to get done using the debugger, we are going to import and then run the module of pdb, which is what we are then able to pass into the command as we showed a bit earlier.

Take a moment to type in the code that we wrote above to see what the output is going to be. When we look at the output, the first line that we see is going to tell us the current name of the module with the directory path. And then we are going to find that the printed line number is going to follow this. In this situation, we are going to have the number 1, but if we find that there is a common, or some other kind of line that is not executable, then this could end up being a higher number.

Then we are able to move onto the second line. this one is going to show us the current line of a source code that is going to be executed here, as a pdb, and will provide us with an interactive console that is going to help us to do the debugging that we want. You are able to work with the help command to help us to learn the commands that are here, and then the help command to help us out with the specific command that we want. Note that the console for pdb is different than what we will find with the interactive shell in Python.

In addition, we are going to find that the Python debugger is automatically going to start over when it reaches the end of the program that you are writing. Whenever you want to be able to leave this console though you are able to type in the command of exit or quit. If you would like the choice to explicitly restart a program at any place within the program, rather than always restarting from the beginning, then you are able to do this with the command of the run.

One more thing that we need to figure out when it comes to working on the debugger in Python is how to use this in order to move through a program. When we are working with some of the programs of the debugger, we are going to work with a variety of commands like next, list, and step to help us get through the code in the manner that we will like.

Within the Python shell that we are working with, we are able to type in the command of the list to help us get some of the contexts that is around the line we are currently in. from the first line of the program, that we did above, we are going to see that it is going to look like the following:

```
num_list = [500, 600, 700]
alpha_list = ['x', 'y', 'z']


def nested_loop():
  for number in num_list:
    print(number)
    for letter in alpha_list:
      print(letter)

if__name__ == '__main__':
  nested_loop()
```

The current line is going to be seen with the ->, which in our case is going to be the first line of the file that we are working with, but it can definitely be found in some of the other parts as well.

Since we are working with a program that is pretty short here, we are going to basically receive most of the program back when we do the list command. This is not going to be true when we work with some of the longer ones, but it works for some of the codes that we are trying to work with right now. Without going through and providing the exact argument that you want to work with, the list command is going to provide us with 11 lines around the current line.

It is also possible for us to go through and specify which lines we would like to be able to include in the process. Some of the codes that we are able to do in order to make this work for our needs, and to not get the whole code to show up at once will include the following:

```
(Pdb) list 3, 7
  3
  4
  5    def nested_loop():
  6        for number in num_list:
  7            print(number)
(Pdb)
```

Now we need to take a quick look at the step and the next function. The step is going to stop within a called function. But then the next one is going to execute all of the called functions, and it is only going to stop at the next line of the current function. We are going to see the difference of this when we work with the functions, even though it may seem like it is not telling us much right now.

The step command that we are talking about is going to iterate through a few loops once it is able to get to the running of the function, and it will be able to show us exactly what loop it is doing, as it will first print a number with print(number). Then it is able to go through and print out the letters that you have with the function of print(letter) to return the number and more.

There is some coding that we are able to use to make this happen. Some of the coding that we are going to use to help make sure that we are able to see the best results with some of the coding, and to show us how the step command is going to work for us will include:

```
(Pdb) step
> /Users/sammy/looping.py(5)<module>()
-> def nested_loop():
(Pdb) step
> /Users/sammy/looping.py(11)<module>()
-> if __name__ == '__main__':
(Pdb) step
> /Users/sammy/looping.py(12)<module>()
-> nested_loop()
(Pdb) step
--Call--
> /Users/sammy/looping.py(5)nested_loop()
-> def nested_loop():
(Pdb) step
> /Users/sammy/looping.py(6)nested_loop()
-> for number in num_list:
(Pdb) step
```

```
> /Users/sammy/looping.py(7)nested_loop()
-> print(number)
(Pdb) step
500
> /Users/sammy/looping.py(8)nested_loop()
-> for letter in alpha_list:
(Pdb) step
> /Users/sammy/looping.py(9)nested_loop()
-> print(letter)
(Pdb) step
x
> /Users/sammy/looping.py(8)nested_loop()
-> for letter in alpha_list:
(Pdb) step
> /Users/sammy/looping.py(9)nested_loop()
-> print(letter)
(Pdb) step
y
> /Users/sammy/looping.py(8)nested_loop()
-> for letter in alpha_list:
(Pdb)
```

On the other hand, the next command is able to go through and execute the entire function, without having to show us each of the steps that we are able to do in the process. In order to help us to get this finished up and to quit the current session that we are in, we are able to use the exit command to help finish off.

There are so many things that we are able to do with the debugger that we are using, and making sure that we are using it in the proper manner, and understand all of the things that it is able to do to help us out, can ensure that we are able to handle some of the work that we are going to see in our codes.

As a beginner, it is likely that we are going to need to work with some of the debugger tools that are there on a regular basis. This will ensure that we are going to see some of the best results with the code and that it is going to help us to really see some codes that will work as strongly as we would like, rather than ones that aren't going to work at all. It may seem like it takes a lot of our time and is kind of a hassle, but it can save us a lot of issues later on because we know that the programs are going to work for us.

Now, sometimes the debugger that you are working with is not going to provide you with some of the results that you are looking for, or it will not solve the problem.

And maybe you have gone through and tried out a few other options and they are not working out for you either. This can be frustrating when you are a beginner, but sometimes the best thing that we are able to do for this is to ask someone who has some more experience with coding to help us out.

If you have gone through all of these steps trying to troubleshoot your program and you still can't seem to find the error or you worry that you are just making things worse, then it is fine to ask someone else for help. But before you ask someone to help you go through the code and figure out what is wrong, you need to make sure that you have all of the following parts in place to help them understand what is going on, what you have tried, and what they can do to help you out.

1. Explain what you want the program to do for you and where the error is occurring.

2. Show the other person the code that is sending you an error so they can see it for themselves.

3. Show the other person the stack trace, all of it, including the message you got stating the error.

4. Explain everything that you have already tried on the error. This helps the other person have a good idea of what you have tried and what they should try to get the code to work.

Another thing that we need to spend some time on is remembering that you should go through and run your code after each small bit or block of code that you are working with, rather than handling a huge amount at once. Do not start out with a blank file, sit down, and spend an hour coding before you even try out the code for the first time. You will just make the work harder for yourself and when there are a whole bunch of little errors that pop up, you won't know where to start. It can take forever to go through it all and fix whatever is going wrong.

Instead, every few minutes, you should run the updates and test the code to see if something comes up. That way, when a bug does show up in the code, you only have a few lines or so of the code to check for the issue rather than a whole bunch of code. It really isn't possible for you to test out your code too often so do it as much as you can.

Always remember that the more code that you write before you test it again, the more places where errors can occur and the more code that you will need to go search through again. And each time that you do go through and run the code, you will get some more feedback on your work so you can learn as you go.

Along the same lines, you may find that printing out a lot of the things that you work with can help you to really see what is going on as well.
As you look through your code, you should be able to look at each line and have a sense of what values are associated with each variable. If you are unsure, then stop and print them out. Then, when it is time to run that program, you can look at the console and see how the values are going to change or how they get changed to null values in a way that you wouldn't expect.

You may find at times that it is helpful to print a fixed string right before you print out a variable. This ensures that all of your print statements won't run together, and then you can tell what is being printed from where. There may even be some times when you aren't sure whether or not the code is being run in the first place. A simple *print "got here"* can often be enough to help you see whether you have a mistake in your loops or in your if statements.

You may find that the process of thinking through these items in your mind and then getting them written down on paper can help make a brand new solution obvious. If that doesn't work, try to find someone who may be able to look through the code and tell you what is going wrong and what you can do to fix the error.

As a beginner, you may be worried that you won't be able to do any debugging or troubleshooting with your own code. But this just isn't true. You have the ability to look through the error messages that the compiler sends to you, you can look up solutions, and you can make sure to test out the code every few minutes or so to ensure that you are getting the results that you want for your code without any of the errors. And if nothing seems to be working for you, it may be best to work with someone who has a bit more experience to help you find the solutions that you need.

Conclusion

Thank you for making it through to the end of *Python Programming*, let's hope it was informative and able to provide you with all of the tools you need to achieve your goals whatever they may be.

The next step is to set up one week where you would like to start learning Python and go through each day of this guidebook to help you get that done. Many people are worried about starting out with a new coding language because it may seem complicated and like something that they would never be able to catch up on. But with the help of this guidebook, you will be able to master some of the basics, and even some of the more advanced, parts that come with the Python language.

In this guidebook, we have set it up so that you can go from a beginner to a pro in no time with the Python language. Each day of the week is divided up to help you to really learn some of the parts that you need to know, to ensure that you are going to be able to learn about the Python language and even write out some of your own codes along the way.

We spend some time learning how to install the language on your own computer system, how to work with the basics of the code that will show up later the importance of the different types of data and how each of them is going to work in your own code, and even some of the work with classes, inheritances, files, and more. We will also end with some information on how you can go through and debug one of your own programs in no time, ensuring that you will get things done, and will not end up with a code that can't be used.

When you are ready to learn how to master some of the basics of Python so you can do some of your own programs, you don't want to spend months, and even years getting it all down. This is where you will find this guidebook to be healthy. When you are ready to get started on the Python language and you are ready to see how working with this language is simple and easy enough to learn how to use and write out in just one week, make sure to check out this guidebook today!

Finally, if you found this book useful in any way, a review on Amazon is always appreciated!

Python Programming

The Ultimate Advanced Guide to Python Coding Language, Machine Learning, and Data Analysis, Become an Expert with Hands-On Projects and Step-by-Step Exercises

John Russel

Introduction

Congratulations on purchasing *Python Programming* and thank you for doing so.

The following chapters will discuss all of the different parts that you need to know in order to get started with Python programming, and how we are able to make this kind of program work for our needs. There may be a variety of coding languages out there that we are able to work with, but none of them are going to be as easy to use, or provide us with as many benefits, as we are able to see with the Python language.

This guidebook is going to start out with some information on the Python language and how we are able to work with it. We are going to focus mainly on some of the more advanced parts that come with the Python language, but we will first look at what we are able to do with the help of the Python language, and even how to make sure that we get the language installed and ready to go with any operating system that you choose. We will even take a look at some of the benefits that you will be able to enjoy when it is time to choose this coding language over some of the others.

Once we have some of those basics down, it is time for us to move on to some of the more advanced types of coding that we are able to work with. We will take a look at how we can use Python to help us with inheritances, creating our own classes, handling exceptions, and working with loops as well. All of these can be combined with some of the basics that you already know and love when it comes to Python and can help us when it is time to move on to things like machine learning and data analysis.

With those topics in mind, it is time for us to take a look at them as well. Machine learning and data analysis are becoming big names when it comes to the world of business. There are many companies who are going to work with these topics in order to see some results and help them to beat out the competition as well. This guidebook is going to take some time to look at the different parts that come with machine learning, the different types of machine learning, and how Python can be combined with machine learning in order to help us create the models and the algorithms that we need.

We will also spend some time looking at a good data analysis and how to get this process started, and the different steps that come with this as well. We can then end this guidebook looking at some of the best data science and data analysis libraries that are out there, ones that will help you to really get some of your models done and handled, and that works well with the Python coding language as well.

There are so many neat things that you will be able to do when it is time to work with the Python language, especially when it comes to working with this language along with machine learning and data analysis. When you are ready to see what the Python language is able to do for you, make sure to check out this guidebook to help you get started!

There are plenty of books on this subject on the market, thanks again for choosing this one! Every effort was made to ensure it is full of as much useful information as possible, please enjoy it!

Chapter 1: What is the Python Language

This guidebook is going to spend some time exploring how you are able to work with the Python language. There are a lot of benefits that are going to be able to help you choose the Python language, but we need to learn more about how to make this language work the way that we would like. In this guidebook, we are going to spend some time learning how this language works, and exploring how it is able to work with things like data analysis and machine learning as well. But first, we need to start with an explanation of what the Python language is all about and some of the benefits that come with this language as well.

What is the Python Language?

There may be a lot of different languages that you are able to work with when it comes to the coding that you would like to work with, but none are going to provide you with the benefits that you are working with. This language is so popular and used so often that there are a few different operating systems that already have some version of Python found on them for you to use. This can make it easier to get some of the coding done that you would like, and will ensure that you will get the best benefits out of it in no time.

There are going to be many different things that you are able to love when it is time to work with the Python language. Many people are going to be a bit wary when it comes to starting out with a new coding language because they feel that it is hard for them to focus on any of it, or to learn how it works without spending years doing it. They may not even think that they will have the time or the resources necessary to get it done. Or they may worry that each time they want to work with the code, they have to begin again from scratch.

This is part of the beauty that comes with the Python language. You will be able to handle all of these issues and more in no time, and you won't have to feel like you are lost when you start as a beginner. In addition to some of the benefits that you are going to find because Python is an OOP language, you can also enjoy that it is open-sourced and can handle a lot of the different types of programming that you want to get done in the process as well.

What this open-source means in your coding is that Python is able to allow you to get the coding for free, and allows you to work with the program and more without having to worry about copyright issues or more. This is going to encourage more advanced programmers to join the game and make some of the adjustments, developments, updates and more that are needed to keep this coding language modern and ready to go.

When you add this into the fact that Python is able to handle a lot of the different options that you would like, and that it has the capabilities to handle all of the coding that you want to do, you can easily see why this is a language that a lot of programmers want to work with. It can handle anything from some basic coding while you are learning how to do it, and can go all the way up to handling a data analysis or machine learning as well. And when you can make choices in the features that you would like to add to this, and which third-party IDLEs and more that you want to use, you can see why you may benefit from working on this kind of language overall.

The Benefits of Working with Python?

There are a lot of great options for working with the Python language, and it is not going to take very long before you will be able to work with this kind of language. There are also a lot of benefits to this language, even when we spend some time comparing it to some of the other coding languages out there.

Keep in mind that there are a lot of different coding languages out there that you are able to focus your attention on. And sometimes all of these options can make it hard to know which one is the best for your needs. Even with these options, the Python language is going to provide us with a lot of power to handle most of the coding that we want to do, while still being easy to read and learn, and can work with all of the operating systems that you would like. There are a ton of benefits out there when it comes to why you would want to choose to work with this language rather than some of the other options out there and these will include:

- *Lots of support libraries:* It won't take long researching through Python before you see that there is a ton of libraries and extensions that you can use with it. This provides you with a lot of help when you first get started and can make things so much easier in the long run. You will be able to find a ton of functions, objects, classes, and more inside this language to help you create your codes. You can also choose to add in some of the third party libraries to the mix if you would like to get some extra power, or if there is something in particular that you want to be able to do with your code that the current library can't help with.

- *Integration features:* Python can be great because it integrates what is known as the Enterprise Application Integration. This really helps with a lot of the different things you want to work on in Python including COBRA, COM, and more. It also has some powerful control capabilities as it calls directly through Java, C++, and C. Python also has the ability to process XML and other markup languages because it can run all of the modern operating systems, including Windows, Mac OS X, and Linux through the same kind of byte code.

- *More productivity for the programmer:* The Python language has a lot of designs that are object-oriented and a lot of support libraries. Because of all these resources and how easy it is to use the program; the programmer is going to increase their productivity. This can even be used to help improve the productivity of the programmer while using languages like C#, C++, C, Perl, VB, and even Java.

- *The Python code is going to be easy for you to learn:* Python was originally developed so that it was easy to adapt and easy to use. This is good for the beginner because it translates into this language being easy for everyone to learn. This guidebook is going to take the Python language to the next level and look at some of the more advanced features that you are able to enjoy with this kind of language, but when you look at some of the codes, even some of these that are more advanced than what you may have worked with in the past, you will find that it is easy to write some codes that have a lot of power, and even easy to complete your own projects.

- *The Python language is easier to read:* If you take a look through some of the codes that we have later on in this guidebook, you will find that this is an easy task to read through some of the different parts of the code. Even if you have not been able to work with this language before, you will still be able to look at some of the codes and notice that you recognize the parts as well.

- *The language comes with a large community that you are able to work with.* Python is considered one of the most popular coding languages to work with throughout the world. The fact that it has all of the benefits above, and that this is going to be easy to work with means that people around the world are coding with Python. This provides you with a lot of opportunities to learn about this kind of coding language and what it is able to do for you. You can watch tutorials, look for others to answer your questions, and more. For someone who is just starting out with coding, this is going to be welcome news.

- *The program is open source.* This means that you won't have to worry about someone taking over the code and ruining it. It also means that the original Python is free and available to anyone who wants to download it. Of course, there are some parties that have taken parts of Python and developed them to meet certain specifications and then try to sell them. But you can always just work with the basics of the Python code without having to purchase anything else to get the program and its components to work.

As we can see through this section, there are a ton of benefits that we are going to be able to see when it is time to work with the

Python programming language. There are a ton of parts that come together to make sure that this is one of the best languages, at least the best general-purpose languages, and will ensure that you are able to get the best results out of the process possible. When you are ready to handle some things like machine learning and data analysis, you will find that the Python language is going to be able to get all of it done for you.

Chapter 2: Installing Python On Your Computer

Now that we know some of the basics that come with the Python language, it is time for us to take this to the next level and start learning how we are able to install the Python language on your own computer. You are not able to start any of the coding that you would like if the Python language is not even found on your system at the time. You instead need to make sure that you are able to go through and work with this language on any computer or any operating system that you would like.

The good news is that Python is really versatile, and it is going to work on all three of the major operating systems that you would like to focus on, no matter which one is your preference. And the steps that are needed to make this happen is simple enough to learn. This chapter is going to take some time to look at the steps that you need to take in order to install the Python language on any operating system that you would like.

How to Install Python on a Mac Computer

The first place we are going to explore when it is time to handle the Python installation is on a Mac computer. If you are working with a computer that has the Mac operating system on it, you will be happy to find out that there is already some version of Python 2 on it and ready to use. These versions are going to vary based on how old the operating system is on your computer, but you will be able to check out the one that is there with the following prompt on your terminal app of the computer:

Python – V

This is going to be a useful thing to learn how to do because it allows you to see the Python version number show up. You are also able to take this a bit further and install Python 3 on this system if you want to work with a newer version of Python. Most of the codes that you will find online, and in this guidebook, are going to rely on Python 3 and higher, so it is usually a good idea to change it up and make sure that this version is found on your computer. To check whether Python 3 is found on your Mac computer or not, you can open up that terminal app again and then type in the command below:

Python3 – V

The default on OS X is that Python 3 is not going to be installed at all. If you want to use Python 3, you can install it using some of the installers that are on Python.org. This is a good place to go because it will install everything that you need to write and execute your codes with Python. It will have the Python shell, the IDLE development tools, and the interpreter. Unlike what happens with Python 2.X, these tools are installed as a standard application in the Applications folder.

Being able to run the IDLE and the Python shell is going to be dependent on which version you choose and some of your own personal preferences. You can use the following commands to help you start the shell and IDLE applications:

- For Python 2.X just type in "Idle"
- For Python 3.X, just type in "idle3"

As we mentioned before, when you download and install Python 3, you are going to install IDLE as a standard application in the Applications folder. In order to start this program from your desktop, you simply need to open up that folder and then double click on the IDLE application.

Installing Python On a Windows Computer

The next operating system that we need to spend our time here is going to be the Windows operating system. This is one that a lot of people like to work with already and it is going to be easy to use when you would like to handle the Python language along the way. Python is able to work well with Windows, but some of the steps that you have to take to install it are going to be more in-depth then what you will find with the Mac computer.

The reason for this is that Windows has developed its own coding language, and this is going to be the default that is found on a computer that has this kind of operating system on it. This doesn't mean that you can't go through and work with the Python language though. It simply means that there are a few more steps that you need to add in to make sure that it is going to work for your needs. With this in mind, some of the steps that you need to work with when it is time to download Python on your Windows operating system and Windows computer includes:

1. To get started, we need to go through and visit the official Python download page at www.python.org, and then grab the installer that you want to work with for your version of Windows. It is usually best to go with the latest version of Python and the default of this is going to be the 32-bit version. There is also a 64-bit version so you can decide which one of these you would like to work with.

2. When you click on the installer, you will have to select that you would like to run this as the administrator. There will then be two main options that show up for you to choose from. Our choice is going to be to do the Customize Installation.

3. On the following screen that comes up after you click on this, you need to make sure that each of the boxes under “Optional Features” is clicked, and then click that it is time to move on.

4. Then you are going to end up under the Advanced Options. While we are there, you will need to pick out the location where you would like Python and all of its folders to be installed. When you are in the right location, you can then click on Install. This will take a few minutes to finish so give it some time. When it is all done, you will be able to close the installers.

5. Next, it is time for us to set up the PATH variable that we want to work within this system. This is going to include all of the directories that you would like to have in the packages, as well as all of the components that come with Python and will be useful later on. To make this work for

your needs, we need to go through the instructions that are below:

a. Open up the Control Panel. Do this by clicking on the taskbar and typing in Control Panel. Click on the icon.

b. Inside the Control Panel, search for Environment. Then click on Edit the System Environment Variables. From here, you can click on the button for Environment Variables.

c. Go to the section for User Variables. You can either edit the PATH variable that is there, or you can create one.

d. If there isn't a variable for PATH on the system, then create one by clicking on New. Make the name for the PATH variable and add it to the directories that you want. Click on close all the control Panel dialogs and move on.

6. The final step that we need to take a look at is to open up the command prompt. You are able to do this by clicking on the Start Menu that comes with Windows, then click on Windows System, and then on the Command Prompt as well. Type in "python" at this time. This is going to help us open up the interpreter of Python and will get it all to work.

When we are done with all of the steps that are above, the program should be set up and ready to go on the Windows system. You can then choose to open up the parts of the language that you would like to use, and you can start getting some practice with all of the coding and the features that come with Python as well.

How to Install Python On a Linux System

Now that we have had some time to look at how to install the Python language on a few other options like the Mac operating system and Windows operating system, it is time to take a look at the steps that we want to use when it is time to install this language on your Linux system. There are a lot of programmers, especially those who would like to get into things like ethical hacking and more advanced types of coding, who are interested in learning how to work with Python on this operating system as well.

The Linux system may not be as well-known and as widely used as we see with the other two systems, but there are still a lot of situations where you will want to work with this kind of language for some of your own needs as well. This is why we need to take a look at some of the steps that are needed to make sure that we can get the Python files uploaded and working well on this language. Some of the steps that you need to use to make all of this happen includes:

The first thing to do here is to see if there is a version of Python 3 already on your system. You can open up the command prompt on Linux and then run the following code:

```
$ python3 - - version
```

If you are on Ubuntu 16.10 or newer, then it is a simple process to install Python 3.6. you just need to use the following commands:

```
$ sudo apt-get update
$ sudo apt-get install Python3.6
```

If you are relying on an older version of Ubuntu or another version, then you may want to work with the deadsnakes PPA, or another tool, to help you download the Python 3.6 version. The code that you need to do this includes:

```
$ sudo apt-get install software-properties-common
$ sudo add-apt repository ppa:deadsnakes/ppa
# sudo apt-get update
$ sudo apt-get install python3.6
```

The good news that comes with this one is that if you have worked with some of the other distributions that come with Linux on that computer, then it is likely that one of the versions of Python 3 is already going to be installed on that system. However, it is pretty easy to go through and install the Python program on your computer without a lot of effort either, so you can always go through this process and do some of the work as well when you want.

As we can see here, working with Python and getting it installed on all of the operating systems that you would like is going to be really important when it is time to handle some of the work that you want to do with it later on. No matter what kind of operating system you like to use, whether you like the Linux, the Windows, or the Mac operating system, Python is one of the best options that you are able to work with. Make sure to check out the steps that are above to ensure that you are able to get it all set up so that you can start some of the programming that you would like to do with the Python language.

Chapter 3: How to Install Homebrew

While we are looking at some of the basics that are needed to handle this Python language and the steps that we need to follow in order to do an installation of Python on any operating system, we also need to take a moment to look at how to install the Homebrew browser on our computers as well. This is going to take a look at how we are able to download and install this program. Some of the steps that we need to use to make all of this happen for our own needs will include:

Downloading and Configuring This Browser

The first thing that we need to focus on doing when it comes to handling this process is to download the installation folder for this browser. To do this, we need to visit the website http://wiibrew.org/wiki/Homebrew_Browser on the web browser of the computer that you are using. You can then click on the link for Download that is under the heading of "Links" on the right side of the page. You can then find the zip folder for this browser is downloaded. Depending on the settings that you have with your own particular browser, it is likely that you are going to get prompted to pick out the same location so that you can find the file later on.

When that step is done, we want to take a moment to extract the downloaded file that we just worked on. There are going to be some different steps that we need to follow here depending on whether we are using a computer with the Mac operating system, or a computer that has the Windows operating system. The steps that you need to use to make this happen will be the following:

1. Windows: If you are using a Windows computer, you can double-click on the zip folder. Then click on the Extract tab at the top of the window. You can then click on Extract All and then click on that same thing again in the pop-up window that shows up on the computer.

2. Mac: If you are working with a Mac computer, the process is going to be a bit different. For this one, you can double click on that zip folder, and then give it a bit so that the extracted folder is able to open up for you.

From here we want to copy the folder that says "homebrew_browser". To do this, you can click once on that folder in the extracted folder to select it and then click either Ctrl + C for a Windows computer or Command + C for a Mac computer in order to copy that folder over.

We are then going to work with an SD card. You can use this to place it into another computer or work to add this to another device depending on what you would like to use. Many gamers like to install this browser onto a gaming console, like the Wii, and this process can definitely help make this happen if you are using an SD card on that device.

When we have the SD card that we want to work with, we need to then go through and plug it into our computer. You want to make sure that the SD card is fitting into the computer with the gold connector side down into the card slot for the SD. If your computer does not have this slot, then you will need to go through another step. You will need to go out and borrow or purchase an SD to USB adapter that is able to fit into the computer. If you are working with a Mac and this does not fit in, then you may need to work with an SD to USB-C adapter to make it all work.

From here, we want to open up the SD card. If the window doesn't open up automatically for you, there are a few steps that you can do, depending on the operating system that you would like to focus on. These will include:

1. For a Windows computer, you can open up the File Explorer, and then click on This PC. You can then double click on the name for the SD card that shows up below the heading of Devices and Drives

2. The work for the Mac computer is going to be a bit different. in this one, we need to open up Finder, then click on the card name for the SD. This name should show up in the lower-left side of the window that you are working with at the time.

Then we need to spend some time opening up the apps folder. This is where you are going to click on the apps folder that is on the SD card. If you do not see that there is an apps folder there,

there are a few steps that we are able to do to make this happen. Again, the steps are going to be a bit different based on whether you are working with a Windows computer or a Mac computer. The steps that we can use in order to create one of these apps folders on this card include:

1. On a Windows computer, we need to find some empty white space on the SD card and right-click on it. Then select New and click on Folder. Type in apps, and then press in entering to make it finish.

2. On a Mac computer, we can click on File, then on New Folder. Again, we can type in the word apps and then press on Return.

Now that we have that apps folder in place, it is time for us to go through and paste the folder that is on your computer so that it is then available to go on the card. We will press down on either Ctrl + V or Command + V to make this happen and to ensure that the Homebrew folder that we created earlier is going to end up on the apps folder, no matter which option we went with above.

When you see that this folder is found on the SD card, you will want to open it up. This simply requires you to double click on that particular folder to get it opened. From here, we want to open up our settings file. You will be able to use the default text editor that comes with your computer in order to make this happen. The steps that we are able to use to make all of this happen for our needs will include the following:

1. On the Windows computer, we need to first click the right button on the settings file. Then select from the drop-

down menu the Open with and click on Notepad. This is going to be the default text editor that we want to use here.

2. For a Mac computer, we want to click just once on our settings file, and then click on File. Then we can select on Open With and click on the TextEdit.

This is where we are going to want to change up the settings file's server value. Due to some of the updates that are done on the software of Wii and other systems, we need to take the time to change the server value from 0 to 1, but doing some of the following:

1. Find the setting_server_"0" line of text.

2. We can then go to this line and replace the 0 that is there with a 1.

3. Make sure that the update has happened and then press on Ctrl + S in Windows or Command + S on Mac to make sure that this file is saved.

4. Then we can close out of the TextEdit or the Notepad when we are done.

We can then eject and remove the SD card from the computer. You will need to use the proper method outlined by the computer that you are working with at the time. this is going to make sure that the process is done in the proper manner, and that the card is ready to use whenever you would like.

You can definitely choose to work with the Homebrew browser on any computer that you would like, and it is just fine if you would like to just do some of the beginning steps that we talked about before and then use it on your own computer. But with some of the steps that we talked about in this chapter, you will be able to take that information and use it on any system that you want. It is all downloaded and ready to go on the SD card, so you can then take it and make sure that it works on any other system that you would like to focus on as well.

Chapter 4: The Importance of Data Types and Variables

Now it is time for us to take a moment to look at some of the work that can be done with the data types and the variables that come with the Python language. Both of these are going to be important and will tell us a lot when it is time to work with the Python language as well. We are not going to get very far in some of the programming that we want to do if we aren't able to learn some of the different types of data that are out there, and we aren't able to have a good understanding of how the variables work as well. Let's take a look at some of the different types of data that come with Python, and how these variables work, so we are able to put it all together and see some great results in the process.

The Python Data Types

The first thing that we need to focus on here is the data types that come with Python. Each of the values that we are going to work within Python is going to have a datatype. Since everything in this programming language is going to be an object, the types of data are actually going to be classes, and then the variables are going to be instances, or objects, of these classes. This is how all of the work is going to be tied in together.

Now, you will find that there are various types of data that can show up in Python. Some of the ones that are the most important ones, and the ones that you are likely going to spend the majority of your time on in Python will be discussed below:

First on the list is the Python numbers. These are going to include floating-point numbers, complex numbers, and integers. These are going to be brought out with the help of the function of type(), which can help us to know which class a variable or our value is going to belong to. This helps us to make sure that we are able to pull out the numbers that we would like in this coding language.

We can also send out the Python list. This list is going to simply be an ordered sequence of items that we can work with. It is going to actually be the type of data that we are able to work within Python that is used the most, and it is very flexible. All of the items that are on the list do not need to end up being the same type of data either. In addition, the lists are going to be mutable, which simply means that the elements that are on the list can be altered in any way that you want.

The Python tuple is also going to be important. The tuple is going to be an ordered sequence of items just the same as we see with the list. The biggest difference that you are going to see with these tuples is that they are immutable. Once you create one of these tuples, you are not able to make modifications to them. Tuples are going to be there to help us write-protect the data, and are usually going to perform faster than a list because it is not going to change dynamically at all.

The Python string is the next thing that we are able to focus some attention on. The string is basically going to be a sequence of Unicode characters. We are going to have the option of working with either a single quote or a double quote to help represent strings. You can also work with some multi-line strings.

The Python set is going to be another type of data that we are able to work with and it is basically a collection of items that are unique and will not be ordered. The set is going to be defined by values that are separated by a comma, and then these items are going to be inside of braces. Items in a set are not going to be ordered at all.

And finally, we are going to take a look at the Python dictionary. The dictionary is basically going to be an unordered collection of key-value pairs. This is the one that is generally going to be used when we have to handle a very large amount of data. Dictionaries are going to be optimized to help us retrieve the data we want. We also have to make sure that we know the key before the data is going to be available. With the Python language, we are going to be able to define these dictionaries within braces, with each item being a pair in the form of key: value. You are able to have the key and the value of any type that you would like.

The Python Variables

The next topic that we need to spend some time on in this guidebook is going to be the variables. Their variables are basically anything that is able to hold onto a value or one of the data types that we talked about from before, that is able to change. Often we are able to think about these variables as a box that is able to hold onto the values that we are using in Python. These are important for us to focus on because they will save some space on our memory, and then allow us to pull that variable back out at a later time.

These variables are something that all programmers need to learn about because they will basically be saved spaces in the memory of the computer, and then you are able to tell the computer that it is time to pull them out at any time when you are ready. The variables that you take the time to create are going to be found in certain locations in the memory of the system you are using, and then they can be found and executed when the code is running. Depending on the type of data that you would like to focus on, the variable is going to be the part that will tell the compiler where to save that information to make it available when needed.

One of the most important things that we need to focus on when it comes to working with these variables is making sure that we assign a value to it. If you do not assign one or more values to your variable, you are going to end up saving some empty space on your memory and nothing is going to come up in the code when you pull it up. If the variable has some kind of value that has been assigned back to it, and sometimes it will have more than one value on it, then it is going to react in the manner that you would like in this code.

Any time that we are working on some of these variables, you will find that there are basically three main options that you are able to choose from for it. Each of these is going to be useful, and it is often going to depend on the codes you are trying to write, and the type of value that you are sending over to the variable. The options that you are able to pick from include:

- Float: this would include numbers like 3.14 and so on.
- String: this is going to be like a statement where you could write out something like "Thank you for visiting my page!" or another similar phrase.
- Whole number: this would be any of the other numbers that you would use that do not have a decimal point.

When you are working with variables in your code, you need to remember that you don't need to take the time to make a declaration to save up this spot in the memory. This is automatically going to happen once you assign a value over to the variable using the equal sign. If you want to check that this is going to happen, just look to see that you added that equal sign in, and everything is going to work.

Assigning a value over to your variable is pretty easy. Some examples of how you can do this in your code would include the following:

x = 12 #this is an example of an integer assignment
pi = 3.14 #this is an example of a floating-point assignment
customer name = John Doe #this is an example of a string assignment

Another option that you can do here, and that we have mentioned a little bit in this chapter already, has a variable assigned to two or more values. There are some instances when you are writing code and you will need to take two values and place them with the same variable.

To make sure that you are able to go through this, we simply need to work with some of the same procedures that we talked about through this section. We just need to make sure that we are putting in the equal signs in the right spots so that the compiler knows which values are going to the variable. So, you could write out something like a = b = c = 1 to show the compiler how each of these variables is going to equal 1. Or you could write out something like 1 = b = 2 to show that this variable is going to have two values assigned to it.

One of the most important things that we are able to focus on here is that the variable has to be assigned over to a value in order to work the way that we want in the code, and that these variables are basically just an empty spot in the memory that is reserved for the value that you decide to assign to the variable. Then, when it is time for the compiler to call up some of these values, it is going to be able to call up the variable, and all of it is going to show up the way that you want.

There are many times when you will need to work with these variables in your code, and they are often going to be assigned with some of the types of data that we were talking about earlier in this chapter. When we are able to make all of these parts fit in with one another, we will find that it is so much easier for us to get the results that we would like in the process. Make sure to learn about these variables, and how to properly set it up with the right value in order to get the code to work the way that you would like.

Chapter 5: How to Create a Class

The next step that we need to take a look at is the idea of the classes that are found in the Python language. Classes and objects are very important when it is time to write some of the coding that you have with Python because they are going to make sure that everything stays organized and that each object is going to stay right where it should for the execution of the code. The objects are going to be there to help us define parts of the code so that they are easier to understand, and then the classes will also be important because they help to store all of those objects.

The idea of classes and objects is a really important one when it comes to working with the Python language, and knowing what these mean, and how they work will ensure that our codes behave the way that they should. Let's take a look at how we can work on creating these classes and how we can make them work well within our Python code:

Creating Our Own Classes

When we are working with Python, we are going to find that we will need to create some of these classes for our own codes because this helps us to make sure that the codes we have are organized and that the objects and other parts of the code will not get lost. To make one of these classes though, we need to make sure that we are relying on some of the right keywords to help us name the class. You get the benefit of naming the class anything that you wish, but we have to make sure that the name shows up right after the keyword, and that it is a name that you are able to recall and use later on.

After naming the class, it is time to name a subclass, which will be placed inside parenthesis to stick with proper programming rules. Make sure that at the end of that first line, whenever you create a class, that you add in a semicolon. While this isn't technically needed with most newer versions of Python and the code is going to work even if you forget this part, it is still considered part of coding etiquette to do this so make sure that you put it in.

Writing a class sounds more complicated than it really is, so let's stop here and look at an example of how you would write this out in Python. Then we can discuss what the parts mean and why they are important. A good example of creating a class with Python includes the following:

```
class Vehicle(object):
#constructor
def_init_(self, steering, wheels, clutch, breaks, gears):
self._steering = steering
self._wheels = wheels
self._clutch = clutch
self._breaks =breaks
self._gears  = gears
#destructor
```

```
def_del_(self):
    print("This is destructor....")

#member functions or methods
def Display_Vehicle(self):
   print('Steering:' , self._steering)
   print('Wheels:', self._wheels)
   print('Clutch:', self._clutch)
   print('Breaks:', self._breaks)
   print('Gears:', self._gears)
#instantiate a vehicle option
myGenericVehicle = Vehicle('Power Steering', 4, 'Super Clutch',
'Disk Breaks', 5)

myGenericVehicle.Display_Vehicle()
```

It is a good idea to take a moment here and try out the code. To do this, just open up the text editor that is available and type in the code that we just listed out. As you are typing out this code, you may notice that a few of the other topics and basics that we have discussed in this guidebook are already showing up. But we do need to take a moment to divide this up a bit and see exactly what we were doing through that code as well.

Class Definition

The first part of the code that we need to take a look at is the class definition. This is the part where we are going to work to instantiate the object, and then it will provide us with the definition that we need of the class. This will ensure that we can stick with the right syntax of the code.

When you are working with this one, make sure to pay special attention here because it is the one that is responsible for telling the compiler what you would like to see happen, and it will highlight some of the commands that it sees as the most important. It is also possible to bring out a brand new definition of the class in your chosen code. To do this, you can work with the functions of object_method and object_attribute to help

Special Attributes

In addition to working with the class definition and making sure that it is set up the way that you would like, we also need to look at some of the special attributes that are important to your code. These are the special attributes that will provide all programmers, new and more advanced, with some peace of mind because they can ensure that their code is going well and that when these attributes are used in the manner that they should, that nothing is going to get messed up.

You will find that there are going to be a few of these attributes found in the codes that you can write, and there are even a few options in the code above. However, there are going to be some other special attributes that show up in the code as well, and these will include:

__bases__: this is considered a tuple that contains any of the superclasses
__module__: this is where you are going to find the name of the module and it will also hold your classes.
__name__: this will hold on to the class name.
__doc__: this is where you are going to find the reference string inside the document for your class.
__dict__: this is going to be the variable for the dict. Inside the class name.

How to Access Members of the Class

Now that we know a bit more about some of the parts of the code that we had above, it is time for us to move on to another thing that we are able to do when it comes to working with classes and objects in the Python language. In this part, we need to explore how we can access the members that are in any class that we create. You want to make sure that the compiler, as well as the text editor that you are working with, are able to properly recognize any of the classes that you work with.

This is so important because it will ensure that your code is going to execute in the proper manner. There are a few methods that we can use with this one to help us make sure that the code is going to execute properly, but we are going to focus on how to work with the accessor method. The accessor method is the one that you will see the most often, and it is the most efficient, making it easier to work with overall.

To make the process and the steps of accessing the members in a created class a little bit better, we are going to take a moment to look through the following code to see how it will work:

```
class Cat(object)
        itsAge = None
        itsWeight = None
        itsName = None
        #set accessor function use to assign values to the fields or
member vars
        def setItsAge(self, itsAge):
        self.itsAge = itsAge

        def setItsWeight(self, itsWeight):
        self.itsWeight = itsWeight
```

```
def setItsName(self, itsName):
self.itsName =itsName

#get accessor function use to return the values from a
field
def getItsAge(self):
return self.itsAge
def getItsWeight(self):
return self.itsWeight

def getItsName(self):
return self.itsName

objFrisky = Cat()
objFrisky.setItsAge(5)
objFrisky.setItsWeight(10)
objFrisky.setItsName("Frisky")
print("Cats Name is:", objFrisky.getItsname())
print("Its age is:", objFrisky.getItsAge())
print("Its weight is:", objFrisky.getItsName())
```

Before we move on, type this into your compiler. If you have your compiler run this, you are going to get some results that show up on the screen right away. This will include that the cat's name is Frisky (or you can change the name to something else if you want), that the age is 5 and that the weight is 10. This is the information that was put into the code, so the compiler is going to pull them up to give you the results that you want. You can take some time to add different options into the code and see how it changes over time.

There are many times when you will want to work with classes inside of some of the codes that you are trying to write in Python. Being able to work with these classes, and make sure that they work the way that you want is going to be a critical part of getting your codes to function properly as well.

You do have some freedom with this one because you are able to create any of the classes that you would like, and you get the benefit of adding in any kind of object that you would like as well. It is just important that the class holds onto objects that make the most sense, rather than a bunch of random objects that should not go with one another. If we are able to do that and use some of the codes that we listed out earlier in this chapter, you will be able to create your own classes in no time.

Chapter 6: Working with an Inheritance and Why These are Important

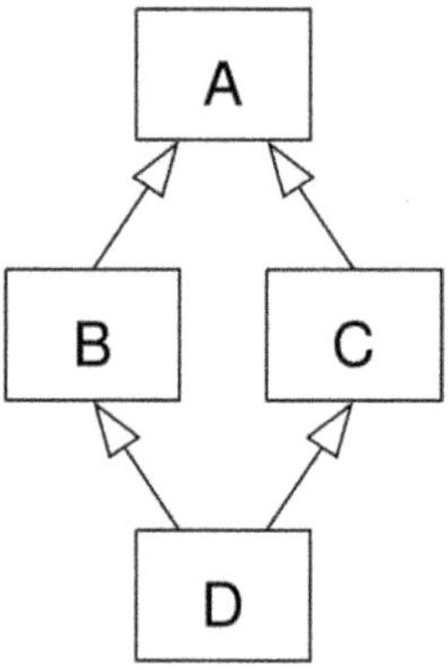

Another topic that we are able to spend some time on is the idea of inheritance when you create some of your codes. These inheritances are nice because they are going to work at making the code look a bit cleaner and more organized in the long run. These inheritances are going to help us to reuse parts of the previous code we have already written, without having to actually go through and rewrite it again. This can help save time and makes the code look more organized than before. Inheritances are a unique part of the OOP languages, like what we see with Python, and it is definitely worth your time to learn how to work with them.

Basically, when we decide to add in one of these inheritances to our code, we are able to take some of the original code, or the parent code, and then we will change up some of the parts that come with it, before reusing that as the derived code. You can use it to help add in some strength to the codes you are writing, or you can find another purpose of reusing the code as well. Even as someone who is just getting started with the world of Python and all that it can offer, you are able to use the idea of these inheritances to help you work with the code over and over again, without having to spend the time and energy to rewrite the code each time that we need it.

During the inheritance, you take your original parent code and copy it over to another part of the program. This becomes the child code, one that you can make changes to as you wish, without it affecting the original parent code at all. Sometimes you just need to copy it down once, and other times you will need to do it many times, but the process is the same.

To help make more sense out of these inheritances, how they work, and how they can help to keep your code clean and tidy and save you time, let's take a look at an example of how they look in your code:

```
#Example of inheritance
#base class
class Student(object):
        def__init__(self, name, rollno):
        self.name = name
        self.rollno = rollno
#Graduate class inherits or derived from Student class
class GraduateStudent(Student):
        def__init__(self, name, rollno, graduate):
        Student__init__(self, name, rollno)
        self.graduate = graduate

def DisplayGraduateStudent(self):
```

```
        print"Student Name:", self.name)
        print("Student Rollno:", self.rollno)
        print("Study Group:", self.graduate)

#Post Graduate class inherits from Student class
class PostGraduate(Student):
        def__init__(self, name, rollno, postgrad):
        Student__init__(self, name, rollno)
        self.postgrad = postgrad

        def DisplayPostGraduateStudent(self):
        print("Student Name:", self.name)
        print("Student Rollno:", self.rollno)
        print("Study Group:", self.postgrad)

#instantiate from Graduate and PostGraduate classes
        objGradStudent = GraduateStudent("Mainu", 1, "MS-
Mathematics")
        objPostGradStudent = PostGraduate("Shainu", 2, "MS-
CS")
        objPostGradStudent.DisplayPostGraduateStudent()
```

When you type this into your interpreter, you are going to get the results:

```
('Student Name:', 'Mainu')
('Student Rollno:', 1)
('Student Group:', 'MSC-Mathematics')
('Student Name:', 'Shainu')
('Student Rollno:', 2)
('Student Group:', 'MSC-CS')
```

Override the Base Class

Now that we have had some time to take a look at an example of how this inheritance is supposed to work, it is time to understand a bit more about why we would want to override one of our base classes, which can also be known in this case as the parent class. There will be times in coding when we are working with one of our new derived classes and we may find that it is best to not use the base class completely but instead change it up a bit to work with what we want.

To keep it all as simple in this process as possible, this means that you will take a look at what we are able to find inside of the base class, and then we will move it down to be a derived class before we make some changes. We will keep some parts and get rid of the other parts based on what we think we are able to do with that class. The child class is then going to be able to use some of that new behavior to complete the job it is doing.

This may sound a little bit complicated to get started with but you will find that it is nice because you will be able to choose and then pick out which of the parental features from that first part of the code that you would like to have shown up in the derived class. You can take the stuff away, keep it there and move things around the way that you would like in this derived class. This whole process is going to make it so much easier for you to end up with some changes to your new class, while also keeping some of the parts of the parent or the base class that you think is important to your needs.

Now, the number of times that you would like to go through this process and do some of these steps, and how much you would like to override in the long run is going to depend on what you are looking to make the code do in the first place it can be as simple as some of the steps that are above in the code, or you can add in some more steps and make things a bit more complex. It all depends on what you would like to see happen in your code. However, no matter how you plan to use the inheritance, you will find that it can help you to write some stronger codes without having to worry about all of the clutter as much.

There are many times when we will want to rely on these inheritances to help us get things done. They speed up the process that is needed to handle parts of your code. They will help you to reuse some of the older codes that are in your program so you don't have to rewrite parts of the code again. And they are one of the best ways for your program to look nice and basically is a great way to keep the code going and speeding up the coding process.

Chapter 7: Raising Your Own Exceptions

Another topic that we need to spend some time on in this guidebook is how to raise and handle exceptions. As you are working with some of the codes in Python, you may find that you run into times when the compiler is going to raise up an exception for you, or maybe you would like to create one of these exceptions in that particular program. Sometimes these exceptions are going to be seen as a more complicated piece of coding, but there are a lot of times when we are going to use them, so learning the basics, how to handle them when they show up, and even how to raise some of your own can be so important.

Now, you will find that these exceptions can be raised in a lot of different scenarios, and sometimes they are going to look like an error message that you may have seen on projects in the past. Make sure that you really read through some of the errors that show up so that you can handle them and make sure to get them fixed. These are not scary things that should make you nervous.

It is just important to learn what they mean and start handling them in the proper manner along the way.

You will notice pretty quickly that there are already a few different types of exceptions that will be found naturally in the Python library. If you try to write a code that has these things in them, or the user tries to do something that is not allowed by the compiler or the Python library, then these are automatically going to show you an exception. In some other instances, you may find that the program you are writing is going to need an extra exception, and you will choose to raise one for your own.

For example, one of the exceptions that you are going to find that is automatically in the library is when the user tries to divide by zero. The compiler that you are using is going to already recognize that this is something that can't be done, and they will raise up an alert when it sees that this exception is there. in addition, if you try to call up one of the functions and you do not spell the name well, then the exception is going to show up as well.

As we mentioned, there are going to be quite a few different exceptions that are going to show up automatically with the Python library. It is a good idea for us to really look through these and learn when to recognize them as well. Some of the most common types of exceptions that we are able to focus on in this language will include:

- Finally—this is the action that you will want to use to perform cleanup actions, whether the exceptions occur or not.

- Assert—this condition is going to trigger the exception inside of the code.
- Raise—the raise command is going to trigger an exception manually inside of the code.
- Try/except—this is when you want to try out a block of code and then it is recovered thanks to the exceptions that either you or the Python code raised.

Raising an Exception

Now that we have a pretty good idea of what the exception is going to be all about, and how we are able to use these, it is then time for us to learn how to write out one of these exceptions on our own. This will also help us to figure out what we should do if one of the exceptions shows up in our own code. If you are writing your own code and you notice ahead of time that a particular issue is going to show up in the code, then you know that the compiler is going to raise this exception as well.

The good news here is that in most cases, the exception is going to be something simple to work with, something that you will be able to figure out quickly and learn how to fix in no time at all. But there are some instances where these are going to be more complicated to work with, and you may need to mess with the code a bit to make it work. One example that we can look at when it is time to raise one of these exceptions in Python includes:

```
x = 10
y = 10
result = x/y #trying to divide by zero
print(result)
```

The output that you are going to get when you try to get the interpreter to go through this code would be:

```
>>>
Traceback (most recent call last):
        File "D: \Python34\tt.py", line 3, in <module>
        result = x/y
ZeroDivisionError: division by zero
>>>
```

Taking a look at this example, the program is going to bring up an exception because you are trying to divide a number by zero, and the Python code is not going to allow you to do this. If you keep it the way that it is, and try to run the program, you may end up with an error message at this point. The code will tell the user the problem, but it's not likely the user will have any idea what the problem is about. You can make some changes in these exceptions and put in the message that works best for the situation.

With the example that we did above, you will find that it is often better if you are able to add in some kind of message that will tell the user why that exception was raised in the first place. This message is going to make it easier for the user to figure out what went wrong and will look a lot nicer than working with a messy string of numbers and letters that the user likely has no idea what they mean. A good example of how we are able to take some of the coding that we did above and change it into something that is easier to read through and understand will include the following:

```
x = 10
y = 0
```

```
result = 0
try:
        result = x/y
        print(result)
except ZeroDivisionError:
        print("You are trying to divide by zero.")
```

Take a look at the two codes above. The one that we just did looks a little bit similar to the one above it, but this one has a message inside. This message is going to show up when the user raises this particular exception. You won't get the string of letters and numbers that don't make sense, and with this one, the user will know exactly what has gone wrong and can fix that error.

How to Define Your Own Exceptions

In the previous section, we spent some of our time taking a closer look at some of the exceptions that are already found in the Python library, and how we are able to handle these. But there are sometimes when you may want to take these a little bit further, and you would like to raise some of your own that are specific to the code you are writing.

For example, if you are working on a code that is only going to allow your user a certain number of chances to make a guess, or to only guess a certain number overall, then you would want to raise up an exception during this. This is going to be a good option to use in things like games that you are creating. You would be able to set it up to only allow the user to have three guesses at the game, or only give them so many chances to guess right.

With these kinds of exceptions that we are going to look at raising, the compiler is not going to really recognize that something is wrong with the number of guesses that the user gives, or the numbers that they provide us. Technically the user should be able to guess as many times as they want in the code until they can get it right. But we are raising the exception to help keep the program going.

These exceptions are going to be ones that are just unique to your code, and without you adding these exceptions into the code, the compiler would not do what you would like. We get the freedom here to add in any type of exception that is needed to make our codes work properly, and you can even take the time to add in any message that you want, in a manner that is similar to what we did in the section above. The code that we will want to use to make all of this happen will look like the following:

```
class CustomException(Exception):
def_init_(self, value):
        self.parameter = value
def_str_(self):
        return repr(self.parameter)

try:
        raise CustomException("This is a CustomError!")
except CustomException as ex:
        print("Caught:", ex.parameter)
```

In this code, you have been successful in setting up your own exceptions and whenever the user raises one of these exceptions, the message of "Caught: This is a CustomError!" is going to come up on the screen. This is the best way to show your users that you have added in a customer exception into the program, especially if this is just one that you personally created for this part of the code, and not one that the compiler is going to recognize on its own.

Just like with the other examples that we went through, we worked with some generic wording just to show how exceptions are able to work. You can easily go through and change this up so that you get a message that is unique for the code that you are writing and will explain to the user what is going on when they get the error message to show up.

There are many times when you will be able to work with the idea of exception handling and it can help you to handle some of the more advanced coding options that you want to work with. Whether you want to handle the exceptions that are already found in the Python library, or you would like to create one that works just for your own program, then this chapter is going to be able to help you to get this done.

Chapter 8: Creating Loops in Python

Loops are going to be another great topic that we are able to work with when it comes to Python. Loops are a good way to clean up some of the code that you want to work with so that you can make sure that enough shows up in your code, without having to write out as many lines. For example, if you have a code that you would like to work with that lists out the numbers gong one from fifty, you do not want to actually write out that many lines of code in the process. You can work with these loops instead to make sure that it is able to write out the lines, but it is really just a short amount of code. These loops are then able to hold onto a ton of information and will only use a few lines of code to make it happen.

There are a lot of things and a ton of data that we are then able to add into the loop, but you will find that these are actually pretty easy for us to work with anyway. These loops are going to be there to tell the compiler that it needs to continue reading through one or two lines of code over and over again until the conditions that you add into it are met.

So, if you are working on a program where you ask the compiler to write out numbers that go from one to ten, then the loop will tell your compiler to read through the numbers going from one to ten, then the loop will be set to go through the same line of code until it reaches ten. This can simplify the code while making sure that you are still able to get the things done that you would like.

When you work with all of these loops, it is important to remember to set up so that you have the condition in place before you ever try to work on the program. If you just go through and write out your loop, without adding in the condition that is needed, then the loop will start, but it will not know when to stop. The loop will just keep going through itself and will freeze the computer. Double-check before you run the program that the condition is in place before starting.

As you go through and create some of your own code with Python, there is going to be a few different loop types that you are able to work with. There are actually going to be many options, but we need to focus on the three main ones known as the while loop, the for loop, and the nested loop.

The While Loop

The first type of loop that we are going to work on is the while loop. This loop is one that you can choose for your code when you know the specific number of times you want the code to cycle through that loop. You would use it to finish counting to ten for example. This one will need to have a condition, in the end, to make sure that it stops at the right point and doesn't keep going forever. It is also a good option if you want to ensure that your loop occurs at least one time before it moves on to the next part of the code. A good example of the while loop is the following code:

```
#calculation of simple interest. Ask the user to input the
principal, rate of interest, number of years.

counter = 1
while(counter <= 3):
        principal = int(input("Enter the principal amount:"))
        numberofyeras = int(input("Enter the number of
years:"))
        rateofinterest = float(input("Enter the rate of interest:"))
        simpleinterest = principal * numberofyears *
rateofinterest/100
        print("Simple interest = %.2f" %simpleinterest)
        #increase the counter by 1
        counter = counter + 1
        print("You have calculated simple interest for 3 time!")
```

With the example that we did above, you will find that the user is able to place in the information that makes the most sense for them and the program. The code is then going to give them the interest rate based on the information that the user provides to it. For this one, we are going to set up the while at the beginning of the code and then told it to only go through the loop a maximum of three times. You will then be able to change up the code as well to make sure that it will go through the loops as many times as you would like.

Working on the For Loop

The while loop can help us out with a lot of the different things that you want to accomplish when you are working on loops in this part of the code. In addition to handling some of the work with loops that the while loop can do, it is possible to work with them for a loop. When you are working with the for loops, you are working with the method that is considered the more traditional out of the two, and you can even make this the option that you use all of the time.

When you work with one of the for loops, your user will not go in and provide information to the code and then the loops start. Rather, with the for loop, Python is set up to go through an iteration in the order that it shows up on the screen. There is no need for input from the user because it just continues through the iteration until the end occurs. An example of a code that shows how a for loop works is the following:

```
# Measure some strings:
words = ['apple', 'mango', 'banana', 'orange']
for w in words:
print(w, len(w))
```

Write this code into your compiler and then execute it. The for loop is going to make sure that all the words in the line above it are shown up on the screen, exactly how you wrote them out. If you want them in a different order, you need to do that as you work on the code, not later on. You can add in any words or other information that you want to show up in this kind of loop, just make sure that you have it in the right order from the beginning.

The Nested Loop

We can also finish this out with a look at how the nested loop is going to work. This is a more advanced type of loop that is going to combine two of the other loop types together in order to get them to run at the same time. There are a number of instances where you can work with this nested loop, and it is often going to depend on the kind of code that you would like to complete and what you are hoping to get out of it.

The third type of loop that we are able to work with here is going to be known as the nested loop. Any time that you are working with this loop, you are basically going to take one of the other types of loops and then you will place it inside of a different loop. Both of these loops will end up running in the code at the same time, and they will both continue on until they are complete. There are a number of situations where you will want to focus on these nested loops to help you finish your code.

For example, you may find that you would like to work on a nested loop that can create a new multiplication table, the nested loop is going to be a good one to get it done. The code that we need to use in order to make this one work for our needs and to see how a nested loop is going to work will include:

```
#write a multiplication table from 1 to 10
For x in xrange(1, 11):
        For y in xrange(1, 11):
        Print '%d = %d' % (x, y, x*x)
```

When you got the output of this program, it is going to look similar to this:

```
1*1 = 1
1*2 = 2
```

1*3 = 3
1*4 = 4
All the way up to 1*10 = 2
Then it would move on to do the table by twos such as this:
2*1 =2
2*2 = 4

And so on until you end up with 10*10 = 100 as your final spot in the sequence

Any time you need to get one loop to run inside another loop, the nested loop will be able to help you get this done. You can combine together the for loop, the while loop, or each combination based on what you want to get done inside the code. But it definitely shows you how much time and space inside the code that these loops can save. The multiplication table above only took up four lines to write out and you got a huge table. Think of how long this would take if you had to write out each part of the table!

The for loop, the while loop, and the nested loop are going to be some of the most common loops that a beginner is able to focus on when it is time to write out their own codes in this language. You are able to use these codes to make sure that you can get a ton done in some of the programs that you have chosen, without having to focus as much on writing out a ton of lines. You are even able to do this in a manner that will make sure that certain parts of the code will read through themselves again, without you having to rewrite it at all. There are many times when you will want to handle writing loops in your code, and learning how to make each one work can help make your code stronger.

Chapter 9: What is Machine Learning

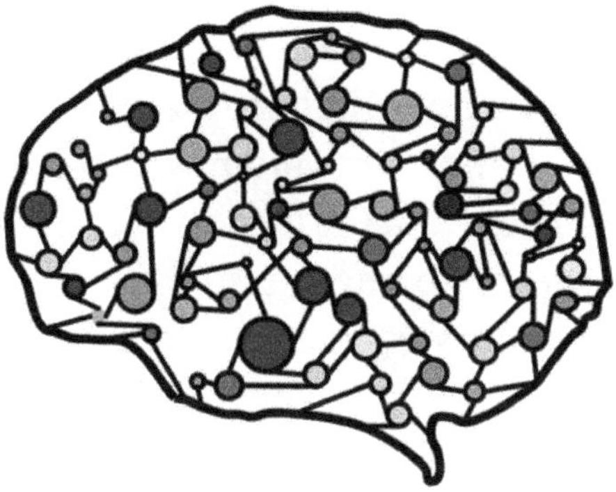

Now that we have some of the basics down that go with Python and we know how to handle some of the things that come with some of the more advanced features of Python, it is time for us to dig a bit more into some of the cool things that we are able to do with this language, and we are going to start out with machine learning. There is so much that we are able to do with machine learning when we want to really dig in, and that is why we are going to devote a whole chapter to what machine learning is, and what we can do with it when we add in some Python.

The first thing that we should spend some of our time here is the basics that come with machine learning. Machine learning is going to simply be a process that is able to automate the process of machine learning, and some of the analytical models that we need to build when we want to complete a data analysis process. We will look at data analysis in a bit, but you will find that machine learning is going to be one of the parts of artificial intelligence and it is going to be based on the idea that a system is able to take the data it has, and learn from it. This system, when it can learn in the proper manner, is able to use the data to help it make some decisions, and even find patterns in large sets of data. The best part about all of this is that this can happen without any intervention from the programmer.

In the beginning, researchers who were interested in some of the different parts of artificial intelligence wanted to get started by seeing if a computer or another system was able to learn from the data that we tried to present to it. The neat thing here is that machine learning is going to have an iterative aspect that will help it to learn. This is important because as the models are exposed to more and more data over time, they will be able to make the necessary adaptations along the way.

What happens with machine learning is that the model is trained to adapt and to learn as needed along the way. these models are going to learn from some of the computations that happened earlier and the hopes are that they are going to come up with some results and decisions that are repeatable and reliable. It is a science that may not be brand new, but it is gaining a lot of popularity as time goes on.

While a lot of the algorithms that are available for machine learning have been around for a number of years, the ability out there to automatically apply some big and complex calculations over to the big data that we want to use, and do this in a faster method each time that we do it, is something that is more recently developed. However, even though it is recent does not mean that a lot of companies have not taken the time to learn more about it and how it is able to work for their needs.

We are going to be able to find a ton of these machine learning examples everywhere that we go. And it is likely that as more time goes on, many businesses are going to hear more about data analysis, big data, and more, and will want to work with machine learning as well. There is just so much potential that is going to come with this machine learning, and it is important that we learn as much about it as possible along the way.

Why Is Machine Learning So Important?

One topic that we need to spend some time on here is the idea of why machine learning is going to be so important to our world today. There has been a lot of interest from companies in all sorts of industries when it comes to what machine learning is, and it is something that we definitely need to take a look at. Things like the growing amount and the growing types of data, and the idea that we are able to process both of these faster, for less money, and with more accuracy to learn something new out of the data have been big benefits of machine learning, and big reasons why companies want to use this as well.

All of these factors are going to come together and will show us that it is possible to quickly and automatically produce the algorithms and models, with the help of Python, that we need. Today, and in the future, we are going to find that these are the same models that we can use to help analyze the growing and more complex types of data that we are going to find later on, and still provide us with some of the results that we are looking for.

Mainly, many businesses are working with machine learning because they know it is one of the best ways to grow their business. And many of the algorithms that we are able to create when it comes to machine learning and Python working together will ensure that we are able to get some of the best results possible out of this as well. When those two pieces of technology can come together, we will find that it is easier than ever to find patterns and insights into the world of business that we can use in the future as well.

How Does Machine Learning Work?

With this in mind, we also need to take a look at how all of this machine learning is going to work for our needs. Working on algorithms and more with machine learning can seem like a really complex thing to handle, but you will see that a lot of the steps are going to seem easy. To help us get the most out of this process though, we need to make sure that we are not only picking out the right algorithms but that we also come up with the right tools and processes that will get the work done as well.

When you are able to combine together the good data that you have collected, the right tools and processes, and a bit of Python to help run the right algorithm that you want to work with, you will find that machine learning will be able to help your business out more than anything has been able to do in the past. And maybe that is a big reason why machine learning has become so important to so many businesses over time.

Medium and large businesses are able to use data analysis and machine learning to help them reach their customers and stay as successful as possible. But this doesn't mean that they want to sit around and wait forever in order to get that data set up and ready to go. This is why we need to make sure that the tools and processes are paired with the right algorithm are able to keep up with them, and that they will not have to wait around to see the results. This doesn't mean that machine learning is going to be an instant solution and that it doesn't take some time. but we need to make sure that it all fits together and that we are able to get some good results out of it without having to wait months or years to get it done.

So, the first thing that we need to have in order to get machine learning to do the work that we would like is the right algorithm. Most of these algorithms are going to run thanks to the Python coding language, which makes them one of the perfect ways to handle all of that data. But you will quickly find that when you are working with data analysis and all of the parts that need to come with this, you will find that there are a lot of different algorithms that we are able to pick from.

Keep in mind wit this one that there are a ton of algorithms that you are able to choose from, and the one that you choose for your needs is going to depend on the data that you have collected, the kind of questions that you want to ask along the way, and what you are hoping to find out when the process is done.

The variety of algorithms can be great though because it helps us to make sure that we are able to find the one that works the best for our needs. There are many choices though including random forests, neural networks, clustering, decision trees, support vector machines, and so much more.

While we are here though, we need to also make sure that we are using the right tools along with the algorithms in order to handle the data and provide us with the insights and data that we are looking for along the way. this is important because it ensures the algorithm is actually able to handle the data that we want. Some of the tools that are available for programmers to choose when it is time to work on a data analysis along the way will include:

1. A comprehensive amount of management for our data, and high-quality data.

2. GUIS to help us to build up the models that we want to use with machine learning. And a good process flow.

3. A way to compare some of the different models that come with machine learning so we have a better chance of figuring out which one is the best for our needs.

4. Interactive exploration of any data that we want to handle so that it is easier to see what small changes are going to do with our information and also a visualization of our model results.

5. Automated ensemble model to make it easier to identify some of the performers who are doing the best.

6. A platform that is integrated to handle some of the automation that we need in our data, speeding up the process that we need for the data to decision selection.

7. A model deployment system that is easy so that we are able to get results quickly that are reliable and repeatable.

As we are able to see here, the algorithms that we want to use for our data analysis are going to be important, but it is even more critical to our process if we are able to take those algorithms and combine them with the right tools to get the work done. Having these together, and ensuring that they are compatible and going to work for the data that we have will make a difference in whether or not you are going to be able to use that data to make some smart business decisions along the way.

There is so much that we are able to work with when it is time to handle data analysis and machine learning as we go through this process. Learning how machine learning is going to work for some of your needs, and making sure that you pick out the right algorithm with this, along with the right Python codes, can help you to get the most out of any data you have collected.

Supervised Machine Learning

There are three main types of machine learning that we are able to work with. Learning the differences and how we are able to work with each one is going to make a big difference in the amount of success that we are able to see when it comes to taking care of our machine learning techniques.

In supervised learning, we are going to spend our time training a machine with some data that is labeled. This means that some data is already tagged and has the right answer attached to it. It can be compared to the learning that we see in school with a teacher or a supervisor showing us the answers that we need to know. An algorithm that is considered supervised is going to learn from the labeled training data, and this helps us to predict the outcomes for some data that we can't see.

Successfully building, scaling, and deploying these accurate supervised machine learning models takes time and some technical support as well from data scientists. In addition, these professionals are going to work wot rebuild models to make sure that the insights given remain true until the data does change.

Now we can look at how this supervised learning is going to work. Let's say that you would like to train a machine so that it is able to help you predict how long it will take you to drive home from where you work. You would be able to do this by creating a set of labeled data. This data might include holidays, the time of day and the conditions of the road. All of these details are going to be your input, and then the output is going to be the amount of time that it takes you to drive back home on a certain day.

You already know that if there is rain outside, then it does add a few minutes or more in order to drive home. But your machine, in order to get it to work properly is going to need statistics and data. You can then go through and create a model that will help you figure out the commute time.

The first step here is to create your training set. This is going to contain the total commute time and then some of the other factors that you need to consider like time and weather. Based on this training set your machine might see that there is a direct relationship between the amount of rain that happens and the time that it will take you to get home. When you put in all of the data that you have about these various factors, you will better be able to train the algorithm so that it knows how long it will take you to get home.

There are going to be a few advantages to working with machine learning. Some of the benefits that you are able to get with supervised learning will include:

1. This kind of learning is going to allow you a way to collect data or even to produce the output that you want to form the data using the experience from the past.

2. It is going to help you to really optimize the performance criteria with experience.

3. This type of learning is going to help you to solve a lot of real-world computation problems that you need to get done.

While there are a number of different options and benefits that come with this kind of learning, there are going to be a few disadvantages that we need to work with as well. Some of the disadvantages that you may see when it comes to working with supervised learning can include:

1. The decision boundary can be overtrained if the set you are using for training doesn't come with examples that you want to have in your particular class.

2. You need to make sure that you are picking out a lot of good examples from each class when you do the training to ensure that the process works well.

3. Classifying your big data can end up being a real challenge.

4. Training for this kind of learning needs a lot of computation time.

As we can see, there are a lot of different ways that we are able to work with the supervised machine learning algorithm, and you will find that there are many times that you will want to work with this kind of learning algorithm to get your data science project done.

Unsupervised Machine Learning

In addition to being able to work with supervised learning, there is also a type of learning that is known as unsupervised machine learning. This type of learning is going to be where we will not need to supervise the model that we are working with. Instead, we need to allow the model to do the work on its own in order to discover the information that should be there. It is mainly the kind that will deal with any unlabeled data that we have.

This kind of learning algorithm is going to be helpful because it will ensure that we are able to handle more complex processing tasks compared to what we were able to do with supervised learning. Although we may find that these algorithms are going to be more unpredictable than some of the other learning methods, there are still plenty of times when we may decide that these are the best options for our needs.

Let's take a look at an example of how we can work with this. We can look at the case of a baby and her family dog. The baby knows and is able to identify the dog. A few weeks later, there is a family friend who brings along their own dog, and that dog tries to play with the baby. IN this situation, the baby has not seen this particular dog in the past, but they do recognize that there are a lot of features that are similar to their pet dog as well.

The baby is going to be able to successfully identify this new animal that is in their home like a dog. This is an example of how unsupervised learning is going to work, where you are not taught, but you are going to be able to learn from the data. Had this been supervised learning like what we talked about above though, then the baby would have had to been told that the new animal was a dog.

There are a lot of reasons out there why you should choose to work with unsupervised machine learning for your needs. Some of these benefits are going to include:

1. This kind of learning is able to find all of the patterns that are in your data, even the ones that you don't know about.
2. Unsupervised methods are going to help you find features that can be really useful when it is time to work on a categorization project.
3. This is all going to take place in real-time, so all of the data you use for the input can be analyzed and then labeled in the presence of the learners.
4. It is much easier to get unlabeled data from a computer than it is to get the labeled data, which is going to need some manual intervention to get things to work out.

Of course, there are going to be some disadvantages when we work with unsupervised machine learning as well. Some of these are going to include the following:

1. You are not able to get precise information regarding data sorting, and the output that is used in unsupervised learning is going to be unlabeled and not known so you are not sure what you are getting into when you get started.
2. There is not always as much accuracy in the results with this because the input data is not going to be known, and it will not be labeled by people in advance. This means that the machine will be required to do all of this on its own.
3. The spectral classes are not always going to correspond back to the informational classes that you have.

4. The user will then need to spend some time with this one interpreting and labeling the classes that are going to show up after the classification.

5. Spectral properties of classes are also going to change over time so you will not be able to have the same class information while moving from one image to another.

There are a lot of really neat things that you are able to do when it comes to working with machine learning that is unsupervised, but it does add in another level to the process that can be difficult to work with. Some companies like to work with the supervised machine learning algorithms because it provides more ease of use and accuracy than unsupervised, but there are definitely a lot of cool things that we are able to do with this kind of learning that we will want to spend our time working with it as well.

Reinforcement Machine Learning

And finally, we need to take some time to look a bit at what reinforcement machine learning is all about. It is often going to seem like it is the same thing as what we talked about above when it comes to unsupervised machine learning, but these are two very different topics to work with based on what you are hoping to get out of the information.

Reinforcement machine learning, to help us get started, is going to be the process by which an agent of the computer is going to be able to learn how to behave in an environment that will reward its action with either negative or positive results. When we are talking about some kind of computer agents, we are going to refer to a program that is able to act on its own, or on behalf of the user autonomously. This is going to be very different from what we are used to seeing with the other two types of algorithms as well.

However, this is going to end up being the algorithm that feels the most familiar in many cases, simply because it is based on the methods that humans use when they learn. Compared to the other three categories that come with machine learning, this is the one that is going to mimic the cognition of humans the most.

One of the biggest differences that you are going to see this kind of learning is that it is going to take a bit of training that is different. for example, for reinforcement learning, the data scientist simply needs to provide an environment and some kind of reward system for the agent of the computer. You do not need to work with training data to do this at all. The training is all going to be experimental with this one, and with an iterative approach that is able to run the simulation over and over again, the algorithm is going to learn what the right responses are and how you would like it to behave.

We can use the example of a game of Tic-Tac-Toe to see how this is going to work. The algorithm for reinforcement learning is going to work with a loop in general. This is going to work with a virtual environment being set up. Then each unique frame of reference is going to be referred to as a state. Prior to any of your own engagement with that environment at all, the state is going to be So.

The algorithm will then go through and perform a finite set of operations in this state that you specified on your own. Based on the consequences that are found in this operation, the algorithm will then be rewarded, either in a positive or a negative manner, and will then retain this information to use the next time that it needs to interact with the state, and in the next episode that it encounters with the environment. This can either loop through the process an indefinite number of times, or it can go through a finite amount of times predicated on the type of learning a task that you would like to use.

This kind of learning is basically going to be a kind of trial and error process that you are able to follow. When you are able to put it all together, the algorithm is going to try things out, similar to how a human does. If it works, it will be rewarded. If it does not reward, there will be some kind of punishment. And over time, the computer is going to learn which actions you would like it to take, and the proper way for it to do what you would like.

Machine learning is really starting to take over the world of computers and business, and being able to put all of this together, and ensure that your business is able to use it in the proper manner is going to help you to get ahead in so many ways. There are so many applications that we can work with on machine learning, and the three learning algorithms are going to make it easier than ever for us to work on creating the right models and algorithms to get our data analysis done in no time.

Chapter 10: How Can Python Work with Machine Learning

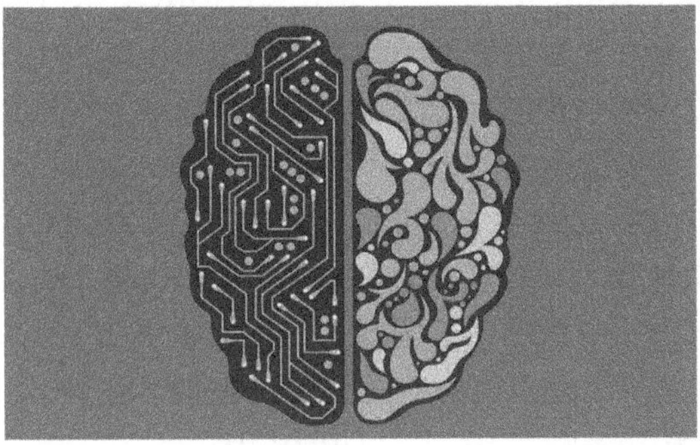

When it comes to completing your own modules and algorithms in machine learning, you will find that there is just one language that can help you get it all done. Sure, other programmers may spend time talking about how another language is the best, but Python has the libraries and extensions, the features, the ease of use, and all of the power that you are looking for all in one place. There are so many reasons why you should choose to work with Python when you want to undertake a project that has machine learning, and we are going to explore some of those benefits here.

Python has the libraries that you need to handle your machine learning algorithms and get things done. We will take a look at some of the libraries that you are able to work with when it comes to the Python language and machine learning or data science in a bit. But there are quite a few that you can focus your attention on. This is great news for someone who is just getting started with this kind of process because you are certain to find the library that works the best for your needs. You can find Python libraries that work for all parts of the data analysis and machine learning process, from gathering up the data you need all the way to show the visuals at the end.

Python has a lot of power behind it that will ensure that we can get some of our data analysis modules done and ready to go. While we have spent some time talking about how easy Python is to learn and how all programmers can figure this one out, whether you are someone who is just getting started with coding or you have been doing it for a long time with other languages. Even though this is a simple language that we are able to learn and that we can catch onto quickly, that doesn't mean that we will have to give up on some of the power that is necessary for some of the coding we want to complete.

As you can imagine, machine learning is going to require some power in order to be successful. If you go in with a wimpy language that is not able to handle complex coding and more, you are going to end up with a lot of issues along the way. This is not a problem that you need to worry about with Python. Despite the ease of using and learning, you will find that this language still has all of the power and strength that you are looking for in order to get all of the different algorithms and modules that you want with machine learning done.

The Python language is easy enough to work with that even a beginner is able to learn even some of the more complicated parts that come with machine learning. If you have never done coding and this is the first step that you have taken to work on machine learning and making it work for you, it may seem like this is all too complicated to handle. But as you go through some of the codings that we have talked about already in this guidebook, and use that to help with machine learning and creating some of your own codes in the process, then you will quickly see that it is not as hard or as scary as you may have thought. Python will make all of this easier to handle.

Many of the algorithms that we will use to handle our data and make it do what we would like in the process work the best with the simple and easy to understand codes of Python. We already know that Python is going to come with a really easy to use and read code, and this can be beneficial when we are working with some of the more complicated parts that come with machine learning. It can be reassuring to see these recognizable codes in Python when we have to handle our own data analysis, and learning some of the simplicity that comes with Python can help prepare us for some of the work that we need to do with machine learning.

Python is also able to work with a lot of the other coding languages out there. With some of our data analysis libraries, we will find that it is best to execute the work with another language. But because Python is able to handle doing some of the work, and it is compatible with other languages, we can still use the Python language in order to help out with writing the codes, but then switching it over, with the help of the Python library that we choose like TensorFlow, in order to have the stronger language finish things up.

The good news here is that the Python language is able to handle a lot of the work and the algorithms that you want to do with machine learning. And many times, you will not need to go through and make any adjustments or add Python to another language to get the work done. This makes it so much easier for us to write out the modules we want, while also training and testing them, to ensure that we can work with the data and really understand what it is trying to tell us.

Python is able to handle all of the different parts that come with machine learning and good data analysis. As we go through the idea of data analysis, you will find that there are actually a number of steps that need to be followed in order to figure out what is inside of all that data. For example, you will need to gather and sort through the data, you will need to clean it up and deal with all of the different parts that are there, and you will need to consider which algorithms to use and then train and test it.

All of this needs to be done before we are even able to put the data through and do the analysis. Then, when we get to the analysis, we may need to trial and error again to make sure that it is working the way that we want, and then we can use Python again in order to create some of the algorithms that we want with our analysis. All of these steps are important to the process of data analysis and will ensure that you are able to get the information that you need, and you can definitely work with Python in order to make this happen.
There may be other choices that we can make when it is time to handle machine learning and all that it entails, but you will find that one of the best languages out there that are able to handle all of the work, from finding and gathering the data to cleaning it off to getting the module done, and so much more, you will find that the Python language is able to take on the work.

Chapter 11: Adding in Some Data Analysis to the Mix

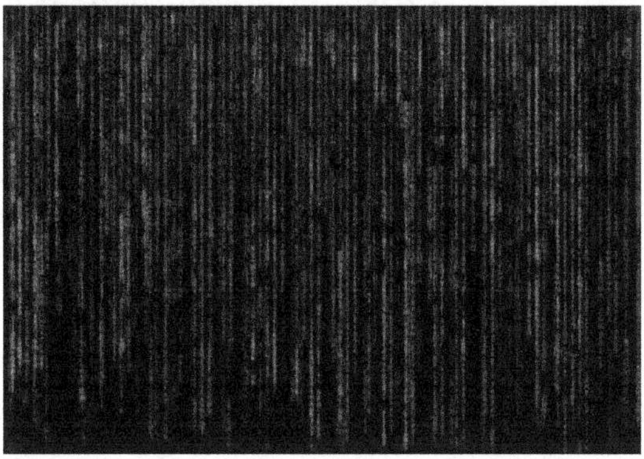

We have mentioned data analysis a bit in this guidebook already, but now it is time for us to take this to the next level, and make sure that we are able to work with the data analysis in the proper manner. There are a lot of parts that come with data analysis, and a lot of benefits of working with this kind of process overall, so now it is time for us to spend some of our time looking at the data analysis and some of the things that we are able to do with it.

Now that we know about the Python coding and some things about machine learning, it is time to look more at what data analysis is all about. Often when a business has a lot of big data that they are trying to work with, they will find that all of that data is overwhelming, and they can't imagine actually going through the process and figuring out the patterns and insights that are in that data. They need to find some other method that will help them to get through that data and figure out what information and insights they are able to use from it.

To keep it simple, data analysis is going to be the practice where a company can take their raw data and then order and organize it. When the data is organized in this manner, and run through a predictive model, it is going to help the company extract useful information out of it. The process of organizing and thinking about our data is going to be very important as it is the key to helping us understand what the data does and does not contain at any given time.

Many companies have been collecting data for a long time. They may gather this data from their customers, from surveys, from social media, and many other locations. And while collecting the data is an important step that we need to focus on as well, another thing to consider is what we can do with the data. You can collect all of the data that you would like, but if it just sits in your cloud or a data warehouse and is never mined or used, then it is going to become worthless to you, and you wasted a lot of time and money trying to figure it all out.

This is where data analysis will come in. it is able to take all of that raw data and actually, put it to some good use. It will use various models and algorithms, usually with the help of machine learning and Python, in order to help us to understand what important insights and information are found in our data, and how we are able to utilize these for our own benefit.

There will be many different methods and approaches that we can use when it is time to work with the data analysis, and many of these are good and secure ways to manage that data the way that we would like. With this in mind, we do need to show some care when picking out the data, and when figuring out the way to manipulate it. It is going to be pretty easy for us to go through the analysis phase and manipulate the data to how we want it, but this is not necessarily going to mean that we are doing it right or that we are actually using the data in the proper manner along the way.

There are a lot of different steps that we are going to see when it is time to work with data analysis, and you will find that there are a lot of benefits that come with it as well. We are going to look at this in more depth in a moment, but often you will find that this is going to include all of the steps that are needed to search for the data, clean it off, pick out the algorithm, train the algorithm that you want to use, and then analyze and share the results. When all of this is done in the proper manner, you will find that you are able to get some great predictions and insights about that information in no time.

The Steps of Your Data Analysis

With all of this in mind, it is time for us to take a little closer look at some of the steps that we are able to take when it is time to handle our own data analysis. There are going to be a number of steps that we are able to use to make this happen, and we just need to make sure that we go through all of them, and that we understand the importance of these before we jump in and start using them. Remember also that we need to spend some time on each of these steps. Rushing through them is not going to provide us with the information that we need, and could project our biases on the information as well. This is never a safe or smart thing to do with data analysis.

With this in mind, some of the different steps that you can take in order to get started with your own data analysis will include:

1. Figuring out what business problem we would like to solve. Whether you have already done a lot of the

gathering that is needed of your chosen date, or you are just starting out and you want to know which type of data is the best to gather, you first need to go through and figure out which business problem you would like to solve. This can help to direct the way that this process goes, and ensures that you keep on track with the kind of information that you bring in.

2. Searching for the data that we want to work with. Once we have a good idea of the information that we need, and the business problem that we would like to solve, it is time for us to go through and look for the data. There are a number of places where we are able to find this data, such as in surveys, social media, and more, so going out and searching for it here is going to be the best way to gather it up and have it ready to work with on the later steps.

3. Cleaning and organizing our data. Since we are usually gathering our data from a lot of different places, and it is often going to come to us in a more unstructured form, it is always a good idea to go through and clean and organize that data. This will make it easier for us to putt that data through the algorithm that we want to use and to make sure that it will all work out.

4. Getting rid of the outliers, the duplication information, and the missing values. These are all going to be found in the data that you are working with because it is raw data, and this happens. But you do need to go through and do some work to clean these up so that they are accurate and will work well in the algorithm you want to focus on. Your results are not going to be very good if you don't take care

of this and make sure that the information is organized and makes sense for what you want to do here.

   a. In some cases, you may want to spend a bit of time taking a look at these outliers and deciding if they are important. If you see that there is a significant number of outliers that all converge together in a general area, this could be a breakthrough that you can use. It may help you to figure out a new niche to get into, or a new demographic that you could offer your product to. Not all outliers are going to be important, but paying a bit of attention and seeing if they have a similar place they fall out of the normal is a good way to get ahead

5. Creating the right algorithm with Python and machine learning. There are a lot of great algorithms out there that you are able to choose, and many of them are going to work with Python as well. You need to take your time to figure out which of the algorithms is going to work the best for your needs and will help you to get the best predictions and insights out of the information as well. You will then need to go through and train and test the algorithm to make sure that it is going to learn along the way and that it is ready for the analysis when you are.

6. When you are done with the training and the testing, it is then time for you to go through and run the analysis. Then you will get some hidden patterns and insights about what is in the data. The whole point of this kind of process is to make sure that we are able to take a large amount of data and then figure out what is inside that is important. The more that we spend or time studying the data, and the

stronger the algorithm that we choose, the easier it is going to be to find the hidden values and the insights that are actually present in that data. We are then able to use this information, when it is analyzed in the proper manner, to make better and more informed decisions for us and our business.

7. Create some visuals: This is something that we need to make sure that we take our time on. These are the visuals that are going to help make it easier for those who need to make decisions based on this information to really see what is there and to find the connections that are in the data. This is really a good way to tell at a glance what is in the data and what we are able to do with that information.

    a. You will find that there are a number of different visuals that we are able to work with here, but the one that you choose is going to vary based on the kind of data that you would like to look at, the comparisons that you are looking to make, and more. There are charts, graphs and more so picking the right one for your needs should be fairly easy to work with.

As we can see, there are a lot of different parts that come with our data analysis and what we are able to do with this process. Taking the time to go through and learn more about the data analysis can make a big difference when it comes to how you will run your business. You will be able to use this in order to sort through all of the data you have collected and learned what is hidden inside. These can then be helpful when reaching out to your customers, working on marketing, figuring out how to open up a new niche to explore and more. But we first need to get ourselves through the process known as data analysis before we are able to use the data that we have been collecting.

The Benefits of a Data Analysis

Now that we have had some time to look at what data analysis is all about, it is important to look at some of the benefits that we are going to be able to enjoy when it is time to work with the data analysis that we want to do. As we are working with this kind of process, it is not going to take us a long time before we notice that there are many benefits that come with this process. That is why there are so many businesses and more who are ready to jump on board with their own data analysis.

These companies know that with the right kind of data in place, the right algorithms that use Python and machine learning, and all of the parts working well together, they will be able to use the data analysis in order to help them with a lot of aspects that come with their business, and then they are able to use all of this to help them get ahead in their business and their industry. Some of the benefits that you are going to be able to use when it is time to handle a data analysis will include:

The data analysis is going to help you learn more about the customers you are working with. Taking the time to learn more about your customers is something that you can always benefit from. Learning about the best way to provide good customer service, how you can provide them with the best products, and even how to create a good recommendation program or loyalty program, and more in order to make the customer happier, while still increasing the profits that you are able to make with your customers is never going to go out of style.

Working with your customers is important to all kinds of businesses, and the analysis that we do with this is going to help show us the steps and the processes that you will need to take when it is time to bring those customers back in the future and even getting those customers to spend more when they come back again.

Work on a stronger marketing campaign. When you have the ability to work with your customers and learn more about them, you will find that it is easier to market to these individuals. You can figure out which demographics are the best to market to, where to reach these individuals, and what they like to see in terms of marketing. With the Internet and other choices in technology that is available today, the number of methods that you can use in marketing is just going up all of the time. using data analysis to help you learn more about these customers and where they will see and respond to your marketing can be helpful in reaching more customers, and reducing the waste that you get here.

Figure out a new demographic or niche to focus on. Sometimes the outliers that we find on our charts and in our information can actually tell us something. We may find that there is a significant distribution of the customers or another factor in one location that is not considered normal, and this is something that we need to focus on and look at closer than before. These outliers don't mean something all of the time, but in other cases, it does mean something and could open up some doors to a new demographic or market that we never focused on before. And if you are able to get there before the competition, and see success, it can help to open up new doors for the success of your business.

Pick out the right products to sell. In the past, releasing a new product could be risky. There were a number of steps that you could take in order to limit this risk a bit, but it was still a process that was not always as safe as a business would like. With the help of data analysis, and going through a few steps before releasing the product in full to the market, can help make this a bit easier. By looking at the market, paying attention to customers, and other steps that are important to the data analysis process, you will be able to have more confidence that the products you release are going to do well.

Another benefit that we are able to look at is how to find some of the waste that may be in your company, and then figure out the best ways that we are able to reduce some of this waste as well. No matter what industry you are working in at the time, it is possible that there is some part of your process that has waste, and this waste is cutting into your quality and your profits. There are a ton of places where the waste can happen, and working with your analysis is going to help you figure out where the waste is and what steps you are able to take to reduce some of that waste as well, without cutting out the quality at all.

As we can see, there are a ton of times when you are able to work with the data analysis in order to really see some good results in the process. Each company is going to work with the data analysis with a slightly different goal in mind, so you can use this in the manner that is the best for your needs. You will find that the data analysis can be adapted and used in so many different methods that it makes sense that you will need to pick the one that works for you. And machine learning and Python will be able to help you get this done in no time.

Chapter 12: The Best Machine Learning and Data Analysis Libraries with Python

Python is going to be one of the best options that we are able to go with when it is time to handle data analysis with machine learning. But the standard library that we will see with Python is often not going to have all of the features and the functions that we need in order to handle this process. Learning how to work with the different libraries that come with Python will be one of the best things that you can do overall, so let's dive in and see which libraries work the best with Python and machine learning, and which ones are going to help you to handle your data analysis models.

The NumPy and SciPy Library

The first two libraries that we are going to explore here are going to be the NumPy, or Numeric and Scientific Computation, and the SciPy library. NumPy is a useful library to learn about because it is going to help us lay down some of the basic premises that are needed for any kind of scientific computing that we wish to do with Python. It is also going to be there to help us grab the functions that we need, many of which are precompiled and fast enough to help out with any and all mathematical and numerical routines.

In addition to some of the listed benefits that we have above, NumPy is also able to help us optimize some of the programming that we want to do with Python. The way that it can do this is to add in a few powerful data structures along the way. what this does is makes it easier for us to efficiently compute the arrays and the matrices that we have, especially when one or both of these are considered multi-dimensional.

Then we have SciPy, or Scientific Python, which is going to come with NumPy in many cases. Often you can't get one to work well without the other because they share many features. When you are working with SciPy, you are able to gain that competitive edge even more than just using NumPy on its own. This happens when you try to enhance some of the useful functions for regression, minimization, and so much more.

The Pandas Library

The next library that we need to spend some time on when we are looking for help with one of our data analytics projects is going to be known as Pandas, or the Python Data Analysis Library. You will find that the name gives away why this library is so important, and why we need to spend some time working with this as well.

Pandas are going to be one of the tools that work with Python, and it is also open-sourced so you can download it and start working with it without any problems. It is going to provide us with some great and easy data structures to work with, and it has a lot of high-performance abilities that will help as well. In fact, you will find that the Pandas library is able to help us out with all of the different programming things that we want to do when it comes to finishing the data analysis.

You are able to work with this library in particular when you want to add in some new structures of data and some new tools to help with the data analysis. And you will find that this work regardless of the kind of project that you would like to complete. There are many industries and companies that are fond of working with this kind of library to help them with things like finance, social science, engineering, and statistics to name a few.

The best part about using this library is that it is adaptable, which helps us to get more work done. It also works with any kind of data that you were able to collect for it, including uncategorized, messy, unstructured, and incomplete data. Even once you have the data, this library is going to step in and help provide us with all of the tools that we need to slice, reshape, merge, and more all of the sets of data we have.

Pandas are going to come with a variety of features that makes it perfect for data science. Some of the best features that come with the Pandas library from Python will include:

1. You can use the Pandas library to help reshape the structures of your data.

2. You can use the Pandas library to label series, as well as tabular data, to help us see an automatic alignment of the data.

3. You can use the Pandas library to help with heterogeneous indexing of the data, and it is also useful when it comes to systematic labeling of the data as well.

4. You can use this library because it can hold onto the capabilities of identifying and then fixing any of the data that is missing.

5. This library provides us with the ability to load and then save data from more than one format.

6. You can easily take some of the data structures that come out of Python and NumPy and convert them into the objects that you need to Pandas objects.

The Matplotlib Library

When you are working with some of the visuals that are needed in data analysis, you will find that the matplotlib library is one of the best ones that you would like to work with. This helps you to really visualize and understand all of the information that you have collected and really helps you to figure out the relationships that are going to come up with your models. It is also going to make it more efficient to see how the insights are going to be worth your time.

Working with these visuals is going to be so important. Depending on the kind of data that is in your models and that you have been working with the whole time, you will find that these visuals are going to make it easier to see what information you have gathered, and how the different parts are going to work when you try to combine them together.

This is one of the areas where you will see that this library is going to be useful. It is basically going to be a 2D plotting library that you are able to use with Python, and it can really help us by producing figures that are publication quality in a lot of formats. You will also see that it can offer you a variety of interactive environments to work with that can handle many platforms based on your needs. This library can be used with scripts from Python, Jupyter, IPython, and more to help get things done.

The way that this library is going to be able to help us with data science is that it is able to generate a lot of the visualizations that we need to handle all of our data, and the results that we get out of the data. This library is able to help with generating scatterplots, error charts, bar charts, power spectra, histograms, and plots to name a few. If you need to have some kind of chart or graph to go along with your data analysis, make sure to check out what the matplotlib option can do for you.

The Scikit-Learn Library

While we are on the topic, we need to spend a few minutes looking at the Scikit-Learn library and how well it is able to handle some of the machine learning and data analysis work that you want to do with Python. This one is going to have a ton of algorithms that work well with machine learning and these algorithms can often fit under the idea of supervised and unsupervised machine learning problems that are low to medium scale. This means that there are a lot of potential uses and applications to make all of this work.

Out of some of the other libraries that we have been able to bring up in this guidebook, and this chapter, so far, the Scikit-Learn library is going to be one of the best to help us handle a lot of different things when it comes to machine learning. This package, in particular, is going to focus on helping us to bring some more machine learning to some of those who may not be professionals in coding and the other parts of this that they need to focus on.

When you are working with the Python language, and working with the Scikit-Learn library to help out with some of the machine learning, you will find that the main emphasis that we are going to see will be on things like how easy it is to use, the performance of the model, a bit on the documentation, and the consistency that we are able to get to show up on the API.

Another benefit that we are going to see when it comes to this library is that it is not going to have a lot of dependencies, which makes it easier to work with, and it is relatively easy to distribute. You will find that this is a library that will show up in many settings, whether they are academic or commercial. This library is going to show us an interface that is concise and consistent and that we can use for many machine learning algorithms and help us handle the machine learning and data science that we would like.

The TensorFlow Library

We can also work with the library that is known as TensorFlow. This is actually considered one of the best libraries out there that works with Python and can handle the work that you want to do with data science. This is a library that was originally released by the Google Brain Team. It was written out mostly with the help of the C++ language, which is a bit different but it comes with some of the bindings in Python, so you will be able to still use the language that you have been learning without having to worry about it.

One of the best features that you will see with the TensorFlow library is that it is going to have a flexible architecture that is nice for allowing the programmer to deploy it with one or more GPU's or CPUs on your device whether that is a server, a mobile, or a desktop device. And you can do all of this with the same API the whole time.

Not many, if really any, of the other libraries that we are working with inside of this chapter are able to come close to making this kind of claim. This library can also add in some more unique features in that it was developed by the Google Brain project, and it is not going to miss out on a lot of the features that you want.

One thing to keep in mind with this though is that you will need to spend a bit more of your time on this library in order to learn the API of this library compared to what we see with the other libraries. It only takes a few minutes to find out that you are able to really get the hang of it pretty quickly as well. And it is going to work when it is time to implement the design that you want to have with your network, without having to fight through the API as we will find with the other options.

The Keras Library

Keras is going to be an open-sourced library form Python that is able to help you to build up your own neural networks, at a high level of the interface. It is going to be pretty minimalistic, which makes it easier to work with, and the coding on this library is going to be simple and straightforward, while still adding in some of the high-level extensibility that you need. It is going to work either TensorFlow or Theano along with CNTK as the backend to make this work better. We can remember that the API that comes with Keras is designed for humans to use, rather than humans, which makes it easier to use and puts the experience of the user right in front.

Keras is going to work with all of the best-known practices at the time when it is necessary to reduce the cognitive load. This Python library is going to offer us a consistent and simple API that will help us to minimize how many actions that the user has to do for the different parts of the code that are common, and it also helps to provide feedback that is actionable and clear if you do end up with an error on the code.

In this library, we may find that the model will be understood more like a sequence, or we can change it up and make it a standalone or a graph. You can even work with fully-configurable modules that you are able to put together with only a few restrictions at the time.

Options like cost functions, initialization schemes, activation functions, optimizers, and neural layers are all going to be examples of the modules that can stand alone but then can be put together when you would like to create your own model. You will then find that Keras can help you to create some of these new modules, and the existing modules that are already there can provide us with examples to work with as well if we are just starting with it.

The Theano Library

Theano is another great library to work with during data science, and it is often seen as one of the highly-rated libraries to get this work done. In this library, you will get the benefit of defining, optimizing, and then evaluating many different types of mathematical expressions that come with multi-dimensional arrays in an efficient manner. This library is able to use lots of GPUs and perform symbolic differentiation in a more efficient manner.

Theano is a great library to learn how to use, but it does come with a learning curve that is pretty steep, especially for most of the people who have learned how to work with Python because declaring the variables and building up some of the functions that you want to work with will be quite a bit different from the premises that you learn in Python.

However, this doesn't mean that the process is impossible. It just means that you need to take a bit longer to learn how to make this happen. With some good tutorials and examples, it is possible for someone who is brand new to Theano to get this coding all done. Many great libraries that come with Python, including Padas and NumPy, will be able to make this a bit easier as well.

As we can see, there are a ton of great libraries that work well with the Python language that can also be added to the project that we do with machine learning and data analysis. Each of these will have their own benefits to work with, and you can pick and choose which ones have the features, the algorithms and the other parts that you need to have a really strong data project in no time.

Conclusion

Thank you for making it through to the end of *Python Programming*, let's hope it was informative and able to provide you with all of the tools you need to achieve your goals whatever they may be.

The next step is to start with some of the different programs and codes that we took some time to explore in this guidebook so that you can get more experience with the Python code. There are a lot of different things that you are able to do when it comes to the Python language, and being able to bring all of this together and getting it to work for your needs is going to be very important. This guidebook took some of the time that was needed to go over some of the basics of the Python language, as well as some of the more complex parts, and put it all together to help you see some results.

In addition to looking at all of the cool things that you are able to do with the Python language, we also spent some time in this guidebook looking at how to work with machine learning and data analysis. While there are many things that you are able to do with the help of Python and its various libraries and features, you will find that it is often used to help out with those two topics. Many companies and individuals want to learn how to use Python so that they can really see results with machine learning and data analysis, and this guidebook will help you to get started with some of that in no time.

When you are ready to learn more about what the Python language is able to do for you, and how you re able to combine it together to get some of the best projects possible, then make sure to take a look at this guidebook to help you get started!

Finally, if you found this book useful in any way, a review on Amazon is always appreciated!

Python for Data Science

The Ultimate Beginner's Guide to Learn Data Science from Scratch, All You Need to Know About Data Analysis, Big Data Analytics, and Machine Learning for Business

John Russel

Introduction

Congratulations on purchasing *Python Programming,* and thank you for doing so.

The following chapters will discuss all of the different parts that you need to know in order to get started with your own data science project. There are many companies who are interested in learning more about this process and what it is able to do for them and figuring out what this all means and how this kind of process can propel us to the future with our smart decisions and more, can ensure that you are going to actually be successful when it is time to handle yourself in the future.

There are so many parts that come with a data science project, and we are going to take some time to discuss them all in this guidebook. We are going to look at some of the basics that come with this data science project, and why it is so beneficial to so many companies to at least check it out and see what it has to offer them. At the same time, we are also going to explore how to set up your own environment to get started with data science, and some of the best libraries that are out there to help us succeed with the use of data science and Python put together.

From there, we need to get into some of the details that come up when we are working on a data science project. We will look at how we are able to gather up some of the data we need, the importance of cleaning up all of that data and getting it to work where we would like, how to handle some of the NumPy arrays to get the work done, and the basics of working with a data analysis in this process. The guidebook will also finish up with one final stop looking at some of the benefits of creating data visuals so that we can take all of the information and trends that we learned bout in the other chapters, and put them into a form that is easy to read through and comprehend.

We will then finish up with a good look at how to work with machine learning and what this is able to offer to us as well when it comes to programming in Python. There are so many different parts that come with machine learning, but we will quickly find that this is going to be the best place for us to learn more about the data we are exploring and can help us to actually create some of the algorithms that we need in this language.

Many businesses are able to benefit when they work with data analysis for some of their own needs. It will help them to learn more about their customers, their industry, and so much more. When you are ready to learn more about what data science can do for you and to figure out whether this is a process your business should spend some time on, make sure to check out this guidebook to help you get started.
There are plenty of books on this subject on the market, thanks again for choosing this one! Every effort was made to ensure it is full of as much useful information as possible, please enjoy it!

Chapter 1: What Is Data Science?

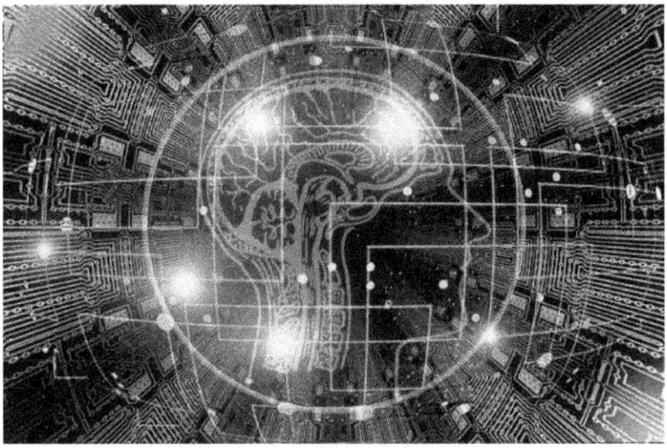

One of the very first things that we need to spend our time on and explore here is the idea of data science and what this is all about. You will find that data science is going to be a very detailed study of the flow of information, which comes from a large amount of data that a company is presented with. When we take a look at our modern world, there is an overabundance of data that we are able to use. Whether it comes from social media, websites, surveys, or somewhere else, there is always a lot of money that we are able to gather up and use. But the trick here is to figure out the right way to use all of this data for our needs.

While the process of gathering up all of this information from all of those different sources may seem like a goldmine, the problem is going to come when we try to figure out what to do with this data. It isn't going to help us out that much if we just gather it and leave it in a database with no plans for that information. It also doesn't help us if we never figure out what is inside of that data either. And because we have so much data that we are gathering, it is pretty much impossible to go through and manually sort through this information on our own.

This is where the process of data science is going to come in. this process is going to be what we use, and all of the steps that are needed, so that we can learn the patterns and insights in all of that data that we are gathering. It works along with machine learning and artificial intelligence to help us figure out the information and make predictions that we are able to use later on.

When it comes to using the process of data science, we will find that there are a lot of techniques that we are able to use in order to obtain some meaningful insights from the data we have, data that is often unstructured and raw. We can then process these to learn something out of them and use that to help enhance our business overall. With this in mind, it is time for us to take a closer look at what we are able to do with data science and why it is so important for us.

Why Is Data Science So Important?

To start with, we need to figure out why this data science industry is so important. In a world that is turning more to the digital space than it ever did before, organizations are going to deal with a ton of data, data that is unstructured and structured, on a daily basis. Some of the evolving technologies that we can look at have enabled us to save a lot of money, and smart storage spaces have come up in order to store a lot of this data until companies are able to get to it.

Currently, there is a huge need for skilled and certified data scientists to help go through this information and see what is found inside. In fact, when it comes to the IT industry, these data scientists are going to be among the highest-paid professionals out there. In fact, According to Forbes, the annual salary for the average data scientist is almost $110,000.

Why is this industry paying so much? Because it is in high demand and many companies are looking to find qualified professionals who are able to gather, store, and look through all of the data that they have available and provide them with predictions, information, and help in using this information to make good business decisions. And the number of professionals who are actually able to process and derive valuable insights out of the data are few and far between, so they are in high demand.

To make this process a little bit further, there are going to be some requirements that have to come into play so that someone who handles this data because of all of these issues, there is actually about a 50 percent gap in the industry when it comes to the demand for a data scientist versus how many of these professionals who are out there. This is another reason why it is so important for us to learn a bit more about the world of data science and how this is going to be a topic that many businesses will want to work with as well.

When we keep this in mind, it is still important for many companies to focus a bit more on the beauty of data science and some of the different steps that we are going to need to focus on as well. As we go through this guidebook, you will find that there are actually quite a few steps that we need to follow in order to see some success with data science along the way, which is why it usually takes a professional in order to go through and handle all of this.

In the past few years, we have found that there has been a huge growth in the amount of data that is out there and available for us to use. And this is the same information that companies are going to try and use in order to get ahead and learn more than their competitors. And it is likely that this growth of data is not going to die out any time soon, which means that we are going to see more and more data that a company is able to use.

Right now, each day we are going to see 25 quintillion bytes of data generated for companies to use, and it is going to grow at an even faster rate as IoT continues to grow this is an extraordinary amount of growth in data, which can be useful for a lot of companies to learn about their customers, figure out the best products to release next, and work the best with the customer service they would like to provide. All of this data is going to come from a variety of sources that will include:

1. Sensors are set up in shopping malls in order to gather up the information of the individual shopper.
2. Posts on the various platforms of social media can send back information to the company.
3. Videos that are found on our phones and digital pictures are taking in more data than ever before.
4. Companies are able to even get some good information when they look at some of the purchase transactions that come when people shop online and through e-commerce.

All of these different data, no matter where we are going to see it from, is going to be called big data. As you can imagine here from all of the various sources of data and what we have talked about so far in this chapter, companies are going to search for data, and find that they are basically flooded with more data than they really know what to do within the first place. It is a ton of data, and assuming that one individual person, or even a small group of people, can go through it manually and effectively is pretty much foolish.

If you did have a team go through and try to do this all on their own, you are going to end up with a mess. They will take too long, miss out on things, or misread these things, and by the time they came up with the insights, especially with how fast the world of data is being created, the insights and predictions are going to be old.

This is why data science is going to be so important for us to focus our attention on. We will find that when we work with this data science, we are going to be able to learn better what we are able to do with all of this data, and some of the best ways that we are able to utilize this data in order to make some good decisions about our business in the future.

It is here that the idea of data science is going to start showing up into the picture. Data science is going to bring together a ton of skills that we can find in the world of business, including business domain knowledge, mathematics, and statistics. All of these are important because they are going to help an organization out in a variety of ways, including:

1. Helping the company learn new ways where they can reduce costs each day.

2. It can help the company figure out the best method to take to get into a new market that will be profitable for them.
3. This can help the company learn about a variety of demographics and how to tap into these
4. It can help the company to take a look at the marketing campaign that they sent out there and then figure out if the marketing campaign was actually effective.
5. It can make it easier for the company to successfully launch a new service product.

These are just a few of the things that this big data is going to be able to help us out with. This means that no matter what kind of industry will be able to use the ideas of data science in order to help them learn about their customers, their marketing campaigns, their products, and more and lead up to more success for the company.

As a business owner, you will find that there are a ton of ways that we are able to work with data science to help us out. We will take a look at some of the specifics of this in the next chapter, but you will find that this is something that all companies, in a variety of industries, are going to be able to benefit from as a whole. Let's explore some of the different things that we are able to do in order to handle our data science project, no matter what kind of company we are in the first place.

Chapter 2: How Can I Use Data Science?

One of the first things that we will have questions when it comes to data science is the idea of how we are able to use it. It may seem like a really neat thing to learn about and like we are able to work with it just for fun, but there are actually quite a few practical purposes that are going to come with using data science, no matter what industry you are in or how you plan to use it. Some of the different ways that we are able to rely on data science will include.

It can help with marketing. Marketing is all about data, and when we are able to use all of the big data that is needed for data science, we will find that we are able to really learn more about our customers and how we are able to reach them to make a sale. There are different ways that a company will be able to use data science in order to help them get ahead of the game, and it can help with knowing how to reach the customers, placing heads in the right places for the right customers, and more.

Helps the company to learn more about their customers. As a company, the more that you are able to learn about your customers, the better off you will be. Learning about what your customers want out of your business, where your customers are located, their demographics, and how you are able to serve them better will ensure that they will continue to pick out your business, rather than working with someone else along the way. it can even help you to determine which products you are going to sell next.

It can help to reduce waste. All companies want to learn about and reduce the amount of waste that is going ton in their company. This waste can be resources, time, machine parts, and even part of the process of making the product. When we are able to cut down on some of this waste, it can help the company to become more efficient and will increase the profits that the company is going to experience. When you are able to use data science in the proper manner, you will find that it is easier to cut out some of this waste and see the results that you would like.

Financial institutions use it to help them fight off fraud. Fraud can cost these financial institutions a lot of money overall. If they are not careful with how they handle their money and they don't learn how to watch out for transactions that are legitimate and the ones that are fraudulent, there are going to be some problems along the way. When the financial institution can come up with algorithms and programs that can recognize and stop fraud, it can end up saving them millions of dollars a year.

This is where data science can come in, as well. Using a lot of different factors, as well as training the algorithms on past transactions that were fraudulent, it is easier for one of these systems to figure out when a transaction is fraudulent or not. And the more times that the algorithm goes through the process, the better it is going to be at doing that work, and the fewer instances of fraud that are going to happen.

It can speed up loan applications. There are often a huge amount of loan applications that come into banks and other financial institutions on a regular basis today. This is a lot for a loan officer to handle, and the resources of the financial institution to do on their own. Data science can come into this to really help.

With the help of data science, the financial institution is able to go through the applications and figure out which loans are the best bets and not. You can set up a few of the different criteria that the application needs to meet, and then work from there. If the application meets some of the requirements, then it is going to be a good option to work with. The loan officer will get these and can make the final determination on it. But if the loan application doesn't meet with the requirements, it will get ignored and not be seen at all. This helps to speed up the loan application process and can allow the loan officer a chance to actually keep up with their work and focus on the customers who will bring that financial institution money.

It helps out in the medical field in a variety of ways. There are so many ways that the process of data science would be able to help out the medical field. To start with, we can see that data science is going to help out with doctors and finishing up their surgeries. With the use of machine learning and other algorithms that come with data science, doctors are going to be able to make the right incisions and get the surgery done with minimal issues and with less recovery time.

In addition, these algorithms are going to help doctors make a prognosis about their patients. With the ever-increasing workload that is on doctors and the limited time, they have to be with each patient, having these can be beneficial. They will be able to use data science to look through some of the images that are available, such as scans and x-rays, and then get a diagnosis in no time at all.

And finally, we can even find data science in work when it comes to the administrative tasks that come in the medical field. These machines are able to talk to the customers, ask a few questions, and figure out the severity of the issue of the patient, and can direct them to the right location. For fields that are running low on staff to handle some of their patient needs, this can be helpful.

It helps a company learn more about their current competition and the industry they are in. if you want to beat out some of the competition that you have right now, then you need to find out as much information about your industry and your competition. You need to see what they are doing, how customers are responding to it, and how you can use this to your own advantage.

When you have all of this information in place, you will find that it is easier to figure out what is working and what is not working. You can then jump right in and make some of the necessary adjustments to your own business model. You may find a new way to reach your customers that no one else is working with. You may be able to make some modifications to a technique that someone else is working with that can improve your own business, as well.

Many manufacturing companies are going to work with data science because it allows them to make predictions that can save them money. First, you are able to use these kinds of algorithms to figure out when a part on a machine is likely to break, or when you need to do maintenance. Then you can schedule this to be done during the off-hours, ensuring that the machine is always up and running on time, and that production is not going to be halted while you get things figured out.

These algorithms can also work, in pretty much any business, when it is time to work with finding ways to cut down on some of the waste that is present. Every company is going to have some kind of waste, and figuring out how to reduce that waste, and take care of it, will make it so that you can offer the products at a competitive rate, while still making as much in profits as possible. It is really as simple as working with data science to figure out where these wastes are and how you can keep them to a minimum.

When you are online doing some shopping, and you see that there is a recommendation tab on that website, we are seeing some of the work of data science and machine learning coming to life. These are so popular on many websites because they can make it easier for the customer to make some informed decisions on what they want to watch next or purchase next or something else. And businesses are going to enjoy them as well because, with these recommendation systems, it is more likely that the customer is going to make another purchase, which is going to increase the bottom line for that company.

Next on the list is going to be the process of speech recognition. If you have ever talked and asked a question to your smartphone, or you have worked with some of the popular devices like the Echo, Cortana, and more, then you can recognize how this feature is going to be really fun and innovative. And it is run with some of the principles of data science.

In fact, some of the best examples that we are going to find when it comes to data science is this speech recognition. Using these features, even if you are not currently in a position to type out a message, you are still about to talk to the machine or the device and ask a question. However, this may not perform accurately, especially when we are in the beginning. This means that we may have to spend some time working with the program and teaching it how to recognize some of the things that we are saying. And this is the machine learning that is behind the process, where the machine, through experience and some time, will be able to learn how to recognize the speech of the user faster and more efficiently.

If you have ever worked with some of the websites that are out there that help out with price comparisons, then you have seen data science at work as well. At a basic kind of level, you will find that these are websites that will be driven with the use of lots and lots of data that they are able to get with the help of RSS Feeds and APIs. They can then use this information to figure out what the price of the same product from different websites and sources will be so you can make the best decision and save money. This can be used in many industries to help you compare priccs and figure out what is best for you.

We can also take a look at how this kind of technology is going to work when we talk about something like airline route planning. This industry is one that is going to bear a lot of heavy losses if they are not careful. Except for a few of the companies out there, there are many who are struggling to maintain the occupancy that they need and make some profits. And when we add in the higher prices of fuel right now, and the need to offer heavy discounts to many customers, the situation is slowly getting worse.

It wasn't too long before these airline companies started to work with data science to see how they can increase their profits and make more without scaring their customers away. This helped them to figure out some of the strategic improvements that they are able to make. Today, with the help of data science, these airline companies are able to:

1. Make better predictions about a flight being delayed.
2. Decide which class of airplanes they should invest their money in.
3. Whether they should land at the direct destination, or take a halt in between.
4. Help to drive some of the loyalty programs that customers are able to sign up for.

Two of the airline companies who have really embraced these changes will include American Airlines and Southwest, and they are now some of the most profitable of the airlines out there.

And finally, we are going to take a look at the idea of delivery logistics and how these are going to help sure that packages and mail are delivered in a good amount of time and that things don't get lost. Companies like UPS, FedEx, and DHL are going to use data science in order to help improve how efficient they are operational.

With the help of data science, these companies and more have been able to figure out the best routes to ship, the best times that they should deliver, and the mode of transportation that is the best for these as well. This helps them to have more cost efficiency and more benefits along the way as well. In addition, the data that these companies are able to generate with the installed GPS units can provide them with the data they need to explore more possibilities and to learn more with data science along the way.

There are so many benefits that we are able to see when it comes to using data science for a company. In many cases, if you are not willing to use data science at least a little bit, you will find that you will fall behind. No matter what kind of business problem you are trying to work on or what you would like to solve in your business, you will find that working with data science is one of the best and most effective methods to help you out.

Chapter 3: The Best Python Libraries for Data Science

Before we dive into seeing some of the cool things that we are able to do when it comes to working with data science and machine learning with Python, we first need to explore some of the different libraries that we need to focus on to make all of this work. We have to remember with this one that while there are a lot of neat things that we are able to do with the help of the Python language, there are also going to be a few places where it falls behind and may not work as well as we would like. And this is why we are able to add in some of the best Python libraries and extensions that are designed to work well with data science and the different steps it requires as well.

Python continues to take on some of the leading positions when it comes to solving tasks of data science and some of the challenges that come with it. And when we are able to add in some of the libraries that we are going to talk about here, you will find that you are really able to handle all of the different processes that are needed for data science in no time. Let's take a look at these libraries and what we are able to do with them to help us see some amazing results.

Core Libraries and Statistics

The first library we are going to take a look at here is the NumPy library. This is going to be the best library to work with when it is time to process some large multi-dimensional arrays and matrices. It also has a pretty extensive collection of mathematical functions and implements methods that will make it possible for us to perform various operations with all of these objects.

Over the past few years, there have been a number of improvements that have been made to the library. In addition to fixing the bugs and dealing with some of the compatibility issues, some of the crucial changes that we are going to see are the possibilities of styling, namely the printing format that comes with the objects in NumPy. There is also the ability of some functions to handle files of any encoding that you can traditionally do with Python.

Then there is the SciPy library. This is a good one to help out with some of the scientific computing that you want to work with, and it is going to be based on the NumPy library that we worked with, which basically means that we are going to extend out the capabilities that come with NumPy. The package of this one is going to contain some tools that will help when you want to work with integral calculus, probability theory, and linear algebra, to name a few.

We can't go far in our discussion of machine learning and data science without taking a look at the Pandas library. Pandas are going to be one of the libraries of Python that is able to provide us with some data structures that re high-level and a lot of tools to help with the analysis. In fact, if you want one library that is able to handle all of the different parts that come with your data science process, then the Pandas library is going to be the one that you need to focus on.

The great feature that comes with this package is that it is going to have the ability for us to translate some complex operations with data into one or two commands, saving time and making it easier. Pandas are also going to come in with a lot of methods that you can use for grouping, filtering, and combining data and the functionality of time-series. All of this is going to be followed by some speed indicators that are impressive, as well.

There have been a few releases that you are able to use when it comes to Pandas and what it can offer to you. And these updates are going to help us to see some great options when it is time to work with the features and all of the neat things that we are able to work with our data science project. This is a library that you need to work in order to make sure that we are going to be able to handle some of the work that we are doing in no time.

And finally, we need to work with StatsModels. This is going to be one of the modules that come with Python, and it is going to provide us with some chances to work with statistical data analysis. This includes things like a model estimation and helping us to perform some statistical tests when they are needed. With the help of this library, we are going to be able to implement a lot of the methods of machine learning that we want, while exploring some of the different possibilities when it comes to plotting.

Visualization

One thing that we need to focus on when it comes to working with machine learning and data science is figuring out how to take some of the insights and patterns that we find, and turning them into a visual that we are able to handle as well. You will need to work with a specific library to help make sure that you are able to get these visuals taken care of overall.

The first of these data visualization libraries that we are able to work with is matplotlib. This is going to be a library that is able to help us to really work on creating some 2D diagrams and graphs that we are working with. This helps us to create a huge number of charts and graphs that we need to handle and show off some of the complex relationships that are going to show up in our work. In addition, many of the other plotting libraries that are out there and pretty popular are designed so that they can work along with this matplotlib.

There have been a lot of changes to matplotlib over the years when it comes to the sizes, colors, legends, and fonts that we can work with. These are good improvements to work with because they are going to show us a lot of different ways that we can create the graphs and more that we are looking at in a short amount of time.

We can also work with Seaborn. This is going to be a higher-level of API that is going to be based on the matplotlib library. It is going to contain a more suitable default setting to help us to go through and process some of the charts that we want to work with. There is also going to be a rich gallery of visuals that you are able to use, like the violin diagram, joint plots, and time series.

Programmers are able to work with the Plotly library as well. This is going to be something that we are able to use when we would like an easy method to build up sophisticated graphics and more. This is a package that is adapted to help work with web applications that are more interactive. And it is going to include a lot of different visualizations that you are able to work with, including ternary plots, 3D plots, and contour graphics.

Machine Learning Libraries

As you go through this process and you work on some of the projects that come with data science, it is possible that you are going to work with machine learning as well. You need to learn how to work with machine learning because it is going to help us to really see how to take that data and learn from it. And this is definitely where we are going to see some of that Python coding come into play. With this in mind, some of the libraries that we are able to use that can help us use Python for machine learning will include:

Scikit-Learn is a library that we need to focus on. This is going to be a module that works with Python and will be based on SciPy and NumPy and can be a great option to handle when it is time to work with data. It is going to provide us with a ton of the algorithms that we need to work on machine learning and tasks of data mining, including model selection, dimensionality reduction, classification, regression, and clustering.

Deep Learning

Deep learning is going to be a subset of machine learning that takes some of the things that we are able to do with that to the next level. A lot of the unsupervised machine learning tasks that you want to work with, and that we will talk about more later, will be done with the help of deep learning. Some of the different tasks that we are able to handle when it comes to working on deep learning will include:
The first option is going to be TensorFlow. This is going to be a very popular framework when it comes to machine learning and deep learning, and it was developed by Google Brain. It is going to provide us with some abilities to work with multiple sets of data and neural networks all in one. In fact, it is going to be one of the most popular deep learning options, and some of the applications of TensorFlow that you will be able to enjoy, including speech recognition, object identification, and more.

PyTorch is another framework that you are going to be able to work with, as well. This is going to include a large framework that is going to allow us to perform some tensor computations with the help of CPU accelerations, create some dynamic computational graphs, and even to automatically calculate gradients. In addition to all of this, PyTorch is going to provide us with a rich API to help solve applications that re related to neural networks.

This is a library that is going to be based on Torch, which is another library that is open-sourced, deep learning, and implemented with the C language and a wrapper of Lua. The Python API was not introduced until 2017, and from that point on, we are going to see that this is a framework that is really popular and used in many applications by data scientists.

The Keras library is next on the list. His is going to be a library that is high-level that can help us with neural networks as well. It is also going to be one that is able to work on top of Theano and TensorFlow. It is going to be able to take some of the specific tasks that you need to spend your time on, and make them easier to handle while reducing how much monotonous code that you have to deal with in data science. You will find that it is not going to be all that suitable for some of the more complicated things that you want to handle.

These are just a few of the different languages that you are going to be able to work with when it is time to handle all of the data science projects that you would like to work with. Some of these are going to work well together, and others are not going to work the way that you want unless they are done on their own. But often it is going to depend on the kind of project that you want to work with, and what you are hoping to get out of that process, for you to choose which of the libraries that you want to pick form. The goal here is to learn about the libraries, know how your own project is supposed to work, and then move from there when it is time to make some choices on the library that you want to work with.

Chapter 4: Setting Up Your Virtual Environments for Data Science

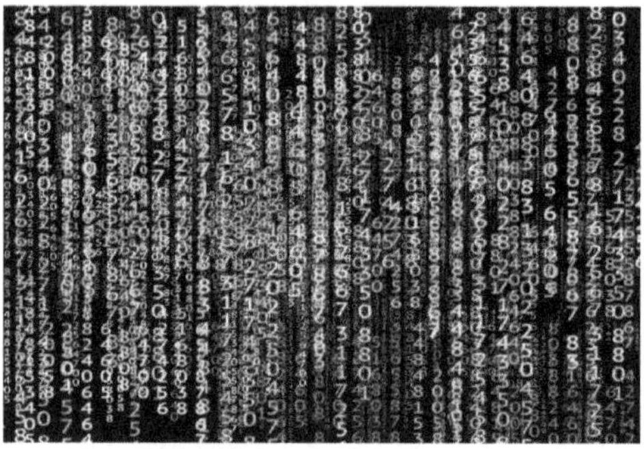

Before we are able to work on some of the projects that we need to use for data science, we have to make sure that we have the right virtual environment in place to help us get it all done. You have to come on board with the right parts working and ready to go, or the program is not going to work the way that you may want in the process either.

There are a few things that we need to focus on when it is time to handle some of the different parts of a data science project, and having these uploaded and ready to go is going to be really important. We are going to take a look at how you can work with downloading and installing the Python language, and some of the ways that you can install the different libraries that you would like to work with as well.

First, we have to focus on the Python language. When it comes to gathering, collecting, organizing, cleaning, analyzing, and more with the data, the number one language that you can use to make it happen is the Python coding language it is important to have this language up and ready to go so that we are able to really get started. You can have the option of working with some other language along the way, but this is one of the most popular options to choose and will ensure that you are going to see some good results in the process as well.

Installing the Python language is going to be easier to handle than you may think, and you are going to love how simple it can be to work with. It will be able to work on any operating system, whether you would like to focus on the Windows, Mac, or Linux system. This is nice for most beginners because it means that they are able to work with the language, no matter what system they are on, without having to worry about learning a brand new system along the way as well.

Another good thing about working with Python is that this is free to use the system to use. This is going to make it easier to do your data science project because you will be able to start on any project without the added costs. You are able to go through and pick out any of the third-party extensions that you would like to work with on this, but some of those may cost you a bit more in order to work with. But when it comes to working with the original Python and some of the parts of the library and more that you want to use, you will be able to do it for free.

It is often best to work with the version of Python that is found on www.python.org. There are a few options for why we would want to work with this version of Python. First, it is going to have all of the versions of Python that you would like to work with.

Most programmers will work with the newest version of Python for some of their programming needs because this is the one that has all of the features that you are looking for, and will make it easier for you to reach your goals and get things done.

However, there are sometimes when you will not want to go with Python 3 or the newest version of Python. This may depend on some of the code that you would like to work on, or what works the best for your system. Depending on what kind of computer or what kind of operating system you are on, there may already be a version of Python on your computer, and you may choose to go with this one instead of one of the others. No matter which version of the Python language you would like to go with, you will find that it is available on that website.

Another benefit is that this website is going to have the installation instructions that you need to add the Python language and its files to any computer that you would like. This means that whether you are working with a Windows, Mac, or Linux system, you will be able to find the link that is needed to handle this and get the Python language set up and ready to go for your needs.

In addition, this website offers the Python language for you to download and install on your computer for free. There are a lot of third party sights out there that will offer you the Python language, and some of them do offer some additional features that you are able to work with as well. But often these are going to cost a bit to use. Depending on what features you want to work with, it may be worth your time to add on some of these features, and you may be fine with paying for that version of Python.

If you are just looking to get some of the basics of the Python language, and you want to keep your costs down, the version of python that is available at www.python.org, is going to be the best option. It is free to use and will come with the standard library that you need to make all of this happen

And finally, when you get your version of Python from the website above, you will be sure to get all of the additional files and the shell that you need with Python. All of these are necessary to make Python work, but some of the other websites are only going to provide you with one part or another. When you click on the download links that are found on that website above, you can rest assured that when the installation is done, all of the parts that you want are going to be in one place and on your computer.

The process of downloading and installing Python from the website above is going to be pretty easy. You can just visit the website, search around for the version of Python that you want to work with, and then click on the operating system that you would like to focus on when it comes to this process. From there, you will have to follow a set of instructions that come up, based on which operating system you are working with, and move through the process until you are done. And it is as simple as that.

Once you have the Python language set up and ready to go, take a few moments to gain some familiarity with how it works and what all you are able to do with it. You want to make sure that you are able to handle some of the codings that are necessary for the project that you are going to work with, and that you see what all you are able to do. If you have time, learning some of the basics of the Python code can be important, too, when it comes to making sure that you are set up for success with this system.

The next step, though, is making sure that we have the right libraries set up for our project. If we want to work with data analysis or any kind of data science project, it is likely that we are going to need more than the standard Python library to help us get it done. There is a ton that this standard Python library is able to help us out with, but it does lack some of the parts that come with a data science project.

The good news here though is that we are able to work with some of the libraries that we have in the previous chapter to help us get this done. There are a ton of libraries that work well with a data science project, and it is going to depend on what we are hoping to accomplish. So, to make this step work, we need to make sure that we pick out the right libraries that we want to work with, and then we need to get it installed.

It is likely that you will need to work with the NumPy library at least a bit. Most of the other libraries are going to rely on the array of NumPy to help them, even some of the more complex libraries, so this is definitely one that you are going to need to spend some of your time downloading. The rest is really going to depend on what you are hoping to accomplish with the project you are on.

We need to spend some time downloading these libraries and making sure that they are set up and ready to work on the projects that we want. You should be able to download these for free from their respective official websites. You can just type in the name of the library that you want to work with, and the website should be one of the top options that we are able to choose. Then you can click on the link that works the best for your needs, and then go through and follow the steps that are necessary to make this happen.

All of this setup process is not going to take too long, and before you know it, the program is going to be ready to go, and you will be able to start some of the coding that you need for machine learning and more. It will probably take a few minutes per the Python language and per the library that you want to work with, to accomplish all of this, so it will depend on the operating system you have, the number of libraries that you would like to work with, and how fast your computer speed is at the time.

Once you have all of these downloaded and ready to go on your system and you are ready to open them up and use them, then it is time to work on a data science project, knowing that you have set up the virtual environment that you need to make all of this happen.

Chapter 5: The Importance of the NumPy Arrays

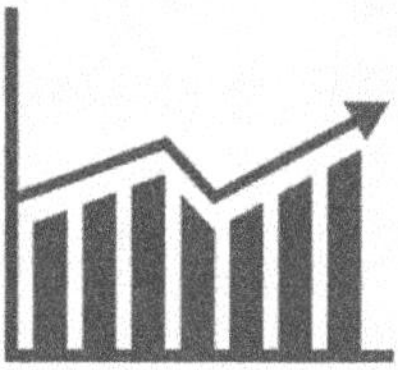

One thing that you will quickly notice when it comes time to work with the different libraries that are supposed to work with Python is that many of them are going to be based on the NumPy array. This means that we will need to spend at least a little bit of time learning about these arrays and how we are able to make them work for some of our needs as well. These arrays are going to help to lead us in many of the other parts that we want to do with data science, so learning how to make them work, and what they are able to do is going to make a big difference.

The first thing that we need to take a look at is what the NumPy array is all about. Often we are going to work with what is known as a structured NumPy array. This is going to be an array of structures, which are going to be similar to what we see with the C language structure. We will also see that these arrays are going to be homogenous, which means that they are only going to be able to contain data that is the same type. So instead of creating an array that is an integer or a floating number, we can go through and create one of these arrays with some homogenous other structures as well.

The best way to see how this is going to work is to take a look at an example of this. Let's say that we are going through some work and we want to be able to create our own NumPy array with elements of the following structure:

struct
{
char name[10];
float marks;
int grade level;
}

What this is going to mean is that each element that is going to show up in the array that we are trying to make is going to be of the above type of structure. This one is going to be called a structured NumPy array in case you need to use this later on.

Now, if you have spent some time working with the Python language, you may look at some of these arrays and wonder how they are going to be any different than what you are able to see with the Python list. There are going to be a few different reasons for this, and we are going to take a bit of time exploring these to gain a better understanding of what is going to happen with both the array and the list when we use them.

To start with, the array in NumPy is going to be more compact than what we are going to see with the lists in Python. A regular list of Python is going to take about 20 MB or more of data in order to handle, and this can go up if you are working with a longer or a more complicated list on the process. But if you are working with an array in NumPy that is 3D and has a single-precision float in a cell, it is going to be about 4 MB. This can help us to get to the information a lot faster. And when you are already working with data analysis or a data science project that has a ton of information, the less space some of your other coding parts will take, the better off for you.

In addition, you would also find that accessing the array versus the list in terms of reading and writing items is going to be a lot faster and easier to handle when you choose to work with the array. This will help you to get through some of the arrays that you would like to handle a little bit faster and will ensure that you are going to get things done faster. When you have at one of the data to get through, and you are working with machine learning, you will find that all of this can be useful in the long run.

Now, in the beginning, it may not seem like the difference in space or speed that comes with the Python lists and the NumPy arrays would be that big of a deal. But you will find that there are a ton of times when this is going to be super important to what you are trying to get done with some of your codes.

It may not matter that much if you are just working with a million cells, but it is going to matter when you are working with something a lot larger, like a billion cells. Neither approach is going to fit into the architecture that is based on 32-bit, but if you are working with a 64-bit you can build with the NumPy and get it all done with about 4 GB of data while the Python, when it is doing all of the works on its own, would need a minimum of 12 GB to get it done, and many people will say that it takes twice as much as this if not more. And we can imagine that the more space that we need to use, the more we will have to spend on the hardware to take care of it.

The difference that you are going to find with the array is mostly going to be thanks to the indirectness that comes with this. The Python list is going to be an array of pointer that goes back to an object of Python, at least 4 bytes per pointer plus 16 bytes for even the smallest of the objects in Python. On the other hand, the NumPy array is going to be an array that comes with lots of uniform values. This makes it a lot easier to work with and will ensure that you are able to keep things in order and uniform without all of the work.

Not only is NumPy going to be more efficient like we talked about above, but you will also find that it is a lot nicer and more convenient to work with. When you work with this one, you are going to find that you are able to get a lot of matrix and vector options to work for you for free. This is going to be nice because it allows you to avoid some of the work that is unnecessary, but which you have to do to get some of the other parts of Python, like the lists to work. Add into this that you are able to implement them in an efficient manner, and it is no wonder that so many people want to work with these arrays for some of their own data analysis projects.

To take it a bit further, not only are you going to enjoy the convenience that comes with these arrays, but you will like how efficient they are, along with their functionality and the speed. When it comes to sorting through millions and even billions of data points overall, it is important that we are able to do this in a fast and efficient manner along the way. This is something that the NumPy array is going to be able to help us with.

The first thing to look at here is going to be the functionality. You are going to be able to build up a lot of things when you are working with the NumPy array. For example, you can work with things like linear algebra, some of the basic statistics, fast searches, FFTs, convolutions, and histograms, to name a few. And how are you supposed to be able to handle some of the data science projects that you want to do without some of these important parts showing up as well?

And another thing that you will be able to notice and enjoy when it comes to working with the NumPy array is that it has a lot of speed. The speed may not be that noticeable when you are working on a smaller project that doesn't have a lot of data points attached to it. But when you are working with a big project with a lot of data points, you will quickly find that this is going to be something important and something that the NumPy array is able to deliver on.

Some of the other benefits that you will be able to receive when you decide to work with the NumPy array rather than the Python list with some of your data analysis projects will include some of the following:

1. The arrays that show up in NumPy are going to come out at a fixed size at creation. This is different than what we are able to see when it comes to the Python list that is able to change and grow in a dynamic manner. Changing the size of your array when it is done is basically going to just create a brand new array that you are able to work with.

2. The elements that you are going to see with some of these arrays are going to tell us that they must be the same kind of data type. We are able to work with heterogeneous

types as well sometimes, but this makes it impossible to do some of the mathematical operations that you want to do. And as this is going to make it so that you can't do some of the parts of data science that you want with the arrays, it is not usually recommended. However, because you are using the same types of objects in all of this, you will find that all of them are going to be the same size in the memory of the code that you are writing.

3. The arrays that we are working with are going to be facilitated advances mathematical and other types of operations when it is time to work on large numbers of data. Typically, these operations are going to be executed more efficiently, and often with less code than what we are able to see with some of the different built-in sequences that we are going to see with Python as well.

The final thing that you are going to notice when it is time to work with the NumPy library is that many of the other specialized libraries that work with Python, including those for deep learning, machine learning, data science, and data analysis, are going to be based on these NumPy arrays. It is hard to do any of the functions that you need concerning these topics if you do not have the NumPy array in place first, and to do this. We need to make sure that we have this library up and ready to go as well.

As we are already able to see here, there are a ton of benefits and uses that we are going to be able to see when it is time to work with one of these NumPy arrays. They are designed to handle a lot of different options when it comes to handling our data science project, and learning how to make them work the right way is going to be critical to how much success we are going to be able to see with this process overall. Make sure that when you want to work with some kind of data science project that you make sure to install and important the NumPy library. This is going to ensure that we are able to get the best results out of everything, and will make it easier for us to really get the results that we would like when the project is done.

Chapter 6: Gathering and Collecting Your Data

Now it is time for us to go through some of the processes that we need to work on in order to start our own data science project. And this is going to be all about collecting the data that we need. It is hard to complete a data science project if we don't have any data saved up and ready to look through, but we don't want to collect just any old data, we want to collect the data that is going to help us see results in no time.

If a company is considering whether it would like to collect its data on its own or if they would like to work with another consultant to help them, they need to really have the right kind and amount of information to make an informed decision on the way that they should proceed. This chapter is going to take some time to look at the process of data collection and how we are able to make this work for us. Let's dive in and see how we are able to make this work for us

Where to Get Our Data

The first thing that we need to work on here is how to gather our data. We want to make sure that we are collecting from some good sources and that the data is high quality and will do the work that we want at the right time. There are a number of methods that we are able to use when it comes to gathering our data, and these will include:

The first option is going to be observed. Seeing is believing with this one. It is going to include us making some direct observations of some of the things that are going on around us. You will find that this is going to be effective and fast, a method to help collect the data that we want with just a little bit of intrusion. The important part here is to make sure that we have the right mechanism in place to make the observations, and we are ready. There are a few advantages to working with this method, including:

1. You will not have the issue of your subjects not responding to you when you make a direct observation.

2. If the observation is simple and doesn't require interpretation, this model isn't going to require a lot of training in order to get it to work the way to make it work.

3. The preparation time and the requirements for the infrastructure re minimal to handle the simple observations.

There are a few disadvantages that can come with using these observations, though. For example, when the observation is more complex, it is going to require some more interpretation and could lead to some bias in the process. And the analysis that you are working with could rely heavily on experts who need to know what to observe and how to interpret the observations once you have collected the data. And in some cases, there is the possibility of missing out on the complete picture because there isn't a direct interaction with the subjects of the sample.

Another option that we are able to work with is the questionnaire. This is going to be a kind of stand-alone instrument that helps us to gather data that can be administered out to the sample of subjects. You can send this out through online methods, phones, or mail. These have long been one of the most popular out of the techniques of data collection, and this can really help us to see some good results with them as well. There are a few benefits to using this kind of process, and these are going to include:

1. These can help the researcher have the chance to carefully structure and even formulate the plan of data collection that they should with some precision.

2. The respondents of these are able to take the survey at the time that is the most convenient for their needs. And they can even go at their own pace when it comes to thinking through the answers

3. The reach that you are able to have with this one is, in theory, limitless. These are able to reach every place that you want in the world if the medium you are using allows for it.

There are going to be some disadvantages that come with this one as well. First, if these are done without human intervention, they can quite passive and can miss out on some of the finer points that come with this and can leave some of the responses open to interpretation. This is why adding them with some discussions in focus groups, and interviews can help. The response rates of these can be low as well because it is hard to encourage the participants to actually fill them out and send the results back.

Next on the list is going to be the interviews. Conducting these interviews is a great way to help us overcome some of the shortfalls of the previous two collection techniques of data that we went through earlier because it allows you to have a better and deeper kind of understanding of the thinking that comes with the answers of the respondents. There are a few benefits that we are going to see when it comes to working with the interview, and these will include:

1. These interviews are going to help the researchers to uncover deep and rich insights and learn information that could have been missed out on in other cases.

2. The presence of this interviewer is going to give the respondents some additional comfort when they are done answering the questions and can ensure that you are getting the interpretation of the questions in the right way.

3. The physical presence of a persistent, well-trained interviewer can significantly improve the rate of response that you are able to get.

Of course, along with some of the other options, there are going to be a few disadvantages that come with this kind of option as well. The first issue is that reaching out to all respondents to help conduct the interviews is going to be a massive and time-consuming exercise that is going to lead to a major increase in the cost of conducting the survey. And to ensure that you are making the whole exercise as effective as possible, the interviewers must be trained well in necessary soft skills and the relevant subject matter.

And the final method that we are going to take a look at is the focus group discussions. These are going to take some of the interactive benefits of an interview to the next level because you are going to bring together a carefully chosen group together for a moderated discussion on the subject of the survey that they are working with. The benefits that come with this will include:

1. The presence of several relevant people together at the same time will be able to encourage them to engage in a healthy form of discussion and can help researchers to uncover some new information that they may not have seen in other methods.

2. These can also help researchers to corroborate the facts instantly, and any of the responses that are inaccurate will most likely be countered by other members who are in the focus group as well.

3. This method is going to give researchers a chance to view both parts of the situation and can build up a balanced perspective when it comes to the matter at hand.

One of the disadvantages that you are able to find when it works with these focus groups is that finding the people you would like to include in this method is going to be hard. You want to find those who are relevant to the survey that you are working on, and then being able to get them to come together for a session at the same time can be a hard thing to accomplish. And if there are some members in the group who are excessively loud, it is going to subdue some of the opinions of those who are less vocal.

Another issue here is that the members who are in the focus group can often fall prey to the issue of groupthink. This means that if there is one person in the group who is really persuasive and influential, it can bury up the diversity of opinion that should come out here. The moderator of this discussion has to guard against this kind of thing happening.

Other sources that we are able to use include social media, surveys that we send out to customers who have shopped with us before, and more. It is important to use as many different sources as we can, as long as they are high-quality, to ensure that we are getting the good data that is needed to form some of our analysis later on. But working with the methods that we have been talking about so far can really help to make this a reality.

Getting High-Quality Data

Another thing that we need to spend some time focusing on is the quality of the data that we are going to collect through this process. It is not going to do us much good if we end up with data that is low-quality, even if we have a ton of it to work with. The better the data that we can use, even if we end up having to take in fewer data overall, the easier it is going to be to train our algorithms and models overall.

Often the best thing that we are able to do with this is to make sure that we know what kind of data we want and how to pick out the data that will solve our particular business problem. If you just randomly go and search for and collect data, then this may provide you with a ton of data, but it is not going to provide us with the data that we need necessarily.

This means that we need to make sure that we are going with data that is going to solve our business problem. And knowing what this business problem is, and the one that is the most important for us to solve and work on first, you will find that this will help us to pick out the option that is best for your needs. When you know what business problem you would like to focus on, you will find that it is much easier to work with this process, and we can search through some of the data that we have and the right sources to answer that business question.

It is also important to make sure that you are going with sources that are going to help you to get some high-quality data as well. You don't want to waste your time on getting data that do not form the customers who don't shop with you, or from a source that is going to have a lot of bias that will mess with the results. You need data that is accurate, matches up to the topic that you are looking to work with, and more.

First, we need to make sure that we are picking out data that is accurate and going to help keep our algorithms as strong as possible. If your data is not accurate, it is going to give you some bad results out of your algorithms. You need to make sure that all of the data that you plan to use in your algorithms is as accurate as possible so that you can train the algorithm and get the insights and more that you are looking for.

Then we need to spend some time looking at the sources we are working with and that the data is not going to have a bias or other issues with it. If you are using third-party surveys and information to help you out, you need to use some critical thinking to help out with it. We need to make sure that there is not any bias in it, that we make sure that there aren't any issues with it, and that the sampling size is big enough to help us.
A good place to start is to figure out who did the report, or at least who paid for it. This can sometimes give us some good information on the data and can help us to figure out whether or not this is the data that we are able to rely on for some of our needs.

We also need to focus on making sure that the sample size is big enough, and that it actually reaches the people you want. You do not want to sample people who are in the 45 to 55 group if your customers are 25 to 35 year old's. You may find some good insights into this, but the insights are not going to be what you are looking for, and you will not get the answers that you want for your demographics.

With this in mind, we also have to make sure that we are going through and picking out the right number of people in our sample. If we have 100,000 customers and we only sample 10 of them, we are not going to get a good idea of how our customers are going to feel about something. We need to figure out how large the original size of the individuals are, and then decide what percentage of those people we would like to talk to when it is time to focus on this. That will ensure that the answers that we are working with will be accurate and can actually help us through this process.

When Do I Have Enough Data?

The next question that we are going to come up with here is whether or not we have enough data to work with for our project. This is kind of a tricky process, and it is often going to depend on what you are trying to figure out and how much data you are able to gather in the first place.

The more data, the better in most cases, but you also do not want to go through and gather data for years on end before you get to create some of the algorithms that you want to work with. You have to have some kind of stopping point and know where that is so that you will have enough data, and can still get the algorithm done in a good amount of time.

When you take a look at your data warehouse, and you see that you have a good amount of data at your disposal to work with, you will find that it is time to work with the algorithms that you want to use. You can then split it up into the testing and the training set that you want to work with and can send this through for your needs. You can continue to collect information at this time as well, because you may have to go through and do the training and the testing phases more than once as well.

Then when you are done with the training and the testing, you may find that you need some more data in order to make it easier for us to learn about the insights and the patterns and make some of the major decisions that are needed. When we are able to make all of this come together for our needs, you will be able to see some great results in the process.

Your goal with all of this is to make sure that you are able to gather as much information as you can, but set a limit on when you would like to get the information by. This will help you to stay on track and ensure that you are not going to end up with an endless process of gathering the data without ever getting to use it to make some of the major decisions that you would like.

Gathering up the data that you would like to use when it comes to working on a data science project is going to be important. When you are able to set this up in the right manner, and you are careful with some of the work that you are doing in order to help you get started, and then you are able to use this through in order to learn more from it overall.

Chapter 7: Loading and Preparing Your Dataset

When you decide to work with the process of data analysis, you will find that it is going to work the best when you are able to take all of that data you have collected and then put it into a database that you are able to look through and send through the algorithm later on. And when you have that database in place, it is also important that we are able to go through this and really have a chance at querying the database to find some of the information that we want

When you work with all of this data and even the sets of data that are collected from all of those different sources, it is likely that you are going to take the data and want to put it into one database to use. This is going to make sure that no matter what you are using in order to collect the data in the first place, you are able to go through that data and see it all in one place, as clearly and concisely as possible. But once you have all of that data in one place, it is also important that you go through and find the information that you need out of the database, without wasting time and getting frustrated.

When you have potentially millions of data points or more, you do not want to go into the database and hope that you can find the one single item that you need. And you don't want to try and compare and contrast all of those points either because there are just too many of them, and the database is going to be too large. With this in mind, one of the best things that you can do to make sure you find the information that you want, and something that can be done with your data analysis, is a database query.

This database query is going to help out because it can extract the data out of the database that you collected, no matter how big or small that database may be, and then it can format that data into a form that is readable for anyone. A query has to be written out in the language that is required by that database, and this usually means that we need to work with SQL or Structured Query Language. With Python is often used when it comes to some of the other parts that we need to do with data science, such as the algorithms that come with machine learning, we need to be able to learn how to work with SQL in order to work with any of the databases that we would like.

For example, when you would like to do the data out of a database, you need to start creating a query in order to request the specific information that is needed. Let's say that you have a table with your employees, and you want to be able to track the performance numbers of the sales and see how they are doing. You could do a query of the database for the employees who were able to record the highest amount of sales in a given period.

Now, one of the first commands that we need to take a look at when it comes to completing this kind of process is the SELECT statement. This is a query that needs to follow the query format that will come with your chosen database. The most common format of this is going to be the SQL format because it is easy to work with, it is the most common, and most databases are going to accept this format in their arsenal as well. This is why we are going to spend some time working with this one for this chapter.

To see how simple working with this can be, we are going to go back to that SELECT statement and see how it is going to work for some of our needs. For example, if you would like to go through and get the name and the title out of the database that you are working with, you are able to use that SELECT statement that we are talking about and then the code below to help:

```
SELECT FirstName, LastName, Title FROM Employees;
```

A database is really neat because it has the potential inside in order to reveal some of the more complex activities and trends, but you will only be able to harness some of this power through the help of the query. A database that has more complexity to it will consist of more than one table that will store up all of the data points that you want. This can make it easier to filter out the data that you want, out of the large amounts of data, into one single table, which can help us to analyze what we want, without all of the noise, in an efficient and quick manner.

These queries are going to be there to help us out when we need to perform some basic calculations on our data, or we are able to do some automation of these to make them easier for management to handle. You can even go through this and review some of the updates that are present in our data before we try to commit them to the database. This can help with some of the cleaning up processes that we are going to talk about in another chapter and can get the work done for us in no time.

To keep this as simple as possible, though, we need to know a few of the terms that are going to be used with this. To start with, the query is going to be whatever command we are using to go and gather the needed data out of the database. It is going to do the searching so that you won't have to go through all of those data points manually. Queries are a big thing in databases and often give them the power that we are used to seeing. A query can often refer to the action that is needed to help us retrieve the data from the database that we are using.

In many cases, you are going to be selective when it comes to how much data you would like returned. If you have a lot of data that is present in that database, you probably don't want to look through all of the information. You likely have some kind of criteria that you would like to work with, and you only want to bring up the data that matches.

For example, you may want to take a look through your database and see how many individuals in that database live in one city or in one geographical area. Or you may want to see the time period of when different individuals registered with your database in a given time period. You can do a query to help you find out all of this information.

The database that is used in data science is going to be quite large and making sure that you only get the information that you want out of it, rather than having to search through and figure out what answers fit and what don't, can be so important to get accurate insights. As with many of the other tasks that you can do with programming, you are able to do a query of your database either through the user interface or programmatically.

He first option that we are going to work with here is the programmatical approach. This is going to be like the code example that we used a bit earlier, where we are going to be able to bring out the SELECT command. You would then be able to use that command in the prompt and then add in any information that you are trying to get out of the database. This is going to be one of the fastest methods to work with here and will help you to get the right types of data, without having to spend your time coding or manually looking up the data.

As we talked about earlier, SQL is going to be a powerful language that we are able to use along with the Python language to help us with the database searchers. But it is also like Python in that the syntax is going to be really easy to read through and use as you would like. We did an example of how to write out some of the codings that we needed earlier on, and you are able to use that same information to help make sure that it is easy to understand what you are pulling out.

Then it is time to move on to the second option that we talked about above. You may find that sometimes when you are working with this language of SQL, there are some cases that you are not going to want to work with the coding part. Instead, maybe you would like to work more with the user interface to help generate some of the queries that you want to work with. This is often going to be the programming choice when you are going to work with a query that is a bit more complex than some of the others.

The systems that are there for database management are good for this because they can make things easier by offering a design view for the queries that you would like to work on. This design sort of view is going to enable us to pick and choose which columns we would like to display, and which criteria are needed in order to filter out the data that we are able to find in the database. Working with this kind of view is often going to be easier than some of the other options, and it will ensure that you are really able to sort through that huge amount of data while finding the information that you want.

As we go through this, the user interface that you may choose to work with on some of the queries is going to depend on the database type that we choose to work with. Some of these are going to prove easier for people to use, such as some of the Microsoft Access options, but then there are others that would prefer that you are able to work with the coding, and you will want to work with this option in order to ensure that you're getting some of the results that you want.

When this happens, you may need to stop and then consider which one you are hoping to get to work before you even start. This will ensure that you know ahead of time what options you can work with, and you can choose the one that will let you program in the manner that you want.

The user interface that you are going to use with some of your queries will depend on the kind of database that you are using. Some are going to be easier for people to use, such as the options that come with Microsoft Access, but others may prefer that you work with coding and want you to work with this option in order to get the results that you want. You may need to consider which one you would like to work with before starting to ensure that you know what options you have and can choose the one that allows programming in the way that you would like.

These databases are going to be important to some of the work that you do with data science. They are going to allow you to put your data in a form that is easier to look over and digest. While it may not be able to make it as easy to read through as some of the data visualizations that we talked about, it helps to get all of the information in one place, helps you to see what is there, and can even make it easier to figure out if something is missing out of the information. You can then modify and change up the information and the data that is there, and then use the information to complete your analysis and your visualizations to use later on.

In many cases, when you are working with data science, you are going to run across times when you need to put your information into a database and then search through all of that information in order to find what is most helpful to you. Actively looking through the database when there are hundreds of thousands, and maybe even millions, of points in there can take way too long, and you are going to miss out on the key information that you are really looking for in that database.

When we are able to work with the query as we have done above, either programmatically or with the user interface, this makes this task much easier to handle. You will get to go through and do a search for the relevant information that you need, rather than having to search through all of the listings that are there. This can limit some of the work that you do, keeps the results that you are looking at down to the minimum of what you actually need, and can provide you with a better opportunity to handle your data and get some good insights in the process.

Chapter 8: Data Mining

Another topic that is important for us to spend some time discussing when it comes to data science is the idea of data mining. Data mining is going to be a process that is used by many companies in order to take some of the raw data that they have and then turn it into information that is actually useful for them to use. By using the software, and a few other tools along the way, that can help them to look for patterns in all of the data they have collected, a business is able to learn a lot more about their customers.

So, why would a business want to learn all of this extra information about their customers? When the business does data mining properly, they will be able to develop marketing strategies that are more effective, can help to decrease their own costs, and even increase sales at the same time. Data mining is going to depend on the effective collection of data, along with computer processing and warehousing, to get it all done.

One thing to note here is that the processes of data mining are going to be used to help us build up machine learning models. These models that rely on machine learning are able to power up applications, including the recommendation programs found on many websites, and the technology that is able to keep search engines running.

How Does Data Mining Work?

So, why is data mining such an important process to focus on? You will see the staggering numbers when it comes to the volume of data that is produced is doubling every two years. Just by looking at unstructured data on its own, but just because we have more of this information doesn't mean that we have more knowledge all of the time. With the help of data mining, you are able to do some of the following tasks:

1. Sift through all of the noise, whether it is repetitive or chaotic, that is found in your data.
2. You are able to understand better what is relevant in all of that information, and then make good use of the information to help you assess what outcomes are the most likely for your needs.
3. It can help you to accelerate the pace of making decisions that are informed and driven by data, and more likely to help your business to thrive and grow.

Now that we have that figured out, it is time to take a look at how all of this data mining is going to work. We are not going to just grab the data, and then these trends will show up with us having to do no more work on them. And this is where we will be able to work with data mining. Data mining is a great way for us to explore and then analyze a large amount of information with the goal of finding all of the insights, trends, and patterns that we are able to use out of that information.

For example, we are able to work with data mining to help us to learn more about the opinions and even the sentiment of the users, to help us learn how to properly detect fraud, to help out with risk management, filtering the spam out of email, and even with marketing. All of these are going to be important to many different kinds of companies, and when you use them properly, you will find that they are going to ensure that you can better serve your customers over time.

There are five basic steps that we are going to see when it comes to working with data mining. In the first step, the company is going to spend some time collecting the data they want to use, and then they will make sure that all of this is going to be loaded up in the proper manner to their data warehouse. When this is all done, the company can then store and manage the data. Sometimes this is done on the in-house servers of the company, and other times it is going to be sent to the cloud.

When we go through with this, the management teams, IT professionals, and even business analysts are going to be able to gain access to this data, and then they can determine the way that they would like to organize all of this information. We are then able to work with application software in order to sort out the data based on the results that the user is going to put in. In the last step, our end-user is going to be able to present their findings and all of that information in a certain format that makes the most sense, and that will be easy for those in charge of making decisions to read through and understand.

While we are on this topic, we need to work on something that is known as data warehousing and mining software. The different programs that you decide to use with data mining are going to be responsible for analyzing the patterns, as well as the relationships, that we are able to find in the data, and all of this is going to be done based on the requests that the user sends out. It is possible that a company is going to use this software to help them create some new classes on that information.

We are able to go through and illustrate this point a bit more, as well. Let's imagine that we are a restaurant that would like to work with all of the steps of data mining in order to determine the right times to offer some specials. The restaurant would be able to do this by looking at all of the information they have been able to collect that is on the specials, and then see how the specials do at different times of the days and on different days of the week. They can then go through and create classes based on when the customers visit, and what the customer is most likely to order when they do come to the restaurant to eat.

We are able to take this to the next level as well. In some cases, a data miner is going to be able to find clusters of information based on a logical relationship, or they may take some time to see if there are sequential patterns and associations that they are able to draw some conclusions to learn more about their customers in the long run.

Warehousing is going to be another important part that we see with the data mining process. This is a pretty simple process to work with, and it is basically going to include when a company is able to centralize their data into one database or one program, rather than spreading out the information in more than one place. With the warehouse for data, an organization is able to spinoff some of the segments of the data for the right users to look over and analyze on a regular basis, and for the specific users to gain access to when they need it.

However, there are also times when we will see that the analyst will take the work on a different course during this process. For example, the analyst may choose to start out with some of the data they find the most useful, and then they will be able to create their own warehouse for the data based on the specifications there. No matter how a business wants to organize their data, they are going; they can definitely use it to help support some of the decision processes that the management of that company is going to make.

With this in mind, we also need to take some time to explore examples of data mining along the way. A good example of this is grocery stores. Many of the supermarkets that we visit on a regular basis are going to give off free loyalty cards to customers. These are beneficial to the customers because it provides them with access to prices that are reduced, and other special deals that non-members at that store are not going to be able to get.

But these cards are also going to be beneficial for the store as well because it is going to make it easier for the company to track which customers are buying what, when they are in the store making the purchase, and at what price they are making the purchases for. After receiving all of this data and having a chance to analyze it the stores can then use this kind of data to offer customers coupons targeted to those buying habits, and they decide when to put certain items on sale, or when it is best for the company to sell them at full price.

This is a great way for both parties to win. The customer is going to enjoy that they can potentially save money and so they will sign up for it. The store is going to enjoy that they get a chance to learn more about the customers and set prices at a point that will bring in more people and make them the most money possible.

We have to keep in mind here that there are sometimes a few concerns that data mining is able to bring up for the customer and for a company. Some customers are concerned about this process of data mining because they worry about the company not being ethical with their use of the data at all. It could even be an issue with a legitimate and honest company because the sampling they use could be wrong, and then they are going to use the wrong kind of information to make their decisions.

Most companies need to take some caution when they decide to work with the data mining process to ensure that they are going to be able to reach their customers better and do well in their industry through some useful insights and more that they are able to learn along the way. it is definitely something that you need to focus on when it is time to learn what patterns and insights are found in all of that data.

All of this data is going to be important when it comes to working in the process of data science. But we have to make sure that we really understand how this data is supposed to work and what is actually found inside of all that data. When we are able to learn all of this, we will find that it is easier than we may think in order to handle the data and get it to work for our needs.

Chapter 9: Completing the Data Analysis

While we are on the topic of working with data science, we also need to take a look at some of the data analysis. This is an important part of all the work that we are going to do with the help of a data science project, and it is actually the part that you have probably been waiting for so far in this process. This is basically a subset of data science, and it is going to be where we will handle the data that we are gathering, which comes in from many different sources, and then using algorithms to help us figure out what all of this data means.

You are able to use all of the data that we want, and we can fill up a lot of data warehouses if we would like, but if you don't understand what the data is telling us, then the data is not going to matter all that much, and your company will not be able to use it. This is where we will be able to grab the process of data analysis and make it come into play for us.

To help us get started, data analytics is basically going to be the process or the science of taking the raw data that we have and then analyzing it in order to help us make some good conclusions about all of that information. Many of the techniques and the processes that are used with this have been automated into algorithms and other mechanical processes that are able to work over the data in its raw form before turning it into something that we can read through and understand better than before.

When the techniques of data analytics are used in the proper manner, this data analysis is going to be used to help us see some of the metrics and the trends that we may miss out on in some of the other situations out there because there is just so much data that we are gathering and holding onto. This information is then going to be what we can use to optimize processes to help increase how efficient a system or a business can be overall.

Now that we know a bit about the broad meaning of data analytics, it is time to get into some of the different parts of it, and how we can use it to our advantage. The term data analytics is going to be broad, and it includes many diverse types of data analysis. Any type of information that can be subjected to techniques of data analytics to get inside that can then be used by humans to improve something about their business will fall under this umbrella.

Let's look at an example of this. Many manufacturing companies are going to spend time recording the work queue, downtime, and run time for the different machines that they are working with. They will then take the data that contains this information, and use it to better plan how and when the workloads should happen. This helps the machines get as close to their peak capacity as possible, saving time and money in the process. This is just one of the tasks that data analytics is going to be able to help out with, even though preventing bottlenecks in production is a good thing to pay attention to. Gaming companies are going to be able to use this process in order to set up the right reward schedules for players, which are done in a way that ensures the majority of players stay active in the game rather than dropping off and rarely using it. Another example is a content company. They can use the various parts of data analytics in order to keep their customers clicking, watching, or even reorganizing the content so that they can get the clicks and the views that they need.

As we are working through this process, we always have to keep in mind that the data analysis that we are working on here is a pretty complex process, and not one that we are able to just glance at and come up with the answers that we want. If you do this, then it is likely that you will end up missing out on information that is important, especially when you work with one of the larger sets of data.

Following the right steps along the way can make a big difference in what we are going to see with this data analysis. And some of the different steps that we are able to use here will include the following:

1. We start out this process by determining the requirements of the data or how the data has been grouped together. There are a lot of possibilities here, including the data being separated out by things like gender, income, demographics, and age. The values of the data could also

be numerical, or they may be divided up by category as well.

2. Then in the second step of this is the process of collecting our data. There are a ton of different sources where you can get all of this information. It could be from your employees, from sources in the environment, online sources like surveys and social media, and even from your computer system.
3. Once the data has been collected, and you are sure you have the data that you need, it is time to organize the data Since you are collecting it from a variety of sources, you have to make sure that it is organized in a manner that makes sense, and one that the algorithm will be able to read through quickly and find the trends to make predictions from when you get to that step.
    a. You can choose what method you would like to use when you organize the information. You can work with a spreadsheet or try some kind of software that is good at handling data that is statistical.
4. Once you have been able to organize the data the way that you would like, it is time to clean it all up before the analysis happens. This means that the data scientist has to go through and scrub the data and check that there are no errors or duplications that are found in the information, or that the data is not incomplete. This step takes some time, but it ensures that everything is fixed and ready to go before you even start.

The key thing that we have to remember here is that it is going to be the science that we can use in order to use raw data, analyze it, and then make some good conclusions on this information as well. The processes and the techniques that are used in this kind of thing is going to be automated in many cases, and you will see that when we work with the right algorithm, it will be able to take all of that raw data and turn it into something that humans are able to consume. And the main reason that a business would want to use this kind of process, and to analyze the data, is because it is going to be so useful when it is time to optimize your customer service, your performance, and how you can help your own performance.

Why Does the Analysis of Data Matter?

While we are here, we need to take a moment to look at why this data analysis is going to be so important, and why a business would like to go through these algorithms and more to learn from that data they have been able to gather in the first place. These companies find that they are able to use the insights and predictions that are in the data, but when there is such a large amount of data, and all of that data comes to them from a variety of sources, it is going to need a lot of work to sort through. Too much work to try and do in a manual manner.

The process that of data analytics is something that can be helpful to any business no matter what industry they are in because it will help them to optimize their performance. It can also help them to work on their business model and can make it easier for them to identify some methods that are more efficient for reducing costs and getting things figured out.

In addition to all of this, a company will be able to take that data analysis and make decisions that are going to help propel them into the future. This analysis is also going to help them to learn more about some of the customer trends that are out there and can help you to offer new services and products that are going to work for your customers as well.

Choices in Data Analysis

The next thing that we need to spend some of our time here is to figure out what kinds of analysis are open for you to work with as well. There are a lot of variations that come with the data analysis, and you can pick the one that works the best for your needs. There are a number of these, but we are going to focus on some of the ones that you are most likely to use when you first get started on this whole process. The four basic types that a beginner in data analysis is able to focus on, and that most data scientists are going to work with will include the following:

1. Descriptive analytics. This is one that will take the time to describe what has happened in the data over a chosen period of time. You may look at things like whether the number of views has gone up, or if the sales for your company are higher or lower than they were in the previous month for a product.

2. Diagnostic analytics This is the one that will focus more on why something has happened or the root of how your business is doing. This one is helpful, but it will involve data inputs that are more diverse and a bit of hypothesizing in the process. For example, did you have a slow sales week because the weather was bad and no one went out shopping? Or did something go wrong with one of your marketing campaigns, and that is why sales are struggling?

3. Predictive analytics. This one is going to be used to help predict what is most likely to happen in the near future, based on the information that we have at our disposal right now. What happened to the sales last year when the summer was warm? How many weather models are going to tell us that there will be a hot summer this year, and we should prepare for more of what we saw in the past?

4. Prescriptive analytics. This one is going to be responsible for suggesting a course of action that the company should take. For example, if the likelihood of a hot summer is measured as an average of five weather models and this likelihood is above 58 percent, then it is likely that you should add in more shifts to handle the sales if this is something that has happened in the past.

As we can see, there are some differences that show up with this, even though they are going to focus more on handling the data and helping us to gather some of the useful insights that are there from the data. The demand to be able to handle all of this data and then perform these in an accurate and timely manner through the analysis is going to be higher, even though right now there are not necessarily enough professionals to handle all of this work.

Even without a professional with this, companies can learn how to make the data analysis work and can then use this to leverage a ton of data and learn from it. Companies are seeing all of the benefits of doing this, and they like that this is going to help them to make some smart decisions, ones that are driven by data so that they are going to be able to see a lot of benefits and really see how to beat out the competition.

What Are the Benefits of a Data Analysis?

When it is time to work with data analysis, it will not take you too long to realize that there are a lot of benefits that are going to come with this overall as well. No matter what kind of company you are in and what your goals are, you will be able to receive a lot of these benefits in the process as well. This process may seem like it has a ton of steps and that you are going to spend too long working on it for it to be worth your time. But it can be so worth it if you actually take the time to learn about the data and all of the cool things that it is able to do for you. With this in mind, some of the benefits that you are going to receive when it is time to work with data analysis for your company, no matter what kind of company, will include:

1. It helps you to understand your customers better. All businesses want to understand their customers. This is the best way to make more sales and increase revenue. But how are you supposed to know what the customer wants, and what is going to convince them to come to your store compared to going over to a competitor? This data analysis can take information from customer surveys and customer habits and help you make more informed decisions to provide better customer service to increase sales as well.

2. It helps you to know what trends are going on that you should follow for your business. There are always trends that go on in any market, but these trends are often shifting and changing at really fast rates that are hard to keep up with. Using a data analysis can help you to catch on to some of the trends ahead of time, making it easier for you to really meet the needs of your customers.

3. It helps you to know your product better. Sometimes, this data analysis can be used to help you know which products are doing the best and why. You may find out that one product is actually doing better than you thought, or that you should start selling more of a similar product to increase sales.

4. It can help make smarter business decisions overall. It is always best if you can have data and information behind all of the decisions that you make for your company. The data analysis helps you to comb through all of that information and see what is there before you make any decisions about your company.

5. This data analysis process is going to be one of the best ways that you are able to beat out the competition. Companies who are willing to look through the data and are willing to see what insights and trends are there are the ones who will be able to find these things faster than the competition, and who will be able to win in their industry.

You will find that these benefits are going to help out your company, and are some of the main reasons why this data analysis can be so good for the whole company, and why it is something that is in such high demand for almost every industry that is out there. For some of the smaller companies that are out there, the ones who may not be choosing to work with this kind of process will find that they can still work with it on a local level and get some results as well.

There are so many benefits that are going to come with your data analysis, and being able to figure out how to make this happens, and what you are able to do to really see some of the results when it comes to learning what is in that data, is going to be very important as well. Make sure to go through some of the steps that we talked about in this chapter, and in the rest of this guidebook, and you will see that you are able to make this work for your needs as well.

Chapter 10: How Machine Learning Can Help

When we are talking about data science and some of the different processes that come with it, you will find that we can't get very far in this process without learning a bit more about machine learning and all of the different parts that come with that as well. All of the algorithms that we are going to talk about with data science will rely on machine learning to help them happen. This is why we need to take some time to learn more about machine learning and how this is going to work with our process.

Machine learning is going to be one of the many branches that we are going to see when we talk about artificial intelligence. This means that it is going to be one of the types of artificial intelligence, but it is not the same, and it is not going to encompass all of the parts of artificial intelligence is able to do as well. This branch is going to be used, and based on the idea that a system can learn from the data it is going to be presented with, it can identify patterns, and it is able to make some smart decisions based on the data.

Because of all of the different technologies that are out there to help us with computing and more, machine learning that we rely on today is going to be a bit different than how it was in the beginning. It was originally born from the idea of recognizing patterns, and the idea that a computer and some of the other systems are able to learn on their own, without needing to have a programmer who would tell it what to do with every step.

Think about how amazing this can be! We are able to teach the computer how to handle a lot of different tasks, all on its own. We can train it and test it and then have the system go through the process that is necessary in order to really figure things out without us having to specifically go through and explain all of the steps to it or program it this way, either. This is something that may have seemed impossible in the past, but it is something that we are able to do now with some of our modern technology.

While many of the algorithms that work with machine learning have been around us for a number of years now, there are some changes that have made it even more fun to learn about today. The ability for this kind of learning to automatically apply mathematical calculations that are complex too big data (which is what we really need it to do when we work in data science), over and over while getting faster in the process, is a more recent development. There are a lot of different ways that this machine learning can already be used, and that we are already seeing it used in our daily lives, and these include:

1. The self-driving Google car is one of the biggest examples right now of machine learning at work.

2. Any of the online recommendations offers that we see on various websites as we shop.
3. Machine learning is able to work with something known as linguistic rule creation to help companies know what customers and others are saying on Twitter and other social media accounts.
4. Fraud detection has been in use with financial institutions for some time now, and when it is powered by machine learning, we are going to see some great results.

All of the new interest that has come with machine learning is due to some of the same factors that have made data mining, and other parts of data science, so important in our modern world. Things like the growing amount and the different types of data that companies are able to get their hands on have helped to raise some of the interest. Add in that the processing power for doing the computations is cheaper and more powerful than ever before, and that companies are finding new and innovative ways to store the data, and it is no wonder that machine learning and artificial intelligence are two parts of data science that are really growing.

When we keep this in mind, we have to remember that there are a few things that we must get in place in order to create a system of machine learning that is actually good. We need to make sure, to start with, that the system we are working with has some capabilities to do preparation of the data. We need a combination of more advanced algorithms, and some basic ones, to help go through the data. We need to have a few iterative processes and even some of those processes that are going to work with automation. We need to have some scalability that shows up, too, because we need to make sure that the program is able to handle a large amount of data as well. And then, we need to work with something that is known as ensemble modeling.

Before we move on with this, there are a few other parts that are going to come with this machine learning process that we need to focus on, as well. To start, when we work with this machine learning, the target is going to be known as a label. But in statistics, we are going to call this the dependent variable instead. And the variable that we talk about in statistics is going to be a feature when we go back into the machine learning algorithm and use statistics for that algorithm as well.

The Different Types of Machine Learning

While we are here, we need to spend a bit of time looking at the four main methods of machine learning that we are going to be able to work with. These are going to help us to organize the types of algorithms that we are able to work with when it comes to handling our data with machine learning, and can make a difference in the way that we take over that data.

The four main types of machine learning that we are able to work with will include supervised, semi-supervised, unsupervised, and reinforcement machine learning. All of these are going to handle our data in a different manner, so we are able to take a bit of time to explore them and see the method and manner that they use to help us handle our data and get things done with machine learning.

The first part of machine learning that we need to focus on here is going to be supervised learning. These are going to be the algorithms that we can use that will be trained with lots of examples, and these examples need to be labeled. We are basically going to take these machine learning algorithms and will show them a ton of examples of what we want to see done so that they can learn how to work. We can show them some examples that are true and some that are false, and they are given the right answers from the very beginning, at least with the training data. Then, when we are done going through and sowing the algorithm a ton of examples, we will then go through and do a test to help figure out how accurate the system is and to figure out if we need to show off more examples or not in the process.

In this kind of learning, we are going to find that the input is based on the known output that we wish to get. We will use this to help speed up the process of machine learning and to make it a lot easier for the system to know what it should do. As long as the data and the examples that you choose are high quality, you will find that this one is going to work well and will provide you with some of the best predictions and insights that you are looking for.

From there, we are going to move on to the second type of algorithm, which is going to be known as semi-supervised machine learning. You will find that this is a nice in-between method that works kind of like supervised and unsupervised. It is going to mash up the two together to help us get some of the results that we want. With this one, we are going to find that the algorithm is going to rely on some combination of labeled and unlabeled data in order to learn. Usually, there is going to be more unlabeled data in this mix, though.

The reason for this is that the labeled data is going to be more expensive and harder to gain access to. It would be nice to train everything with this, but depending on what you are trying to do, you may not be able to find the data or afford to use that much of it. When we use just a bit of the labeled data and then finish off the training with some of the unlabeled data, we will find that we are going to be able to get some amazing results with all of this as well. It gives us kind of the best of both worlds so we can see the results that we want and train the algorithm quickly.

Now that we know a bit about the two types of supervised machine learning options that are out there, it is time for us to move onto the third type that we can work with, known as the unsupervised machine learning. This is going to be the one that is able to help provide us with some more power and neat options for the programs that we want to work with, but it is going to work differently than what we are going to see with some of the other options. With this one, we are able to train the model with data that is not labeled for us at all.

The goal that we are going to work with here is that we want to have the algorithm figure out what is being shown, without us telling it what it should see. We want to have the option to explore the data, and then figure out whether or not there is some structure that can be found in it ahead of time. the one method that we are able to see how this is going to work with unsupervised learning is to work with some transactional data. What we are going to see here is that with the unsupervised machine learning, we would be able to segment out our customers who have similar attributes, and can use that information to help out with our marketing goals overall.

Or you are able to use this in order to figure out which of the attributes are the most important when it is time to sort out or separate your customers into the segments you choose. These are just a few examples, but basically, the unsupervised machine learning algorithms are able to go through a lot of data and then figure out what patterns are there for us, even if we do not know what the patterns should be in the first place.

And the fourth type of machine learning that we can focus on is reinforcement learning. To those who have not had much time to explore machine learning and all that it entails, you will find that reinforcement sometimes acts in a manner that is similar to what we discussed in unsupervised machine learning. While the outward appearance is maybe going to look similar, the stuff that goes on behind the scenes and the things that put this kind of algorithm into motion will be different than what you see with the unsupervised machine learning algorithms we talked about before.

This kind of algorithm is something that we see often in gaming, robotics, and navigation. With reinforcement learning, the algorithm is going to be able to discover, using the process of trial and error, which actions out of a set of choices will provide you with the best rewards to the minimum amount of risks in the process.

When we work with reinforcement machine learning, we will find that there are going to be three components that have to show up to make it work. We will start out with the first component of the agent, who is the decision-maker or the learning in this process. Then we have the environment, which will include everything that our agent from before is able to interact with. And finally, we end with actions, which will be what our agent is able to do.

The main point that we are going to see when we are working with this is that we want to have the reinforcement algorithm to go through and determine the right actions while ensuring that the algorithm is able to maximize the expected reward over a given amount of time. The agent, when it is working in the proper manner, is going to be able to do this when it focuses on following a good policy. It will learn what this is over time and can then follow that each time, becoming faster and more efficient at the same time.

The future that comes with machine learning is looking bright, and it is likely that we are going to see this expand and grow more in the future as well. There are many ways that we are going to be able to use machine learning, as well as the other parts that come with artificial intelligence, and learning how to make all of this work and come together, and ensuring that we are going to see the results that we want, will all depend on how we decide to use this in the future.

There are a few different ways that we are able to take some of the features and capabilities that we see with machine learning and use it in our business. Due to some of the jobs that we are going to see impacted through this technology, it is important for us to also stop and address the pitfalls that are potentially there as well. There are a few things that could be considered pitfalls, and as such, we really need to take a look at them as well. Some of these potential pitfalls are going to include:

1. Businesses have to be able to overcome some of the bias and trust issues that are often going to come with AI by achieving an effective as well as the successful implementation that will make it possible for all of the people using the system to benefit in the process.
2. The governments who use this need to ensure that any gains they get from Ai can be shared widely, or as much as possible, across the whole of society to prevent social inequality between those affected and those who unaffected by these developments. For example, this could

be through increased investment in the training to make it happen.

3. With some of the additional cost savings that happen with implementing the AI systems, employers need to also focus on increasing the number of skills that their current and future employees need to have.

Working with machine learning is going to be one of the best things that you can focus on when it is time to complete some of your data analysis and data science project. Without this, it is hard to create some of the models and algorithms that we need in order to handle that data and get it all to work the way that we want. With this in mind, we took a look at some of the different methods that you can use with machine learning and some of the different benefits that come with this as well. When you are ready to get started with data analysis and ready to create some of the algorithms that you need to sort through and understand the data, then working with machine learning is going to become your best friend along the way.

Chapter 11: How to Work with Data Visualization

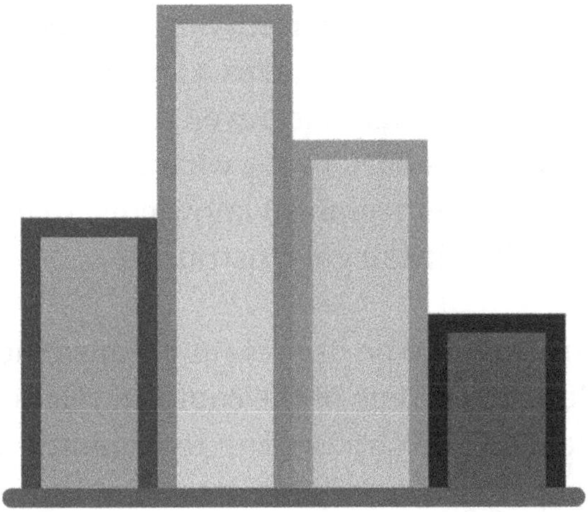

The final thing that we need to spend some time looking at in this guidebook is the idea of data visualization. This is going to be an important step that helps us to finish out the data science project that we are working with because these visuals can provide us with a unique and easy way to take a look at some of the data that we are focusing on, and can ensure that we will really be able to understand some of the more complex relationships that are showing up in some of the data that we have.

There are a lot of times when we are going to think that this step is not necessary. We assume that we are able to just look at the data, and that is good enough. But we are going to find that these visuals are going to help us to really see what is going on, at a glance, compared to trying to read through all of the information and hoping that it is going to make sense.

For most people, we will find that working with these visuals will make it easier to see what is in all of that data and how we are able to understand what is going on. Sure, we can look through the reports and spreadsheets and more and hope that we are able to find the information that we need, but this does not always work in our favor. First off, this takes a lot more time. When you try to look through all of that data, even after the algorithm it could be pages long, it is hard to see what is going on there, and if you do not have the right technical knowledge that comes with these algorithms, then it can get frustrating.

These visuals are going to be important because they will ensure that we are able to take some of the complex relationships that are found in the data and shows them to us in just a few moments instead of having to pour over all of those documents. This doesn't mean that the documents don't have some use in our work either. It simply means that we need to take the right precautions to add in the visuals because they can definitely make the work easier.

Data visualization is basically going to be the presentation of our quantitative information in a form that is graphical. This means that we are able to use these visualizations in order to turn small and large sets of data into visuals that are going to be easier for the human brain to process and understand. You may even be surprised at how common these visuals are going to be in your daily life, but they will also still appear in the form of well-known charts and graphs. A combination of more than one visual and bits of information to help explain what is going on will be known as an infographic.

Data visualizations are going to be used in order to help us to discover some of the unknown trends and facts that are found in the data that we are working with. We could see them in a lot of different forms, though, depending on the kind of information that we are trying to learn from. They could be in the form of a line chart that is going to display some change over time. We may see them as bar and column charts that can help us to make some comparisons and observe relationships. And pie charts are going to be able to showcase parts of a whole that we want to keep track of.

What Makes for a Good Data Visual?

The first thing that we need to take a look at here is what will make a good data visualization. These are going to be created when we see communication, data science, and then also design collides with one another. When we do these visuals in the right manner, we will find that they can offer us some key insights into sets of data that are complicated, and it does this in ways that are meaningful and intuitive.

In order to help us come up with a better data visualization, we need to make sure that we start out with data that is clean, and that comes from a good source, while also being complete. Once the data is set up and ready to visualize, it is then time for us to go through and pick out the right kind of chart. This is sometimes easy and sometimes a bit trickier, but the good news is that there are a ton of resources that you are able to use that will make it easier to pick out the right kind of chart.

After you have had a chance to decide which of the chart types will be the best for your needs, it is time to design and even do some customization of your vision to your liking. The thing to remember here is that simple is better. It is never a good idea to add in any kind of element that is going to distract from the data. When the visual is complete, it is time to publish and share with those who need to know more about the data at hand.

Why Is Data Visualization Important?

Then we need to move on to figuring out why these visuals are going to be so important to the work that we want to get done. There are a lot of reasons that companies are going to work with these data visuals to handle some of their workloads, and the first one is that these can help them to make better decisions. Today, more than ever, companies are relying on various data tools, including data visuals, in order to ask better questions to start with, and then make some good decisions along the way.

With the help of some of the newer computer technologies and software programs that are more user-friendly, it is easier for us to learn more about our own company and make decisions that are going to help our business while being driven by data.

The strong emphasis on some of the metrics of performance, the data dashboards, and even the KIPs, can show us all of the importance that comes with measuring and monitoring the data of the company. And when we are able to sort through all of this data and turn it into a form that we can really understand through the graphs and charts, it becomes so much easier for us to really make the decisions that our business needs.

Another benefit is that the visuals are going to work as a way to tell meaningful stories. These graphics and visuals are going to be so important when we look at places like the mainstream media today. For example, data journalism is on the rise, and these professionals are often going to rely on some good visual tools to make it easier to tell their stories about the work that is going on around us. This can make it easier for viewers, who are just watching this information, to understand what is going on in different parts of the world.

We will also find that marketers are able to benefit from some of this, as well. Good marketers are able to make decisions that are driven by data on a daily basis, but then they need to make sure that when they share this kind of information with their customers, they are going with a more user-friendly approach rather than just showing a bunch of data. With the help of these visuals, the marketer is able to make all of that happen.

Being able to go through and understand, as well as read through these visuals is something that has become a requirement for those who wish to have a professional career in our modern world. Because these tools and resources are available almost everywhere, it is important, and easy to learn how to use them for some of our own needs. This is definitely something that you need to learn how to do if you wish to gain some professional careers in our modern world.

As we can see here, there are a lot of benefits that are going to come when using the data visuals for your business. And there are a lot of choices that you are able to make when it is time to bring some of these visuals out and use them for your own needs. Spending the necessary time on these, and ensuring that you have the right visual for the job at hand, and for the data that you are working with, is going to be so critical to the success that you are able to see overall.

Make sure that you take some care with the data visuals that you want to work with. Choosing the right one and matching it up with some of the work that you are going to do along the way can make or break your project. Think about the method that will make understanding the data as easy as possible, and you will find that you can make all of this work for your needs in no time.

Conclusion

Thank you for making it through to the end of *Python Programming*, let's hope it was informative and able to provide you with all of the tools you need to achieve your goals whatever they may be.

The next step is to go through and work on some of the different topics that we brought up. If you have spent any time in business recently, then it is likely that you have heard about data science and all of the parts that go with this. This is a unique process that allows you to collect a ton of data, and there is more than enough of this data all over the place right now, and then learn from some of the insights and the predictions and patterns that are needed inside of all that data as well.

There are many times when we are going to work with a data science project, and adding in some of the Python languages, and learning how to work with the process of machine learning too can make a difference in the amount of success that we are going to have with this process as well. Putting it all together, though, and being willing to take the time and the talent that it needs, will be so helpful to your business. You will be able to learn more about your competition, figure out what your customers are looking for when they show with you or with the competition, and so much more.

This guidebook took some time to explore the process of data science. We looked at what data science is all about, how to set up the environment that you need to complete one of these projects, some of the best libraries that would help you to get all of this done, and more. We even went through some of the steps that are needed to help out with this kind of programming thing, and how we would be able to gather, clean, analyze, and visualize the data that we are looking for as well. We even had some time to talk about machine learning and how this process is going to fit in with the work that we are doing.

There is just so much that we can do with a data science project, and while it does take some time, some technical knowledge, and some dedication to stay on task, you will find that this is one of the best processes that you are able to do to help your business be successful in the future and to help you make smart decisions that are driven by the data that is around you.

Many companies are jumping on board and learning more about how to work with data science and what all this process can do for them. And with the help of this guidebook, you will be able to do some of the same as well. When you are ready to jump on board and learn more about data science and how you and your business can benefit from this process, make sure to check out this guidebook to get started.

SQL Programming

The Ultimate Beginner's Guide to Structured Query Language Coding for Databases, Including MySQL, Microsoft SQL Server, Oracle and Access

Preface

What is SQL?

The SQL (**the Structured Query Language**, **Structured Query Language**) is a special language used to define data, provide access to data and their processing. **The SQL language** refers to nonprocedural languages - it only describes the necessary components (for example, tables) and the desired results, without specifying how these results should be obtained. Each **SQL** implementation is an add-on on the database engine, which interprets **SQL statements** and determines the order of accessing the database structures for the correct and effective formation of the desired result.

SQL to Work with Databases?

To process the request, the database server translates **SQL** commands into internal procedures. Due to the fact that **SQL** hides the details of data processing, it is easy to use.

You can use SQL to help out in the following ways:

SQL helps when you want to create tables based on the data you have.

SQL can store the data that you collect.

SQL can look at your database and retrieves the information on there.

SQL allows you to modify data.

SQL can take some of the structures in your database and change them up.

SQL allows you to combine data.

SQL allows you to perform calculations.

SQL allows data protection.

Client and Server Technology

When using client-server technology, the application is divided into two parts. The client part provides a convenient graphical interface and is located on the user's computer. The server part provides data management, information sharing, administration and ensures the security of information. The client application generates requests to the

database server on which the corresponding commands are executed. Query results are sent to the client.
When developing distributed information systems in the organization of interaction between the client and server parts, the following important tasks in a practical sense are distinguished:

- Transfer of a personal database to a server for its subsequent collective use as a corporate database;
- Organization of requests from one end of the client over to the company's database will help make sure that the client will receive the right results.
- Development of a client application for remote access to a corporate database from a client computer.

The task of transferring a personal database to a server may arise in situations when it is necessary to provide collective access to a database developed using a personal DBMS (FoxPro, Access). To solve this problem, these personal DBMSs have the appropriate tools designed to convert databases to SQL format.
The preparation of queries to the database on the server (in SQL) from the client-side can be performed using a specially designed utility. To provide the user with great

opportunities and convenience in preparing and executing requests, client applications are created.
To organize queries to a server database in SQL or using a client application, various methods of interaction are possible that significantly affect efficiency. The main ways of such interaction include:

- Interface DB-LIB (database libraries);
- ODBC technologies (open database compatibility);
- OLE DB interface (linking and embedding database objects);
- DAO technologies (data access objects);
- ADO technologies (data objects).

The DB-LIB interface is an application programming interface specifically designed for SQL. Therefore, it is the least mobile among those considered in the sense of the possibility of transferring applications to another environment. In terms of performance, this method allows the fastest access to information. The reason for this is that it represents an optimized application programming interface and directly uses the SQL system query language.
ODBC technologies are designed to provide the possibility of interconnection between different DBMSs and to receive requests from the application to retrieve information,

translate them into the core language of the addressable database to access the information stored in it.
The main purpose of ODBC is to abstract the application from the features of the core of the server database with which it interacts, so the server database becomes as if transparent to any client application.
The advantage of this technology is the simplicity of application development, due to the high level of abstractness of the data access interface of almost any existing DBMS types. Using this technology, it is possible to create client-server applications, and it is advisable to develop the client part of the application using personal DBMS tools and the server part using SQL tools.
The main disadvantage of ODBC technology is the need to translate queries, which reduces the speed of data access. On client-server systems, this drawback is eliminated by moving the request from the client computer to the server computer. This eliminates the intermediate links, which are the main reason for reducing the speed of information processing using the tools of this technology.
When using ODBC tools in a client application, a specific data source is accessed, and through it, to the DBMS that it represents. When installing ODBC tools, the common ODBC

subsystem is installed and the "driver-database" pairs are defined, which are the names used to establish the connection with. database. Corresponding pairs are called named data sources.

Each named data source describes the actual data source and information about access to this data. The data can be databases, spreadsheets and text files. Access information, for example, to a database server, usually includes server location information, database name, account ID and password, as well as various driver parameters that describe how you should establish the right kinds of connections to your source of data.

When processing data on a server using ODBC technology and using a client application, two main stages are distinguished: setting a data source - creating and configuring a connection, as well as actually processing data using queries.

It is usually best if you are able to work with the OLE DB interface to create tools and utilities, or system-level developments that require high performance or access to SQL properties that are not available using ADO technology. Key features of the OLE DB specification provide full data access functionality. In SQL, the server database processor

uses this interface for communication: between internal components, such as the storage processor and the relationship processor; Between SQL installations using remote stored procedures as an interface to other data sources for distributed queries.
When using OJSC technology, work with databases and tables is carried out using collections of objects. This provides great convenience in working with database objects.

At present, the technology of JSC is gradually superseded by ADO technology, which allows you to develop Web applications for working with databases. In general, ADO technology can be described as the most advanced application development technology for working with distributed client-server technology databases.

Chapter 1: A Look At The Basics of SQL

Many companies have to spend some time finding ways to store all of the data that they want to work with. This data is such an important part of how they will run their business and the amount of success that they are going to find, that they know it is one of the best ways to help them get ahead. Thanks to the modern world of technology we are currently in, there are a ton of resources out there to provide us with some of the data that we are looking for. This data can be used by companies in so many ways. It can help them to learn how to reach their customers better, how to make better decisions, how to reduce some of the waste that they see on a regular basis in their business, and how to beat out the competition.

Gathering up the data that is needed is not going to be the hardest part. In fact, often the hardest part of all of this is figuring out the best way to store it, and then figuring out how you are able to take that information and actually sort through it, and make it work for your needs. One of the methods that can help with this is a database.

These databases are able to hold onto large amounts of information and can sort through it as well. But when you have millions of potential points of data that you want to sort, compare, and more, it is going to seem like a huge undertaking. And this is where the SQL language is going to come into play as well. Let's dive into what this language is all about, and why it is so important to helping us to achieve our goals with all of that data.

A Look at SQL

The first thing that you need to ask is what is SQL. SQL is going to stand for Structured Query Language and it is a pretty basic language that you can use in order to interact with the different databases that are on your system. The original version did come out in the 70s, but it had really started to see some changes when IBM released a new prototype that released SQL to the world.

This first particular tool was called ORACLE and it was so successful that the part of the company that worked with ORACLE was able to break off from IBM and started off on their own. ORACLE is still one of the leaders in the programming language field because it works with SQL and continuously makes it easier for people to learn how to work with the database.

Working with the Database

When we decide to spend some of our time looking at these databases and working with some of the neat things that are available with the SQL language, you will find that the database is simple, and will just hold onto groups of information. Sometimes we are going to think of these as mechanisms that will only hold onto the information that the user is able to access when they would like but other times it is going to come into play and will help a business to get ahold of the information that they need, without having to worry about some other potential issues showing up as well.

There are going to be times when you would want to bring out the database, and working with SQL, even if you didn't realize it at the time, can help you to work through this process. For example, if you have gone through and looked for a product on one of your favorite websites, then you are used to some of the ideas that come with this SQL and all that it is able to do to make things easier for you. It will help to sort through the perhaps millions of items on that website and will make it easier for you to really see some of the results that you would like.

With this in mind, we do need to take a look at some of the other information that we can use, and the different parts that are going to come with the databases that we are able to use when it comes to the SQL language.

Relational Database

The first type of database that we are going to talk about is a relational database. These are ones that are going to be segregated into tables or logical units. These tables can be interconnected inside of the database so that they make sense based on what you are working on at the time. The database is going to also make it easier to break up the data into some smaller units so that you are able to manage them easier and they will be optimized for making things easier on you.

It is important to know about the relational database because it is going to help to keep all your information together, but it does help to split it up so that the pieces are small enough to read through easier. The server will be able to go through all of these parts to see what you need because the smaller pieces are easier to go through compared to the bigger pieces. Because of the optimization and the efficiency that is found in this kind of system, it is common to see a lot of businesses going with this option instead of another one.

Client and Server Technology

For quite a while, a lot of the computers that were being used in the business industry were considered mainframe computers. This means that the machines were holding a large system that was great for processing as well as storing information. The user was able to use these computers in order to interact with the mainframe using what was done with a dumber terminal, or one that doesn't think on their own. In order to get all the right functions to perform, the dumb terminals are going to rely on the memory, storage, and processor that are inside of the computer.

While these systems worked and there isn't anything wrong with this setup (many companies even still use them to help get things done in their business), there is a better solution that will get the job done faster and more efficiently than you will find with the mainframe option.

The client/server systems will use a slightly different process in order to get the results that you would like. The main computer, also known as the server, can be accessed by the user that is on the network; for the most part, they are going to have a WAN or a LAN network that will help them to access the network. The user will be able to access this server with a desktop computer, as well as another server, rather than having to use the old dumb terminals. Every computer, which will be known as the client inside of this system, will be able to access this system, which can make it easier to have interaction between any clients and the server to get things done.

Internet-Based Database Systems

While the client to server kind of technology is widely popular and has worked well for a lot of people to use over time, you will also find that there are some programmers who have decided to add in some databases that are going to have more integration with the internet. This kind of system is going to allow the user to access the database when they go online, so they will be able to use their own personal web browser in order to check this out when they would like. Along with this, the customer can go and check out the data if they would like, and they can even go online and make some changes to the account, check on the transactions that are there, check out the inventories, and purchase items. They can even make payments online if this is all set up in the right manner. thanks to acting that we are able to base some of our databases online, we will find that it is possible to go online and let the customer access this database, even from their own home.

To help us work with these databases, we will just need to pick out the kind of web browser that we would like to go with, and then head on over to the website of the company that we go with. At times, you may need to have some credentials to get onto the account, but that is going to depend on the requirements of the company at the time. Then you can work with the search function in order to find some of the information hats you would like on the database.

You may find that a lot of these online databases are going to require us to have a login to have any kind of access, especially if there is some kind of payment requirement that goes with them. This may seem like a pain to work with, but it does add in some of that extra security that you are looking for to make sure your personal and financial information is always safe.

Of course, we have to remember that while this may seem like a simple and easy to handle kind of database, there are actually quite a few things that are showing up behind the scenes in order to make sure that the database is going to work. We have to make sure the database is working properly and that the right commands are being sent out at

the right times to ensure we can reach our accounts, find the products we want, look at our order history, and more.
For example, we may see that the web browser that we want to work with at any given time is able to use and also execute the SQL in order to make sure that it is showing any of the data and information that the user would like to see. SQL is going to be used to help reach the database that the customer is looking for, such as clothing or food that they are interested in seeing, and then SQL is going to send this information right back to the website before showing it to the user in that browser.
This sounds pretty complicated in the beginning, but you will find that it is actually going to be really easy to work with and can get done in just a few minutes if the program is set up in the proper manner. all of the things that we have been able to discuss with SQL so far will ensure that we are able to make a simple search or something else similar happen in no time at all. SQL can really make it that simple.

The Benefits of Using SQL

And finally, we need to spend some time taking a look at some of the advantages that we are going to see when it comes to using the SQL language to help us sort through all of the information that may be found in our database. There are actually a few other options that we can use when we would like to sort through a database that we want to work with. But SQL is going to often be the one that is chosen because it is easy to use, works well with databases in particular, and so much more.

There are a ton of benefits that you will be able to enjoy when it comes to working with SQL for some of your database programming needs. And using this is going to ensure that you are able to make sure that your database is set up and ready to go. Some of the many benefits that you will be able to notice when it comes to working with this kind of language will include:

- **High speed**—if you are looking for something that is a high speed, the SQL option is one of the best. The SQL queries are able to retrieve a lot of information from the database in just a little bit of time and it is one of the most efficient options that you are able to use on the market to get this done.

- **Well defined standards**—the SQL databases have been around for some time and they have some good standards that will help to make it easier to keep the database nice and strong. Some of the other databases don't have these clear standards and it can make it difficult to store the information that you need.

- **No coding needed**—you are able to use the SQL system in order to store some of the information for your business without knowing a lot of coding ahead of time. You will learn a few parts of coding inside of this guidebook to do the right commands, but you don't need to have extensive knowledge of coding before getting started.

- **The emergence of object**-oriented DBMS—the earlier SQL databases were based on the relational databases and while this is not a bad thing, there are some better and faster options. Now they are moving on to some of the newer options to help get the work done, including with object-oriented DBMS to help out.

Now with this in mind, we also have to remember that even though there are a ton of benefits that we are able to see when we are working with this kind of coding languages in our database, there are a few negatives that are going to show up and a few reasons why people may not want to work with this kind of language even on some of their database needs.

The first issue is that sometimes the SQL interface can be difficult to work with. Even though you do not need to know a ton of coding rules in order to start off with this language, it is still hard in some cases to interface with the database when you use SQL. This database is going to be a bit more complex in terms of its interface compared to just working with a few lines of code that we may find with some of the other options out there, so you at least need to take this issue into consideration.

Then there is also the issue that there are some features that come with this that are going to need third-party extensions on them. There are going to be some features that are added to SQL that will have to come with a third-party part in order to get them to work the way that you would like. If you do not want to take all of this effort to make it happen, then you may want to work with another language along the way instead.

SQL is going to be one of the best tools that you are able to use when it comes to handling some of the work that needs to be done with your database. It is a good method to use to store things to the database, make the tables that you want, bring in new information compare parts, bring other parts out, and so much more. When you are ready to work with your database and actually see some of the neat information that is inside, make sure to take a look at some of the different things that you are able to do with the SQL language.

Chapter 2: Some of the Basic Commands We Need to Know

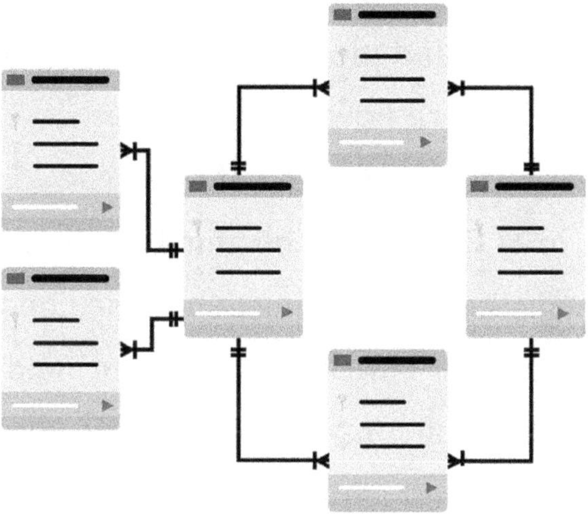

Now, before we are able to get too far into some of the codings that we are able to do with this kind of language, one of the first things that we need to learn a bit more about is some of the basic commands that come with this language, and how each of them is going to work. You will find that when you know some of the commands that come with any language, but especially with the SQL language, it will ensure that everything within the database is going to work the way that you would like.

As we go through this, you will find that the commands in SQL, just like the commands in any other language, are going to vary. Some are going to be easier to work with and some are going to be more of a challenge. But all of them are going to come into use when you would like to create some of your own queries and more in this language as well so it is worth our time to learn how this works.

When it comes to learning some of the basic commands that are available in SQL, you will be able to divide them into six categories and these are all going to be based on what you will be able to use them for within the system. Below are the six different categories of commands that you can use inside of SQL and they include the following.

Data Definition Language

The data definition language, or DDL, is an aspect inside of SQL that will allow you to generate objects in the database before arranging them the way that you would like. For example, you will be able to use this aspect of the system in order to add or delete objects in the database table. Some of the commands that you will be able to use with the DDL category include:

- Drop table
- Create a table
- Alter table
- Create an index

- Alter index
- Drop index
- Drop view

Data Manipulation Language

The idea of a DML, or data manipulation language, is one of the aspects of SQL that you will be able to use to help modify a bit of the information that is out there about objects that are inside of your database. This is going to make it so much easier to delete the objects, update the objects, or even to allow for something new to be inserted inside of the database that you are working with. You will find that this is one of the best ways to make sure that you add in some freedom to the work that you are doing, and will ensure that you are able to change up the information that is already there rather than adding to something new.

Data Query Language

Along with the same kinds of lines and thoughts here are the DQL or the data query language. This one is going to be kind of fun to work with because it is going to be one of the most powerful of the aspects that you are able to do with the SQL language you have. This is going to be even truer when you work with a modern database to help you get the work done.

When we work with this one, we will find that there is only really one command that we are able to choose from, and this is going to be the SELECT command. You are able to use this command to make sure that all of your queries are ran in the right way within your relational database. But if you want to ensure that you are getting results that are more detailed, it is possible to go through and add in some options or a special clause along with the SELECT command to make this easier.

Data Control Language

The DCL or the data control language is going to be a command that you are able to use when you would like to ensure you are maintaining some of the control that you need over the database, and when you would like to limit who is allowed to access that particular database, or parts of the database, at a given time. You will also find that the DCL idea is going to be used in a few situations to help generate the objects of the database related to who is going to have the necessary access to see the information that is found on that database.

This could include those who will have the right to distribute the necessary privileges of access when it comes to this data. This can be a good thing in order to use your business is dealing with a lot of sensitive information and you only want a few people to get ahold of it all the time. Some of the different commands that you may find useful to use when working with the DCL commands are going to include:

- Revoke
- Create synonym
- Alter password
- Grand

Data Administration Commands

When you choose to work with these commands, you will be able to analyze and also audit the operation that is in the database. In some instances, you will be able to assess the overall performance with the help of these commands. This is what makes these good commands to choose when you want to fix some of the bugs that are on the system and you want to get rid of them so that the database will continue to work properly. Some of the most common commands that are used for this type include:

Start audit

Stop audit

One thing to keep in mind with the database administration and the data administration are basically different things when you are on SQL. The database administration is going to be in charge of managing all of the databases, including the commands that you set out in SQL. This one is also a bit more specific to implementing SQL as well.

Transactional Control Commands

The final type of command that we are going to take a look at is going to be the transactional control commands. These are going to be some good commands that you are able to work within SQL if you would like to have the ability to keep track of as well as manage some of the different transactions that are going to show up in the database that you are working with.

If you sell some products online for your website, for example, you will need to work with the transactional control commands to help keep track of the different options that the user is going to look for, to keep track of the profits, and to help you to manage this kind of website so that you know what is going on with it all of the time. there are a few options that you are able to work with when it comes to these transactional control commands, and a few of the most important ones that we need to spend our time on will include:

- **Commit**—this one is going to save all the information that you have about the transactions inside the database.

- **Savepoint**—this is going to generate different points inside the groups of transactions. You should use this along with the Rollback command.
- **Rollback**—this is the command that you will use if you want to go through the database and undo one or more of the transactions.
- **Set transaction**—this is the command that will assign names to the transactions in your database. You can use it to help add in some organization to your database system.

All of the commands that we have spent some time discussing in this chapter are going to be important to some of the work that we want to get done and will ensure that we are going to find the specific results that we need out of our database. We will be able to spend some time looking through them in this book, but this can be a good introduction to show us what they mean, and how we will be able to use them for some of our needs later on.

Chapter 3: Creating Your SQL Tables

We have spent some time here looking at how to create a table in SQL. These tables are going to be there to hold onto the various types of data that we want to work with along the way. These tables are going to be able to make SQL work as efficiently as possible. What this means is that you are going to be in charge of creating the data that will go into these tables and SQL can make this easier than ever before. There are a lot of times when we need to work with creating some of our own tables. We are not going to get very far with some of the databases that we want to create if we do not first work to create a few SQL tables These tables are going to help us to keep the information organized in the manner that we need and will make it easier for some of the searches that we would like to accomplish to happen.

You are able to create any of the tables that you would like, and these can hold onto all sorts of information. Maybe you have a table that is responsible for holding onto your products for sale, and then one that holds onto all of the customer information, and one that holds onto some of the information about the payments and transactions that will happen in your business.

You can then go through and bring up the table that you would like and then search for the information that comes in that table. If you want to look at adding a new product to your system, for example, you would be able to go to the product table and make the adjustments that are needed. Depending on the kind of business that you are trying to run, and what you hope to get out of the process, you may find that there could be just a handful of tables to get the work done, and other times you will need to have quite a few of these tables to see the work be accomplished. You may need to go through ahead of time and figure out how many of these you are going to need before starting. This will help you to stay on track and will ensure that you are going to be able to get all of the ones set up that you want so nothing is going to get missing in the process.

You will not be able to get things to work as well as you would like if you do not add in these tables along the way. this is the best way to ensure that your information and your data is going to stay as organized as possible and that you are going to be able to get some of the results that you are looking for as well when you do a query and more.

The first step that we have to take here is to work with a new list, such as a shopping list, with all of the items that you want to work with found inside one of the tables in the database. We are going to start this off with a simple list to see how this is going to work, including three items, and the number of each item that you would like to work with as well. This will give us a good start to what we would like to see get done on this kind of process and will ensure that we are going to get the results that we want out of it.

The three items that we are going to work with to help us get the table created here is a blouse, underwear, and pants. We will have to go through and make a new command for the table that will then be able to store this particular type of list. So the sample list that you are going to see inside of the SQL that you are working with will look like the following:

/**Shopping list:

Blouse (4)

Pants (1)

Underwear (2)

*****/***

CREATE TABLE shopping_list(name TEXT):

If you place this syntax into the program, you are going to see that the table will have on the right-side column. You only listed that you wanted to have the text inside of the database, and nothing about the amount of the items, so the database at this point is just going to have the list of the things that you want to purchase (the blouse, pants, and underwear). Now it is time to add in the amount of each that you would like to have in the database. We need to add in the integer for this data type with the help of this new code:

```
/**Shopping list:
Blouse (4)
Pants (1)
Underwear (2)
**/
CREATE TABLE shopping_list(name TEXT,
quantity INTEGER);
```

Now you will notice here is that when you look at the table, there is going to be a new column that will be listed out in the database that you worked with before. The first column is going to have all of the different items that you would like to purchase, and then he second one is going to have the amount of each of these items that you would like to purchase as well. This is going to be a nice way to create the table that you want to use because it will ensure that you are able to get the unique identifier that you would like to have for these rows, and can help you when it is time to delete or update the rows later on. If you are reliant on just using the rows for your identification purposes, you are going to find that this causes a mess because these values are things that can change for you later on.

After you have had some time to name the rows that you would like to have in the table, it is time to fill all of this in. You will find at this time that the table is not going to have any of the information inside that you would like, and you will need to use the command of INSERT INFO to help get this started. you will be able to set up the first column that you would like to use and then label it as 1, and then the second one is going to be a blouse, and then the third one is going to be how many are inside, which is four. You are able to continue on with this process until you make sure that all of the information that you would like to use is found in the database as well.

To make sure that all of these steps are going to be done in the proper manner, you will need to spend some time creating a good syntax. This will ensure that the table is going to look the way that you would like. The syntax, or an example of code, that you are able to use to help with that shopping list that we made a bit before, and will ensure that everything is in order in the code, will include the following.

```
/**Shopping list:
Blouse (4)
Pants (1)
Underwear (2)
**/
CREATE TABLE shopping_list(id INTEGER
PRIMARY KEY, name TEXT, quantity INTEGER);
INSERT INTO shopping_list VALUES (1, "Blouse",
4);
INSERT INTO shopping_list VALUES (2, "Pants",
1);
INSERT INTO shopping_list VALUES (3,
"Underwear", 2);
```

Once you have placed this information into your new table, you can take a look back at it any time during this process to see how it is going, make sure that the numbers are still the right way that you want. You can even change the numbers, delete some of the things that you are working on, and even add in some new items if you would like to expand the list. There is so much that you are able to do when it comes to creating your own tables inside this program. While we just started out with a simple formula that has three items inside and a few items of each, you will find that most businesses are going to need tables that are much larger than this. You will still need to go through the same process in order to get this to work. Whether you just need five items or five hundred items inside of your table in order to keep all of your stuff inside the database, you will find that these same syntaxes are going to work, you will just need to use more of them.

As we can see with some of this, creating a table to work inside of the SQL program is going to be something that is fairly easy for us to work with. It is going to bring in a few different parts, and you do have the freedom of adding in the number of columns and rows that you would like in order to make sure that this database is going to work in the manner that you would like. You do have some freedom later on to make some of the necessary changes to your database, such as adding something new in, taking things out and more. There is a lot of freedom that is going to happen when you work with your own table in SQL, and it is one of the best ways to make sure that your data is safe and secure along the way, and that you will be able to pull it out and use it in the manner that you would like.

Chapter 4: Learning Phase One - The Basics

Now that we have been able to get this far, it is time for us to take a look at a few more of the basics that we need when it comes to learning with this language. We have looked at these a bit already, but now it is time for us to take a closer look at how to make it work, and some of the commands that are going to be important in this phase as well. Some of the different things that we need to explore when it comes to working with the SQL basics will include the following.

Extract Data - SELECT Statement

The first statement that we need to look at is the SELECT statement. This one is going to help us retrieve the items that we want out of the database. We can ask the language to bring back anything that we would like to view in the database, and the command that we need for this includes:

SELECT;

With this one, we need to go through and add in what we want to select. You can select a certain part out of a database or something from the computer that you are working with. But you start out with the SELECT keyword and go from there, telling it what you want to select. With this one, we will be able to gather up all of the records that are in that database and match up with our object that is named PC. However, the columns and rows of the result set are not ordered. To help us order the fields in the result set, they should be listed with a comma in the desired order that we would like to see after the command of SELECT:

```
SELECT price, speed, HD, ram, cd, model, code
FROM Pc;
```

When we take a look at the vertical projection of the PC table, we will find that we are also able to obtain this kind of listing when we use only the fields that are the most necessary to it. A good example of this is when we would like to be able to get the information out about the speed, and nothing else, of our processor, or the amount of RAM that our computer holds. We would then be able to work with the following code to make this happen.

```
SELECT speed, ram FROM PC;
```

Elimination of Duplicates - DISTINCT Clause

One thing that we are going to notice here is that the vertical selection that we would like to work with could contain duplicate rows on occasion if it does not contain a potential key ahead of time that will help us to identify the unique record that we want. In the PC table that we work with, the potential key is the code field, which is selected as the main key that we need for this table. Since this field will not be part of the query, the result that we get above has duplicate rows (for example, rows 1 and 3). If you want to get unique lines (say, we are only interested in various combinations when it comes to the processor speed, and memory size, and it will not necessarily be the characteristics of all the computers that are available and that you can use, then you would want to work with the following code:

```
SELECT DISTINCT speed, ram FROM Pc;
```

When we run this code, we are going to get the following output as a result

In addition to DISTINCT, the **ALL keyword** (all lines) can also be used, which is the default.

The ORDER BY Command

To sort the rows of the result set, you can sort by any specific amount of fields that you would like that was originally specified with the SELECT command or clause. To do this, use **the ORDER BY clause**. At the same time, *the field list* can contain both field names and their ordinal positions in the SELECT clause list.

This is going to be a good command that you are able to use when you want to make sure that you are not just getting some random order of information back at the time.

instead, you want to put it in alphabetical or by the age of the data, to help you sort through that information and keep it as organized and easy to work with as possible. With this command, you can tell the database, and the SQL language how you would like things to play out when you are all done.

Sample - WHERE Clause

The horizontal selection is implemented **by the WHERE clause**, which is written after the FROM clause. In this case, only those rows from the record source will fall into the result set, for each of which the *predicate* value is TRUE. That is, the predicate is checked for each record.

Boolean Operators AND, OR, NOT and Three-Valued Logic - Predicates

Predicates are expressions that take on truth value. They can be either a single expression or any combination of an unlimited number of expressions constructed using the

Boolean operators **AND**, **OR** or **NOT**. In addition, the **IS** SQL statement can be used in these combinations, as well as parentheses to specify the order in which operations are performed.
A SQL predicate can take one of three values: **TRUE** (true), **FALSE** (false), or **UNKNOWN** (unknown). The following predicates are an exception: **NULL** (no value), **EXISTS** (existence), **UNIQUE** (uniqueness), and **MATCH** (match), which cannot take the value UNKNOWN.

This can be a good way that we would want to go through and make sure that we are getting the right information out of the database that we are using. You would be able to use this to make sure that the data is only coming back as you would like.

We can take a look at the example of a search engine for this one. You do not want to have a bunch of items showing up that the customer does not want, especially if you have hundreds of items. You can use the Boolean operators to help you determine what items on the database match up to the query from the customer, and which ones do not, providing them with a seamless experience that will help them to get the most out of what you are providing in the website.

Comparison Queries

There are times when you will want to do a comparison between what is found on your database, and the query that you are completing. And maybe sometimes you would even like to go through and compare more than one part of the database to see what is all there. You could try to do this by hand or manually, but it will not take long before you find that, with a potential for millions of data points in the database, this is going to take a long time and be too hard to handle.

Instead, we can work with some of the comparison operators that are present in the SQL language. These will allow us to figure out if the different parts are equal, not equal, or something else. There are a number of these found inside of the SQL language, and this can really help us to find out what is there and whether it is going to work for our needs or not.

Chapter 5: A Look at Queries

While we have spent a little bit of time taking a look at some of the commands and queries that we are able to use when it comes to working in the SQL language, it is time for us to go more in-depth about these queries and what they are able to do for some of our needs along the way as well.

When we are working on our own business database and it is all set up the way that we would like, it is going to be possible that at one point or another you will want to do a search in order to make sure you are able to find the perfect information inside of all that. This is going to make it easier for us to find the easier information and results that we want. But we do have to make sure that the database is set up in the right manner so that we can use the right commands, and see that it is fast and accurate in the process.

Think of this like when someone comes to your website, searching for that particular product that they would like to purchase. Do you want them to get stuck on the website that is slow, and have them see results that have nothing to do with the item they wanted? Or would you like a fast search that was helpful and will encourage the person to make that purchase? Of course, for the success of your business, you are more likely to want the second option, and we can take a look at how to set up your database and work with queries in order to make this happen.

Working with the Queries

When you do set up the query that you would like to use, you will find that you are basically sending out an inquiry to the database that you already set up. You will find that there are a few methods to do this, but the SELECT command is going to be one of the best options to make this happen, and can instantly bring back the information that we need from there, based on our search.

For example, if you are working with a table that is going to hold onto all of the products that you offer for sale, then you would be able to use the command of SELECT in order to find the best selling products or ones that will meet another criterion that you have at that time. The request is going to be good on any of the information on the product that is stored in the database, and you will see that this is done pretty normally when we are talking about work in a relational database.

Working with the SELECT Command

Any time that you have a plan to go through and query your database, you will find that the command of SELECT is going to be the best option to make this happen. This command is important because it is going to be in charge of starting and then executing the queries that you would like to send out. in many cases, you will have to add something to the statement as just sending out SELECT is not going to help us to get some of the results that you want. You can choose the product that you would like to find along with the command, or even work with some of the features that show up as well.

Whenever you work with the SELECT command on one of your databases inside of the SQL language, you will find that there are four main keywords that we are able to focus on. These are going to be known as the four classes that we need to have present in order to make sure that we are able to complete the command that we want and see some good results. These four commands are going to include:

- **SELECT**—this command will be combined with the FROM command in order to obtain the necessary data in a format that is readable and organized. You will use this to help determine the data that is going to show up. The SELECT clause is going to introduce the columns that you would like to see out of the search results and then you can use the FROM in order to find the exact point that you need.
- **FROM**—the SELECT and the FROM commands often go together. It is mandatory because it takes your search from everything in the database, down to just the things that you would like. You will need to have at least one FROM clause for this to work. A good syntax that would use both the SELECT and the FROM properly includes:
    - SELEC [* | ALL | DISTINCT COLUMN1, COLUMN2]
    - FROM TABLE1 [, TABLE2];

- **WHERE**—this is what you will use when there are multiple conditions within the clause. For example, it is the element in the query that will display the selective data after the user puts in the information that they want to find. If you are using this feature, the right conditions to have along with it are the AND and OR operators. The syntax that you should use for the WHERE command includes:
    - SELEC [* | ALL | DISTINCT COLUMN1, COLUMN2]
    - FROM TABLE1 [, TABLE2];
    - WHERE [CONDITION1 | EXPRESSION 1]
    - [AND CONDITION2 | EXPRESSION 2]
- **ORDER BY**—you are able to use this clause in order to arrange the output of your query. The server will be able to decide the order and the format that the different information comes up for the user after they do their basic query. The default for this query is going to be organizing the output going from A to Z, but you can make changes that you would like. The

syntax that you can use for this will be the same as the one above, but add in the following line at the end:

- ORDER BY COLUMN 1 | INTEGER [ASC/DESC]

You will quickly see that all of these are helpful and you can easily use them instead of the SELECT command if you would like. They can sometimes pull out the information that you need from the database you are working in a more efficient manner than you will see with just the SELECT command. But there are going to be many times when you will find that the SELECT command will be plenty to help you get things done when it is time to search your database as well.

A Look at Case Sensitivity

Unlike some of the other coding languages that are out there and that you may be tempted to use on your database searches, you may find that the case sensitivity in SQL is not going to be as important as it is in some of those other ones. You are able to use uppercase or lowercase words as you would like, and you can use either typing of the word and still get the part that you need out of the database. It is even possible for us to go through and enter in some clauses and statements in uppercase or lowercase, without having to worry too much about how these commands are going to work for our needs.

However, there are a few exceptions to this, which means there are going to be times when we need to worry about the case sensitivity that is going to show up in this language a bit more than we may want to. One of the main times for this is when we are looking at the data objects. For the most part, the data that you are storing should be done with uppercase letters. This is going to be helpful because it ensures that there is some consistency in the work that you are doing and can make it easier for us to get the results that we want.

For example, you could run into some issues down the road if one of the users is going through the database and typing in JOHN, but then the next person is typing in John, and then the third person is going through and typing in john to get the results. If you make sure that there is some consistency present, you will find that it is easier for all of the users to get the information that they want, and then you can make sure that you are able to provide the relevant information back when it is all done.

In this case, working with letters in uppercase is often one of the easiest ways to work with this because it is going to make it easier and the user is going to see that this is the norm in order options as well. If you choose to not go with uppercase in this, then you should try to find some other method that is going to keep the consistency that you are looking for during the whole thing. This allows the user a chance to figure out what you are doing, and will help them to find what they need with what is inside of their queries.

As you go through this, you may notice that these queries and transactions that you are able to create for the database that you are working on are going to be important to the whole system and ensuring that it is actually going to work in the manner that you would like. In the beginning, this may feel like a lot of busywork to keep up with and that it is not worth your time or energy to do or that it is not that big of a deal. We may assume that with a good query from the user, they will be able to find all of the information that they need in no time.

However, it will not take long working with the SQL language and more to figure out that this is going to make everyone a bit frustrated. It is always better to go through and set up a good search query with SQL and make sure that your data is organized and ready to go so that everyone is able to find what they would like out of the database each time. This is going to be one of the best ways to ensure that you are going to provide the user with a good experience on your website, so take some extra care when you are working with this.

There are then going to be some times when the user is going to be able to do their searching and look up some information just by doing a search and finding the information that they want to use inside of that particular database. This is when they will want to ensure that the database is set up in a manner so that they are going to find the task or the item that they want right away, rather than having to continue to search and not having to put in many keywords in order to hopefully find the thing that they want along the way.

No matter which method you choose to use, or what seems to work best for the work that you are trying to accomplish with all of this, you will find that it is very important along the way that your commands fall in the right place each time and that they will lead you to the place where you want to be in your database. When you make sure that the table is going to be set up in the right manner so that you, as well as any potential users, are able to find what they want quickly and efficiently, you will find that it is so much easier to enhance the experience and grow your business.

This chapter is important because it shows us how to get all of this done. It helped us to see what was going on in the database and provided us with the right commands in order to bring out that information and make it work for some of our needs as well. While the SELECT command is often the one that is used to help control the database and make it work well, and you can choose the one that you would like to use. Setting up the database in a good and strong manner, and being careful with the commands that you are using is one of the best ways to ensure that you are going to get the best results with this along the way while providing your users and customers with the shopping and transaction experience that they want to enjoy it and that will get them to come back again.

Chapter 5: A Bit About Subqueries

The next topic that we are going to spend some time talking about is how to work with the subqueries in this language. We will take a look at some of the queries in another chapter in this guidebook, but getting a good look at what these subqueries are all about, and how we are able to add them into some of the codes that we are doing is going to be very important as well. Some of the things that we need to know when it comes to the subqueries in SQL will include:

More About Subqueries

Note that in general, a query returns a **plurality of** values. Therefore, using a subquery when you are working with a **WHERE clause** without **EXISTS**, **IN**, **ALL,** and **ANY** statements that give a **Boolean** value can result in a query runtime error.

Example. Find PC models and prices, the cost of which exceeds the minimum cost of PC notebooks:

```
SELECT DISTINCT model, price
FROM PC
WHERE price
(SELECT MIN(price)
FROM Laptop);
```

You will find that this is the right way to work with this kind of request because the scalar value of the price is going to be compared back to the subquery that returns just one value to you.

The result that you will get with this is going to depend on what you are doing, but in this option, we will find that we will get the results of three models of PC's because that is

how we worked on the code. You can input this into your SQL language and see what results you get.
On the other hand, a subquery that returns multiple rows and contains multiple columns can naturally be used in **the FROM clause**. This allows you to limit the set of columns and / or rows when performing the join operation of tables.

In addition, you will find that some of these subqueries are going to be found in the SELECT clause. This is going to make it possible to formulate a query very compactly.
We can take some time to look at how this is done. For this example, we want to be able to find the difference between the average price o a notebook PC, and the PC that we want. Or, we would want to figure out, on average, whether the notebook is going to be more expensive than we will see with the regular PC. A good code that we can use for this will be the following:

```
SELECT (SELECT AVG(price)
FROM Laptop) -
(SELECT AVG(price)
FROM PC) AS dif_price;
```

Type Conversion

In implementations of the SQL language, implicit type conversion can be performed. So, for example, in T-SQL, when comparing or combining values of the **smallest** and **int** types, data of the **smallint** type **is** implicitly converted to the **int** type. Details on explicit and implicit type conversion in MS SQL Server can be found in BOL.

Example. Display the average price of notebook PCs with the preceding text "average price =".

Attempt to execute the request

```
SELECT 'average price = ' + AVG(price) FROM laptop;
```

will result in an error message. This message is going to tell us that we are trying to do what is known as an implicit conversion from the varchar data type over to money, and this is something that we are not allowed to do. This is because the system is not able to move one data type, especially this kind, over to another type, or a money type in this situation.

In these kinds of situations, the process of using an explicit type of conversion is going to help. If you end up in a situation with that error message from before, you can then choose to work with the CONVERT function instead. But we have to remember that even with this, the function you are working with will not be standardized. Therefore, for portability purposes, it is recommended that you use the standard **CAST** expression.

We can go through and make this a little bit easier to see. If we go through and rewrite the request that we want to use, working with the form below:

```
SELECT 'average price = ' + CAST(AVG(price) AS
CHAR(15)) FROM laptop;
```

We will find that it is a lot easier to go through and get the results that we would like. The answer that you get here is going to be that the average price is $1410.44, but this number can change based on the input that we get, or what you are hoping to do with this kind of code.

We used an explicit **CAST** type conversion expression to

cast the average price to a string representation. The syntax of the **CAST** expression is very simple:

CAST (AS)

It should be borne in mind, firstly, that not any type of conversions are possible (the standard contains a table of valid data type conversions). Secondly, the result of the **CAST** function for an expression value of NULL will also be NULL.

We can also take some time to look at another example of how this is going to work to our advantage as well. In this one, we are going to use the same idea in order to figure out the average year that certain ships were launched, working with the Ships table that we are going to work with here. The command that we want to use in order to make this happen includes:

SELECT AVG(launched) FROM ships;

This one is going to give us the result of 1926. In principle, everything is correct, because as a result, we received what we asked - YEAR. However, if you take a look at this, the actual mean of all the years does not quite end up with the same year as above. There are a few decimal points behind it. It should be something that we note that the aggregate functions we are working with, outside of the COUNT function that will provide us with an integer all of the time), will inherit the type of data that is in the possessed values.

Since we went through this and launched a field that was an integer, we are going to end up with an average value. And since the integer is usually not going to have a fraction of a decimal with it, we are going to discard this part of the year to keep things as simple as possible.
And if we are interested in the result with a given accuracy, say, up to two decimal places? Applying
the **CAST** expression to the average will not do anything for the above reason. Really, this will:

SELECT CAST(AVG(launched) AS NUMERIC(6,2)) FROM ships;

...return the value 1926.00. Therefore, **CAST** needs to be something that we are going to apply to the argument that we will get with one of these aggregate functions. The coding that we can use for this one will be below:

```
SELECT AVG(CAST(launched AS
NUMERIC(6,2))) FROM ships;
```

The result is 1926.238095. Not that again. The reason is that when calculating the average, an implicit type conversion was performed. Let's take one more step:

```
SELECT CAST(AVG(CAST(launched AS
NUMERIC(6,2))) AS NUMERIC(6,2)) FROM
ships;
```

As a result, we get what we need - 1926.24. You can guess from here though that we don't want to figure out exactly how long that .24 is supposed to stand for, and it can be kind of a pain, so we want to make sure that makes it easier. This is where we are going to work with more of an implicit type of conversion. The commands that we are able to use to make this one happen includes:

```
SELECT CAST(AVG(launched*1.0) AS
NUMERIC(6,2)) FROM ships;
```

In the option that we did above, you will see that we were relying on the implicit type of conversion to go with our

integer argument to the exact type of number, and then we went through and multiplied it by a real unit. And finally, we were able to apply it to the explicit cast of the result type that would become our aggregate function here.
Similar type conversions can be performed using the **CONVERT** function:

SELECT
CONVERT(NUMERIC(6,2),AVG(launched*1.0))
FROM ships;

This will help us to finish up the conversion that we would like to see with some of the work and will ensure that we are going to really make sure that all of this works in the manner that it should.

The **CONVERT** function has the following syntax:

CONVERT ([()], [,])

The main difference between The CAST function and the CONVERT function is that with the CONVERT function, we are able to do some formatting with our data when we want to change it to a character type, and we can even specify out the format when we want to do some reversing on this.

The different integer values that we see here are going to fall together with some of the formats that we need to make this work.

CASE Statement

Suppose you want to list all PC models that are in your store and you want to make sure that the prices are with them. If you are going through this and notice that the model is not available for sale, which means it is not in the PC table that we create, then instead of the price showing up here, a text that says something like “Not available” will show up. We are able to use SQL to work with SELECT DISTINCT and then find the right PC model that we want to work with.

In the result set, the missing price will be replaced by a NULL value: This happens if we are working with a set that will not provide us with the prices that we need for those PCs.

To replace NULL values with the desired text, you can use the **CASE** statement:

```
SELECT DISTINCT product. model,
CASE WHEN price IS NULL THEN 'Нет в наличии' ELSE
CAST(price AS CHAR(20)) END price
FROM product LEFT JOIN pc c ON product.model=c.model
WHERE product.type='pc'
```

The **CASE** statement, based on the conditions that you decide to specify, can return to us one of many possible values. In our example, the condition is a check the whole thing or NULL. If you meet with this condition, then the text of "Out of stock" is returned; otherwise (**ELSE**), the price value is returned. There is one fundamental point. Since the result of the **SELECT statement is** always a table, ten each of the values that we see in that column must fall into the same type of data (taking into account the implicit type conversion). Therefore, we cannot, along with the price (numerical type), derive a symbolic constant. This is why type conversion is applied to the price field to bring its values to a symbolic representation. As a result, we get:

We have to make sure that any time we use the WHEN statement they fall in the same kind of format, i.e. You cannot mix the first and second forms. When we start with the first form, then the command of WHEN is going to be done as soon as the value that is being tested in our expression turns to something that is equal to the value of any specified expression in that clause.

But if we move it around and work with the second from here, then this command is only going to b satisfied when you can get the predicate to be TRUE. When any of the conditions are satisfied as above, then we can bring out the statement of CASE, which is then going to return to us the value that goes with the clause of THEN that comes back to it. If none of the WHEN conditions if it fails, then the value specified in the **ELSE clause** will be used. If there is no **ELSE**, a NULL value will be returned. If several conditions are satisfied, the value of the **THEN** clause of the first of them will be returned.

In the code that we worked on above, we spend our time working with the second form of our CASE statement.

Note that to check for NULL, the standard offers a shorter form of the operator - **COALESCE**. This operator has a random amount of parameters that we are able to work with and it is going to be working to return to us the first non-NULL value that it finds.

Chapter 6: Transact-SQL Functions for Date / Time Processing

The standard that we are working with here is only going to specify the functions that we are using if they are able to return to us a system date and a system time together. For example, if we work with the function of CURRENT_TIMESTAMP, it is going to return to us both the time and the date of that together. Plus, there are also functions we can work with that will only return one thing to us.

Naturally, due to such limitations, language implementations expand the standard by adding functions that facilitate the work of users with data of this type. Here we look at date/time processing functions in T-SQL. The function that we are able to utilize to make this one happen is below:

DATEADD (datepart, number, date)

This function returns to us the datetime value, which is obtained by adding to the date the number of intervals that are going to be found in the datepart and it will be equal to the number we are looking at. For example, it is possible for us to go through and add in any number of hours, days, minutes, years and so on to the date that works the best for us. Valid values for the *datepart* argument *are* given below and are taken from BOL.

DATEDIFF Function

Syntax

DATEDIFF (*datepart*, *startdate*, *enddate*)

The interval that we work with here is something that we can measure out in different units. The options that we choose will be determined thanks to the datapart argument that we listed out above for the function of DATEADD.

One thing that we need to note here is that the time we are using for departure, which is the function of time_out, and the arrival time, which is going to be used with the function of time_in, will be stored in our Trip table under the type of datetime. This is a bit different if you are using any version that was before 2000 in SQL because these versions did not have the temporal types of data to get things done. For us, that means that only when we take the time and insert it into our field of datetime, then the time is going to be supplemented back to the date value that is the default. Firstly, for flights that depart on one day and arrive on the next, the value calculated in this way will be incorrect. The second thing to consider here is that it is never reliable for us to make assumptions about the day we are on, which is going to be the present only due to the fact that it has to conform in some manner to our datetime type.

But how to determine that the plane landed the next day? This helps the description of the subject area, which says that the flight cannot last more than a day
But back to our example. Assuming that the departure/arrival time is a multiple of a minute, we can define it as the sum of hours and minutes. Since the date/time functions work with integer values, we reduce the result to the smallest interval - minutes. So, the departure time of flight 1123 in minutes:

```
SELECT DATEPART(hh, time_out)*60 + DATEPART(mi,
time_out) FROM trip WHERE trip_no=1123
```

From there we are going to work on the arrival time and how we are able to use this for our needs. Some of the coding that we need to work with to show this will be below:

```
SELECT DATEPART(hh, time_in)*60 + DATEPART(mi,
time_in) FROM trip WHERE trip_no=1123
```

When we get to this point, we need to be able to take a look at some of our times. We need to know whether the arrival time is going to be able to exceed the time of departure. If this does show to be true, then we need to subtract the second number that we have from the first so that we know how long the flight is. Otherwise, we will need to add one day to the difference to get this done.

Here, in order not to repeat long constructions in the CASE statement, a subquery is used. Of course, the result turned out to be rather cumbersome, but absolutely correct in the light of the comments made to this problem.

Example. Determine the date and time of departure of flight 1123.

The table of completed flights Pass_in_trip contains only the date of the flight, but not the time because, in accordance with the subject area, each flight can be operated just one time for the day. To help us figure out this kind of problem, we need to be able to add up some of the time that is in our table of Trip to the data that we stored in there as well.

Take some time to type in the code that we just did above, and see what the output should be. This should tell us a bit more about the time and so on within our output. If you type part of this in the wrong manner, you are going to end up with an error message so check that you write it all out the proper manner for the best results here.

DISTINCT is necessary here to exclude possible duplicates since the flight number and date are duplicated in this table that we are using for all of the passengers of the flight we are looking at.

Datename Function

Syntax

DATENAME (*datepart*, *date*)

This function returns the symbolic representation of the component, which is going to be known as the datepart, which is for our date that we specified before. The argument is going to spend some time specifying for us the date component and will tell us that the data is only able to take on one, and no more, of the values that are found on the table. This is going to give us a lot of chances to work with the process of concatenating the components of our data and getting it in the right format in order to present it to ourselves or to others.

It should be noted that this function detects difference values of *the dayofyear* or the argument tfor day when it comes to the datapart. The first of these is going to be more symbolic in the kind of representation that it is going to provide to the day when we go off the beginning of the year. In some situations, we are going to notice that the function of DATEPART is going to be better served when we replace it with a function that is easier. This will often depend on what we are trying to do within some of the code we use.

All of these parts are going to be important in how we are able to handle some of the codes that we need along the way. Make sure that these are found in these types of codes to get the results you are looking for.

Chapter 7: Data Modification Operators

The DML that we are working within here, or the Data Manipulation Language, is going to come together with the statement of SELECT in order to get the right information from the database and then include other statements that change the state of the data. These operators are:

INSERT - Adding records (rows) to the database table

UPDATE - Updating data in a column of a table in our database.

DELETE - Delete some of the records that are found in the table of our database.

INSERT Statement

When we are talking about the statement for INSERT, we are looking at the command that is able to add in some new rows to any table that we are working with. When we take a look at our current cause, the values of the columns have the potential to be literal constants, but we can also see that they are just a subquery result in some cases. With the first situation, we will work with a separate statement of INSERT to insert each row. the second case, as many rows will be inserted as the number returned by the subquery.

Operator Syntax

INSERT INTO < *table name* [(< *column name* , ...)]
{VALUES (< *column value* , ...)}
| < *query expression*
| {DEFAULT VALUES};

As you can see from the syntax presented, a list of columns is optional. If this is a part that is not present in our work, then the list of all values that are inserted must be done. This means that the programmer needs to be able to provide for us the values for each column that shows up in the table. When we look back at this particular case, the order that we see the values fall in need to correspond to the specific column order that the statement for CREATE TABLE said along the way.

In addition, each of these values has to come from the same type of data, and it needs to also be the same type that is defined in the column or columns that we chose with our statement for CREATE TABLE. This may not seem important now but it is going to make a difference in some of the coding that we are able to do with this.
It would seem that this is a completely redundant feature, which makes the design only more cumbersome. However, it becomes advantageous if the columns have default values. Consider the following table structure:

```
CREATE TABLE [product_D] (
[maker] [char] (1) NULL ,
[model] [varchar] (4) NULL ,
[type] [varchar] (7) NOT NULL DEFAULT 'PC' )
```

One thing to remember with this one is that the columns are going to come to us with default values. The first of the default values is going to be NULL< and then the last column is going to be a type of PC to keep it organized. With this in mind, we are able to write out the following to help us out:

INSERT INTO Product_D (model, maker) VALUES (1157, 'B');

When we look at this situation, the value that is missing when you insert one of these new rows is going to be replaced by the default value that is known as "PC" for this one. One thing to remember with this one is that if the value that is the default is not going to be specified for the statement of CREATE table and it is not a constraint of NOT NULL is specified that prohibits the use of NULL in this part of the table that we are working with, then we are able to assume that the value we are looking for on the default will be NULL.

The question arises: is it possible not to specify a list of columns and, nevertheless, use the default values? The answer is yes. To do this, instead of explicitly specifying a value, use the reserved word **DEFAULT**:

One thing that we can remember with this one is that when we would like to be able to insert a new row into one of our tables, the syntax is going to check all of the restrictions that are already imposed on that table. These could be unique constraints or primary key constraints. We can also work with the constraints for CHECK type to see if this is going to work for our needs.

Consider now the use of a subquery. Suppose we need to insert into the *Product_D* part of the table all of the rows that are found in our table of Products are going to relate back to different models of personal computers. Since these are going to hold onto the values that are needed to get started, the formation of inserted rows manually, firstly, is inefficient, and, secondly, it may allow input errors. Using a subquery solves these problems:

```
INSERT INTO Product_D SELECT * FROM Product
WHERE type = 'PC';
```

The symbol that we used in this query is justified in this case, since the order of the columns is the same for all of the tables. If this were found to not be true, then the list of the column should be used to help us work with the statement of INSERT< or to do a subquery, and sometimes it can do it in both places, which would bring the order of the columns in correspondence:

There are often going to be a few other methods that we are able to work with here to get the same idea, and the option that you choose to go with will depend on the coding that you want to write, and what you hope to get out of the database.

While there are a few options that we are able to focus on here, keep in mind that the one above is going to be able to handle a lot of the work that you want to do, and will work just fine for most of the situations you end up within SQL.

Here, as before, you can specify not all columns if you want to use the available default values, for example:

```
INSERT INTO Product_D (maker, model)
SELECT maker, model FROM Product WHERE type = 'PC';
```

When we take a look at this cause, the default type is going to be found in all of the rows, which is then going to be the part that is substituted into the type of column in our table. Note that when using a subquery containing a predicate, you will find that only the rows that we are inserting and will allow the predicate value of TRUE, rather than any that

are UNKNOWN will be used. What this means is that if the table has the type of a column that is NULL in value, and this value was present in a number of rows, then these are going to be rows that would not be added to the table we are looking at.
To help us get rid of this restriction on taking in a single line in the **INSERT statement** when using **VALUES, the** artificial use of the subquery forming the line with the **UNION ALL** clause allows. It is possible to go through and write this out to meet our needs as well.

It is best to work with the statement of UNION ALL in this case, even if there are no duplicate rows, as in this case, a check will not be performed to eliminate duplicates.

Insert Rows into a Table Containing an Auto-Increment Field

Many commercial products allow the use of auto-incrementing columns in tables, i.e. fields whose value is generated in an automatic manner when we want to put in the new records. These types of columns are going to turn into the primary keys of the table because they automatically provide uniqueness.

A good example of this type of column is going to be known as a sequential counter. With this one, when you do go through and insert a row, it is going to generate out a value of one that is greater compared to the previous value. This previous value is going to be obtained when inserting the previous row.

An auto-incrementing field is defined using the **IDENTITY (1, 1)** construct. In this case, the first parameter of the **IDENTITY (1)** property determines which value starts the count, and the second - which step will be used to increment the value. Thus, in our example, the first inserted record will have a value of 1 in the *code* column, the second - 2, etc.

Since the value is generated automatically in the *code* field, the operator

INSERT INTO Printer_Inc VALUES (15, 3111, 'y', 'laser', 2599);

will lead to an error even if you are not working with any row that is in your table that relies on this kind of *code* field equal to 15. Therefore, to insert a row into the table, we simply will not indicate this field in the same way as in the case of using the default value, i.e.

```
INSERT INTO Printer_Inc (model, color, type, price)
VALUES (3111, 'y', 'laser', 2599);
```

Because of this statement and what it can do, the information about the laser printer of model 3111, the cost of which is $ 2599, will be inserted into
the *Printer_Inc* table. In the **code** field, there will be a value that can only happen to be equal to 15. In most cases, this is enough, because the value of the auto-incrementing field, as a rule, does not carry any information; the main thing is that it is unique.
However, there are times when you need to substitute a very specific value in the auto-incrementing field. For example, you need to transfer existing data to a newly created structure; however, this data is involved in a relationship that is just too many from that particular side. Because of this, we are not going to allow any of the arbitrariness on this one. In addition, though, we have to be careful because we do not want to abandon the auto-incrementing field

because it will simplify data processing during the subsequent operation of the database.
Since the standard of the SQL language does not imply the presence of auto-incrementing fields, there is accordingly no single approach. Here we show how this is implemented in MS SQL Server.
Operator disables (ON value) or enables (OFF) the use of auto-increment. Therefore, to insert a line with the value 15 in the *code* field, you need to write

```
SET IDENTITY_INSERT Printer_Inc ON;
INSERT INTO Printer_Inc(code, model, color, type, price)
VALUES (15, 3111, 'y', 'laser', 2599);
```

Keep in mind here that it has to be written out exactly in the format that is above. If we do not do this in the proper manner, then we are going to end up with some problems in it, and we will get an error message in the code.
It is important to note that if the value 15 turns out to be the maximum in the *code* column, then the numbering will continue from the value 16. Naturally, if you enable auto-increment: **SET IDENTITY_INSERT Printer_Inc OFF**.

When we take a look at the auto-incrementing columns that we want to add in, there are a few things that we need to keep in mind. First, we need to take the last value that shows up in our code to be 16 here. When we are past this, then the line that has this value will be deleted out of it.

This brings up the question of what the value inside of this column is going to be when you are done inserting the new row? The answer is 17 here because the last value of our counter is going to still be there and preserved, even though we are deleting the line that is there at this time.

Therefore, the numbering of values as a result of deleting and adding rows will not be sequential. In addition to some of the other points, this is a good reason for us to insert a row with the missing, or the given, value in this column.

UPDATE Statement

There are going to be a number of times when we need to work with updating our table. If someone else is added to the database we work with, or we are trying to handle some changes to the table for our customers, for example, then handling the UPDATE command is one of the best ways to get this under control. The **UPDATE statement** modifies the data in the table. The command has the following syntax

UPDATE
SET {column name = {expression to calculate the column value
| Null
| DEFAULT}, ...}
[{WHERE}];

Using one operator, values can be set for any number of columns. However, in the same **UPDATE statement,** you can make changes to each column of the specified table only once. If there is no **WHERE clause,** all rows in the table will be updated.

If a column allows a NULL value, then it can be specified explicitly. In addition, you can replace the existing value with the default value that we want to work within our column.

If there is a reference to expression here, then we may find that this command is going to refer to all of the values that are currently in the table that is being edited.

It is also allowed to assign values of some columns to other columns. Suppose, for example, you want to replace hard drives of less than 10 GB in PC notebooks. In this case, the capacity of new disks should be half the amount of RAM available on these devices. This problem can be solved as follows:

```
UPDATE Laptop SET hd=ram/2 WHERE hd<10
```

Naturally, we are going to find that the types of data we use for the ram and the hd columns have to be compatible. If you want to help cast these types, then you would work with the command of CAST to get it done. If you would like to change the data based on the contents that we are seeing in the columns that you want to work with, then you would want to work with the statement of CASE.
If, say, you need to put 20 GB hard drives on PC notebooks with memory less than 128 MB and 40-gigabyte ones on other PC notebooks, then you can write this request:

You can also use subqueries to calculate column values. For example, you need to equip all PC notebooks with the fastest processors available. Then you can write:

```
UPDATE Laptop
SET speed = (SELECT MAX(speed) FROM Laptop)
```

In this case, the code will not be executed because the auto-incrementing field does not allow updates, and we will receive the corresponding error message. To accomplish this task nevertheless, one can proceed as follows.

In Transact-SQL, the **UPDATE** statement ng> extends the standard by using the optional FROM clause. This proposal specifies a table that provides the criteria for the update operation. Additional flexibility is provided by the use of table join operations.

An example. Let it be required to indicate “No PC” in the *Type* column for those PC models from the *Product* table for which there are no corresponding rows in the *PC* table.

This is a good way to ensure that we are able to join together a few of the different tables to each other. There are a lot of different methods that we are able to use to make this one work for us.

An external join is used here, as a result of which the *pc.model* column for PC models that are not in the *PC* table will contain a NULL value, which is used to identify the rows to be updated. Naturally, this problem has a solution in the "standard" version:

```
UPDATE Product
SET type='No PC'
WHERE type='pc' and model NOT IN (SELECT model
FROM PC)
```

DELETE Statement

This is a good statement to learn a little bit about. The statement of DELETE is going to b there to help us get rid of statements from any kind of table or cursor or even view that we want, and in a few of them, the operator's action extends to those base tables from which data was extracted to these views or cursors. The delete operator has a simple syntax:

DELETE FROM [WHERE];

If you are working with the WHERE command here, and it is missing, then all of your rows in the view or the table will be gone. This is true if the table is something we can update. You can also perform this operation (deleting all rows from a table) in Transact-SQL more quickly using the command

TRUNCATE TABLE

However, there are a number of differences in the implementation of the **TRUNCATE TABLE** command compared to using the **DELETE statement**, which should be kept in mind:

1. It is not journalized to delete individual rows of a table. Only the release of pages that were busy with table data is written to the log.
2. Do not work out triggers. As a result, this command is not applicable if there is a foreign key reference to this table.
3. The counter value (IDENTITY) is reset to the initial value.

An example. You want to remove all notebooks with a screen size less than 12 inches from the *Laptop* table.

```
DELETE FROM Laptop
WHERE screen<12
```

All notebooks can be deleted using the operator.

```
DELETE FROM Laptop
```

or

FROM

Using a *table type source,* you can specify the data that is deleted from the table in the first FROM clause.
Using this clause, you can join tables, which logically replaces the use of subqueries in the WHERE clause to identify deleted rows.
Let us explain what was said by an example. Suppose you want to remove those PC models from the *Product* table for which there are no rows that would correspond to it in the PC table either.
When we stick with the syntax that is considered standard in this one, this is something that we are able to solve with the help of the DELETE FROM code if we would like.
An external join is used here, as a result of which the *pc.model* column for PC models that are not in the *PC* table will contain a NULL value, which is used to identify the rows to be deleted.

Chapter 8: Some More Learning Phases to Work With

We need to take some time now to look at some of more of the things that we are going to be able to do when it is time to handle the SQL that we want to work with. We need to take a look at the PL and SQL and how these are able to work with each other, and even how they are supposed to be different in some cases as well.

PL / SQL - “Procedural Language extensions to the Structured Query Language”, which translates as “Procedural Language Extensions for SQL”. Almost every enterprise-level DBMS has a programming language designed to expand the capabilities of SQL:

PL / SQL - in Oracle Database Server

Transact-SQL - in Microsoft SQL Server;
SQL PL - in IBM DB2;
PL / pgSQL - in PostgreSQL.

In these languages, programs are created that are stored directly in the databases and are executed by the DBMS, therefore they are called stored procedure languages. The languages of stored procedures have similar syntax and semantics, therefore, after mastering the PL / SQL language, it will later become quite easy to switch, for example,
to Transact-SQL or PL / pgSQL.

Function in Oracle PL / SQL
Function in PL / pgSQL PostgreSQL

```
CREATE FUNCTION F1 RETURN INT AS
BEGIN
FOR r IN (SELECT * FROM tab1) LOOP
UPDATE tab2 SET at3 = r.at2;
END LOOP;
RETURN 1;
END
```

```
CREATE FUNCTION F1 () RETURNS int AS '
Decare
r RECORD;
BEGIN
FOR r IN SELECT * FROM tab1 LOOP
UPDATE tab2 SET at3 = r.at2;
END LOOP;
RETURN 1;
END
'LANGUAGE plpgsql;
```

Tasks Solved by PL / SQL

PL / SQL, unlike Java, Python or C ++, is not used to develop mathematical applications, games, etc. It is a specific third-generation programming language designed to work with Oracle databases directly in the core of the Oracle server. In fact, PL / SQL programs are wrappers around SQL statements.

- PL / SQL is used to solve the following tasks:

- implementation of server-side business logic in the form of stored programs;

- automation of Oracle database administration tasks;
- web application development;
- development of client applications in the Oracle Developer environment.

We will not dwell on automating database administration tasks and developing client applications but focus on the main direction of using PL / SQL - implementing server-side business logic in the form of stored programs.

Use Case for PL / SQL Programs

Let there be an Oracle database in the corporate network on a Linux server with information about the organization's clients. Connect to the Oracle server from the laptop over the network using the SQL * Plus utility. Starting PL / SQL calc_clients_debt from SQL * Plus to calculate customer debt may look something like this:

```
SQL> BEGIN
2 calc_clients_debt (p_account_from => 100001,
p_account_to => 200000);
3 END;
```

four /

PL / SQL procedure successfully completed.

Only four lines to start the calc_clients_debt procedure will be transferred from the laptop to the Linux server, where the Oracle database server, having received these lines, will execute the PL / SQL procedure. Only information about the successful completion of the procedure will be returned to the laptop - one line. The gigabytes of financial data required for the calculations for a given range of 100,000 personal accounts will not be transferred to the laptop via the network - all client data will be sampled using SQL from PL / SQL and all calculations will be performed in PL / SQL by the Oracle database engine on a powerful Linux server. On the same server, in the same Oracle database, calc_clients_debt will also save the calculation results.

This is how a debt calculation might look if it were run by a technical specialist who knows the database device and prefers to work with it in SQL * Plus. It is clear that accounting or client department employees do not work with the database in SQL * Plus. For them, a client program in C #, Java or another programming language with screen forms and reports should be developed and installed. In this program, on the screen, the user sets the range of processed personal accounts and clicks the button “Calculate debt”.

The client program, through the appropriate programming interfaces that are found in most modern programming languages, launches the calc_clients_debt stored procedure in Oracle and starts showing the user an hourglass or a running bar (progress bar) to the user. The program itself does not carry out data processing, which at this time is on a remote Linux server. As soon as the stored procedure successfully completes and the Oracle server reports this to the client program, it will give the user the message "Debt has been successfully calculated."

This is a typical PL / SQL usage scenario: implementing business logic (in this example, calculating customer debt) as a PL / SQL procedure stored in a database and running it from a client program that connects to an Oracle server via a network. Typically, PL / SQL programs run “under the hood” and are not visible from the outside.

Advantages and Disadvantages of Stored Programs

When implementing business logic, it is quite possible to do without using stored programs. So, the problem of calculating customer debt can be solved in two ways:
to develop one or several (frontend, backend) applications in Java, JavaScript, C ++, Python, etc., that implement only the user interface, and implement the business logic of the debt calculation itself in the form of a stored program that the applications call when the calculation process starts;

* to develop one or several (frontend, backend) applications in Java, JavaScript, C ++, Python, etc. that implement both the user interface and the business logic of debt calculation.

For the second method, the database is used only for storing data. All the necessary data for each client is retrieved by the application from the database, calculated by the application and the received debt information is saved back to the database. An application that reviews data is often placed on the same server as the database — so that the network does not become a system bottleneck.

The choice of the method used to solve the problem is the responsibility of the system architect, and many factors should be taken into account that is formed in each case based on the known advantages and disadvantages of using stored programs.

Advantages of Stored Programs

- portability of stored programs with the database;
- increased processing performance due to the lack of data transfer outside the database server;
- close integration with the SQL execution subsystem (SQL statements in stored programs are executed without the use of additional interfaces and drivers);
- control of access to data based on stored programs (access is not granted to database tables for reading and writing data to them, but to executing stored programs - thereby isolating data from application programs);

- implementation of dynamic integrity constraints and the concept of active databases using the trigger mechanism.

Disadvantages of Stored Programs

- "Smearing" the logic of the system according to several programs written in different languages;
- the need, along with Java, Python, C ++ programmers, to have a database programmer in the team;
- the scarcity of the expressive capabilities of the languages of stored procedures against the background of modern languages Java, Python, C ++;
- intolerance of stored programs between different DBMSs;
- possible problems with scaling.

The most significant drawback of stored programs is their binding to a specific DBMS. For example, when switching from Oracle to PostgreSQL within the framework of the current topic of import substitution, all stored programs will have to be rewritten from PL / SQL to PL / pgSQL, and this will lead to significant costs for reengineering PL / SQL code, which can amount to hundreds of thousands of lines.

As for the problems of scaling, the processing of data directly in the database using the DBMS itself is the advantage of stored programs until the required level of performance is provided. Otherwise, this circumstance will interfere with scaling, since the installation of additional servers will require a large amount of work. We will have to install a DBMS on each new server, create our own database with stored programs and solve the problem of distributing data across several databases. Of the virtues of stored programs, integrating data storage and processing can thus be a drawback. With separate applications that implement server-side business logic without stored programs, there is usually no scaling problem - adding new servers only for computing applications is usually quite easy.

Portability of PL / SQL Programs

Portability of PL / SQL programs along with the database is provided by the PL / SQL language architecture, similar to the Java language architecture.

When programming in C / C ++, Pascal, as a result of the compiler, an executable file is obtained. This file contains machine instructions for a specific hardware platform and is designed to work on a specific operating system. Therefore, if you copy the executable file for Windows to a computer with the Linux operating system, then it will not start there. If the executable file for one hardware platform is transferred to another platform (a computer with other machine instructions), then it will not start there either. As a result, if you need to provide cross-platform, then for the same C ++ program, you have to have a version for Windows and a version for Linux, a version for x86 (32-bit) and a version for x64 (64-bit) and so on.

The situation is different with Java programming. As a result of the Java compiler, the result is not an executable file with machine instructions, but a bytecode file - a low-level machine-independent code executed by a bytecode interpreter. This bytecode interpreter is called the Java

Virtual Machine (JVM). When the Java program starts, a file with its bytecode is fed to the input of the Java virtual machine, which converts the bytecode instructions into machine codes of a specific platform. Thus, in order to run a program in Java in a particular environment, it is enough to have JVM for this environment. For example, in the core of the Oracle server, there is an Aurora JVM virtual machine designed to run Java programs stored in Oracle databases.

As a result of the PL / SQL compiler, the result is not an executable file, but a bytecode called p-code. This PL byte code is interpreted by the PL / SQL virtual machine (PL / SQL Virtual Machine, PVM) located in the Oracle database engine. There is a PL / SQL virtual machine in all versions of the Oracle DBMS for any operating system and for any hardware platform; therefore, PL / SQL programs remain operational when transferring Oracle databases from one computing system to another.

Evaluating PL / SQL

As a programming language, PL / SQL has the following advantages:

- static typing;

- availability of error handling tools and user exceptions;
- the presence of concise and convenient language constructs for executing sentences of the SQL language.

It is believed that efficient high-performance code for working with an Oracle database is easier to write in PL / SQL than in any other procedural programming language. In particular, in PL / SQL there are special means of bulk data processing (bulk processing), allowing to increase productivity by an order or more.

Here is a fairly large quote from the book "Oracle for Professionals" written by Tom Kyte, vice president of Oracle Corporation [18, p. 48]:

"When developing database software, I adhere to a fairly simple philosophy that has remained unchanged for many years:

Everything that is possible should be done in one SQL statement. Believe it or not, but it is almost always possible. Over time, this statement becomes even truer. SQL is a language with a lot of power.

If something cannot be done in one SQL statement, then it must be implemented in PL / SQL using as shortcode as possible. Follow the principle of “more code = more errors, less code = fewer errors”.

If the problem cannot be solved using PL / SQL, we may find that working with the procedure stored as Java is the best to work with. However, after the release of Oracle 9i and subsequent versions, the need for this is very rare. PL / SQL is a full-fledged and popular third-generation programming language.

If the problem cannot be solved in Java, try writing an external procedure C. This is the approach most often used when you need to ensure the high speed of the application, or use an API from independent developers implemented in C.

If you cannot solve the problem using the external procedure C, seriously think about whether there is a need for it.

We will work with PL / SQL and its types of objects to help us work with our problems that are impossible or inefficient in SQL. PL / SQL is actually something that has been around for a number of years - it took more than 27 years to develop it (by 2015); in fact, back to Oracle 10g, the PL / SQL compiler on its own was rewritten a few times in order to make sure that it is as optimized for the work that it needs as possible.

No other language is so closely related to SQL and is not so optimized for interacting with SQL. Working with SQL in this kind of format is actually going to feel pretty natural, while it would be something that is hard in other kinds of languages that you would want to work with, and can be quite burdensome. "

The New Procedural Option - PL / SQL appeared in Oracle 6.0 in 1988. Since then, PL / SQL has written millions of lines of server-side business logic code and developed thousands of client forms and reports in the Oracle Developer environment. For many years, Oracle Corporation has demonstrated its commitment to PL / SQL, and with the release of each new version of Oracle Database Server, PL / SQL introduces new enhancements. PL / SQL is an integral part of Oracle technologies and the corporation plans to develop and support it in the future.

First PL / SQL Program

According to a long tradition dating back to C, textbooks on programming languages begin with the program "Hello, World!" And a description of the data types of the language being studied. We will not break this tradition, but make one change to it. Since the PL / SQL language is designed to work with Oracle databases, we will not set the string "Hello, World!" Statically in the source code, but take it from the database table.

```
CREATE TABLE hello_world_table (message VARCHAR2
(30));
INSERT INTO hello_world_table VALUES ('Hello,
World!');
```

To make this a bit further, we are able to work with the following code, making sure that we do it in SQL Plus, to see what is going to happen.

```
SQL> SET SERVEROUTPUT ON
SQL> DECLARE
2 l_message VARCHAR2 (30);
3 BEGIN
4 SELECT message INTO l_message FROM
hello_world_table;
5 DBMS_OUTPUT.PUT_LINE (l_message);
6 END;
7 /
Hello World!

PL / SQL procedure successfully completed.
```

In the PL / SQL program presented above, using the SELECT INTO command, the value of the message column of the hello_world_table table row is read from the database and assigned to the local variable l_message, the value of which is then displayed in the SQL * Plus window. The l_message variable is previously declared in the declarations section after the DECLARE keyword.

Screen output in PL / SQL is performed by the PUT_LINE procedure of the built-in DBMS_OUTPUT package, which is available in all Oracle databases. We can assume that DBMS_OUTPUT.PUT_LINE procedure in PL / SQL is an analog of the printf procedure in C.

Recall two things that are important when working with the SQL * Plus utility:

To run the PL / SQL program in SQL * Plus for execution, you need to type the / character on a new line and press the Enter key on the keyboard;

in SQL * Plus, the screen output of PL / SQL programs is enabled with the SET SERVEROUTPUT ON command (by default, screen output is turned off).

If you do not execute the SET SERVEROUTPUT ON command, then nothing will be printed in the SQL * Plus console. In the popular Quest SQL Navigator GUI client, the

PL / SQL screen output is also turned off by default and is turned on by the special button "Turn the server output", which after pressing should remain in the "pressed" position.

PL / SQL Data Types

Recall that a data type (data tour) is a named set of data values of a given structure that satisfies the specified integrity constraints and allows the execution of a certain set of operations associated with this set. For example, numbers and dates can be added and subtracted, but strings and logical values cannot.

PL / SQL refers to languages with static typing. Static typing is called data type checking during program compilation. Static typed programming languages include Pascal, Java, C / C ++ / C #. Dynamic typing languages (JavaScript, Python, Ruby) perform most type checks at run time. Static typing can detect errors during compilation, which increases the reliability of programs.

Types of Data Types

Since PL / SQL is a procedural extension of SQL, PL / SQL has all the data types available in the Oracle SQL dialect with some minor differences. In addition to them, PL / SQL also has data types that are not available in Oracle SQL.

PL / SQL has scalar and composite data types:
* data of scalar types consist of one indivisible (atomic) value (logical values, numbers, dates, strings);

* composite type data consists of several values (records and collections).

Scalar PL / SQL Data Types

We also need to take a look at some of the types of data that we are able to work within this kind of language. The good news here is that a lot of the data types are going to look familiar, especially if you have worked with other coding languages in the past.

These types of data are nice to work with because they will provide us with information on what is going on inside of our codes, and what we are able to do with it as well. for example, if we are working with an integer data type, then we are handling a data type that works with numbers.

This is not the only type of data that we are able to handle though. It is possible to work not only with the integers, but with the characters, the varchars, floating numbers, and more. Pretty much any of the options that you will find in other coding languages will be found in this one as well.

It can be seen that the PL / SQL data types declared in the STANDARD package either correspond to Oracle SQL data types (_BASE types) or are entered as their subtypes.

Note the presence of the BOOLEAN data type, which is not available in Oracle SQL. Values of type BOOLEAN can, for example, be used in code of the following form:

```
l_amount_negative_flag BOOLEAN: = amount <0;
IF l_amount_negative_flag THEN ... END IF;
```

A significant difference between the PL / SQL and Oracle SQL data types is *the* greater maximum length of the values of the CHAR and VARCHAR2 types, designed to represent fixed and variable-length strings:

* for VARCHAR2 in PL / SQL, the maximum length of values is in the range from 1 to 32,767 bytes (in Oracle SQL up to version Oracle 12c, the maximum length of VARCHAR2 was up to 4,000 bytes, in Oracle 12c it was also increased to 32,767 bytes);

* for CHAR in PL / SQL, the maximum length of values is in the range from 1 to 32,767 bytes (in Oracle SQL up to version Oracle 12c, the maximum length of CHAR was up to 2,000 bytes, in Oracle 12c it was also increased to 32,767 bytes).

PL / SQL Records

PL / SQL records are composite data types and are defined as sets of attributes associated with specific relationships. Record attributes can be either scalar data types or other composite types — other records and collections.

A PL / SQL record is declared as a user data type using the RECORD keyword, in general, working with PL / SQL records is similar to working with Pascal records or structures in C: If you have worked with this kind of coding language in the past, you should be fairly familiar with what we are able to do with these records and how we can pull them out for some of our own needs here as well.

Purpose of PL / SQL Records

* reading in the PL / SQL records the rows of the resulting SQL query samples (when declaring PL / SQL records based on tables and cursors using the% ROWTYPE attribute);

* combining several parameters of procedures and functions into one structure (instead of a large number of parameters of scalar types it is more convenient to transfer one parameter of a composite type to procedures and functions).

Compactness and extensibility of the source code is the main advantage of using PL / SQL records. Compare the two options for calling the procedure for printing information about a person - with one PL / SQL record parameter and with several parameters of scalar data types:

print (l_person) and print (l_name, l_secname, l_surname, l_born)

The first call option looks more compact. In addition, if it becomes necessary to process new information about a person, for example, TIN and SNILS, then for the second option, you will need to add two new parameters to all calls to the print procedure throughout the code. If you pass the description of the person in the form of a PL / SQL record, you only need to add new attributes to the declaration of type t_person. It is not necessary to make changes to the header of the print function and to its calls by the source

code. By using PL / SQL records, this extends the extensibility of the source code.
Here are the basic rules for working with PL / SQL records:

* the definition of record attributes can specify NOT NULL constraints and set attribute values by default;

* assigning a record NULL assigns NULL to all its attributes;

* to compare two entries for equality or inequality, you need to consistently compare the values of all attributes in pairs.

Since PL / SQL records are similar to table rows, the advantages of using them for compactness and extensibility of the code are especially pronounced when executing SQL statements in PL / SQL. One row of the table - one PL / SQL record. Table rows "live" in the database, PL / SQL records "live" in programs. A row of a table can be considered as a single command in a PL / SQL record, a PL / SQL record can be inserted as a row in a single command, that is, data can be moved in both directions. PL / SQL also has special language constructs that allow you to move between the database and the PL / SQL program not individual PL / SQL records and table rows, but many of them. And all this is done very compactly - with one or two lines of PL / SQL code.

Bind Variable Declarations

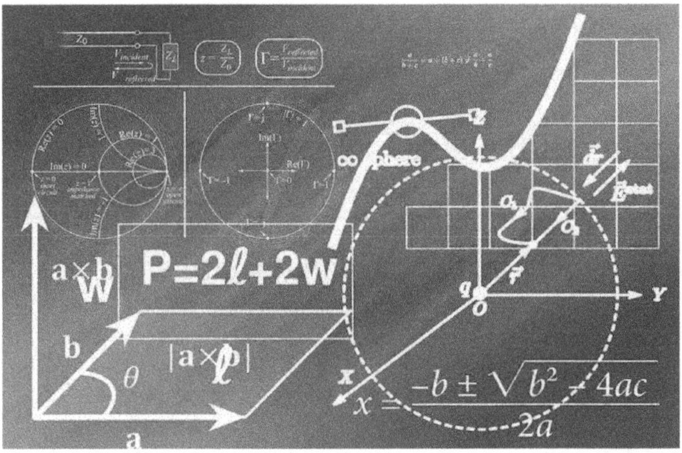

Since the PL / SQL language is designed to process the data that is in the tables of the Oracle database, it provides the ability to declare variables with reference to the schemes of these tables. For example, if some variable is used to read the values of the surname column of the person table into it, then it would be logical to indicate when declaring this variable a data type that matches the data type of the column.

There are two types of variable binding:
* scalar binding (using the% TYPE attribute, the variable is declared with the data type of the specified table column);

* binding to a record (using the% ROWTYPE attribute, a PL / SQL record variable is declared with attributes by the number of columns of the specified table or cursor).

Consider an example. Let the database have a table tab1 with at1 columns of type DATE and at2 of type VARCHAR2 (20). Then in the PL / SQL code, you can declare variables as follows:

```
l_tab1 tab1% ROWTYPE;
l_at1 tab1.at1% TYPE;
```

The variable l_tab1 will be a PL / SQL record with two attributes at1, at2, the data types of which will be the same as the data types of the columns at1, at2 of table tab1, that is, DATE and VARCHAR2 (20), respectively. The l_at1 variable will have a data type that is the same as the at1 column, that is, date.

Benefits of Declaring Bind Variables

* synchronization with table schemas is automatically performed;

* compact extensible code for reading rows of result sets of SQL queries without listing columns.

Automatic synchronization of variable declarations in PL / SQL programs and database table schemas makes PL / SQL programs resistant to possible future changes, such as adding, deleting or renaming table columns, changing their data types. In practice, such table schema changes occur quite often.

We give a concrete example. There was a client table in the CRM system database, in which there was an inn column. At the time of the development of the system, clients could only be legal entities with a TIN of 10 characters. Over time, the company began to serve individuals who have a TIN of 12 characters. The database administrator changed the data type of the inn column of the client's table from VARCHAR2 (10) to VARCHAR2 (12) and rows with long TINs began to appear in the table. Since in the PL / SQL code all the variables for working with the TIN were declared as VARCHAR2 (10), errors occurred when reading individuals from the TIN database in PL / SQL programs. If the variables for the TIN were declared in due time with reference to the inn column using the% TYPE attribute, then they would automatically “expand” themselves and there would be no errors at the execution stage.

Without listing the columns of the resulting SQL query samples, a very compact code is written like:

```
l_person person% ROWTYPE;
SELECT * INTO l_person FROM person WHERE id =
13243297;
print (l_person);
```

The SQL query selects all the columns of the person table, and the variable l_person declared with% ROWTYPE will have exactly the same attributes as the columns of the person table, with the same names and data types, in the same order. The values of all columns of the table row being read are assigned to the corresponding attributes of the PL / SQL record. If a new column appears in the person table in the future, it will automatically be picked up by both the SQL query (SELECT *) and the declaration of the l_person variable in the PL / SQL program. No changes to the code will be required; the program will automatically recompile the first time it is accessed.

Variables can be declared as PL / SQL records using the% ROWTYPE attribute not only on the basis of a single table but also on the basis of columns of the resulting samples of arbitrary SQL queries. For this, PL / SQL records are declared based on explicit cursors.

Chapter 9: PL / SQL Program Structure

Now that we have had some time to take a closer look at the PL and SQL kind of structure from the last chapter, it is time to dive into this a bit more and see what else we are able to do with it. In particular, this chapter is going to explore some of the structure that comes with the PL and SQL program structure. Let's dive right in and see what it is all about.

Block Structure

In PL / SQL, as in most procedural programming languages, the smallest unit of source grouping is a block. It is a piece of code that defines the boundaries of code execution and the scope for ads. Blocks can be nested into each other.

PL / SQL Block Sections

A PL / SQL block consists of four sections:

- heading section;
- announcements section;
- executable section;
- exception handling section.

The heading sections, declarations, and exception handling may not be in the block; only the executable section is mandatory.

The syntax that we are able to find with this kind of process will be below:

heading section
Decare
ads section
BEGIN
executable section
EXCEPTION
exception handling section
END

The heading section indicates:
block type (procedure, function);
block name (name of the procedure, function);
parameter names, their data types and value transfer modes.

The declaration section declares custom data types, variables, and constants, which are then used in the executable section and the exception handling section. The executable section implements the actual program logic. In a degenerate case, there can be only one "empty" NULL command.

The BEGIN and END keywords in PL / SQL are operator brackets similar to the {and} characters in other programming languages and mark the beginning of an executable section and the end of a block. Each command in PL / SQL must end with a semicolon (symbol;).

Types of PL / SQL Blocks

There are two kinds of blocks in PL / SQL:
* named blocks (with header section);

* anonymous blocks (no header section).

Named blocks, in turn, also come in two forms:
* named blocks of programs stored in the database (procedures, functions, packages, and triggers);

* named blocks in the declaration sections of other blocks (anonymous or named).

Stored programs are objects of the Oracle database and are created by the CREATE DDL command, after which the named PL / SQL block is written. The block name indicated in the header section will be the name of the database object.

Anonymous blocks do not have a header section. If a block does not have a header section, then it does not have a name that is indicated in this section; therefore, such blocks are called anonymous.

Anonymous blocks are either embedded in other blocks or stored as text script files. In the latter case, anonymous blocks are usually used to call stored programs or to automate database administration tasks.

Anonymous block script file1.sql
- Anonymous nested blocks in a named block of a stored program

Decare
I INTEGER;
- named block of proc1 procedure
- in the anonymous block section
PROCEDURE proc1 IS
BEGIN
NULL
END
BEGIN
- proc1 procedure call
proc1;
END
- named block of proc2 procedure

Chapter 10: Other Things We Can Work On In SQL

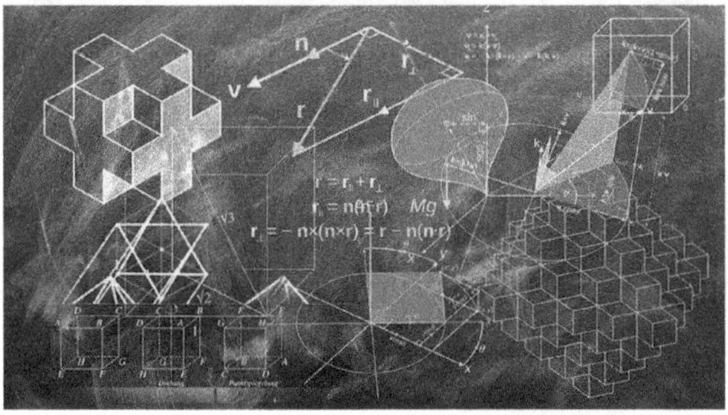

After we go through and do some of the initial loadings of some of the spatial columns that are there, it is time for us to go through and make a request, and then analyze them. MySQL provides a set of functions to perform a lot of the operations that we need when it comes to this kind of analysis. We are able to take these functions and then group them into four new categories based on what they are able to perform for us. These are going to include the following:

1. The first type is going to be the type of function that is able to convert a configuration between more than one type of format.
2. Then we have the type that is going to help provide us with the access that we need in order to work with

quantitative or qualitative details that come with geometry.

3. The next type is going to be any of the functions that are going to help us get a description of a relationship between the configurations that you have.
4. Then the last kind is going to be the functions that are going to be able to create a new configuration from one that is already existing.

All of these are going to be important to some of the things that we are going to be able to do when it comes to spatial analysis. This kind of analysis can be used in a variety of contexts including:

1. Any kind of program in SQL that is interactive, including the SQL query browser.
2. Applications that are done in any other kind of coding language that you would like that are also able to support the client of MySQL API Geometry Conversion Functions.

Geometry Functions

Each of the functions that we are hoping to use in this and that will belong in a group will take the value of that geometry as a parameter, and then will be able to return some quantitative or qualitative property of the geometry that we work with. Some of the functions that you would want to work with along the way will end up limiting the types of parameters that you are able to work with. And these are going to provide us with a return known as NULL if the parameter does not provide us with the right type. Depending on the information that we want to get out of our tables, we will find that these geometry functions, and some of the other options for arithmetic as well, will be useful to get the process done for us as well.

Property Limitations

While we are here, we need to spend some time taking a look at what is known as the property limitations when we work with the SQL language. This will ensure that we are going to be able to take advantage of what is available in some of our codings, and will make it easier for us to use with the database. Let's take a look at how we can make this work for our needs.

Views Limitations

View processing is not optimized: This will mean that it is unable to come in and create a new index on the view.

Indexes are helpful for working on the processed views because it will combine together more than one of the algorithms you want to work with at a time. However, we have to remember the view, which is going to be something we can process with a temptable algorithm, is not going to help us take advantage of the indexes on the tables that are considered on our main ones, even though w can use these when we want to make a temporary table.

Subqueries, on the other hand, can't be used if we work with the clause of FROM. This is going to b a restriction that will be moved later but is in place for now. There is also a good rule in place that makes it hard to modify a table and then do a subquery on that same table so keep this in mind.

The same principle also applies if you select from a view that selects from a table if the selection of view from a table in a subquery and view are evaluated using a combining algorithm. Example:

CREATE VIEW v1 AS SELECT * FROM t2 WHERE EXISTS (SELECT 1 FROM t1 WHERE

t1.a = t2.a);

UPDATE t1, v2 SET t1.a = 1 WHERE t1.b = v2.b;

If we find that the view is something that we are going to evaluate using an ability that is temporary, we are then able to select from the table in view with the help of a subquery and then change around that table with the help of a query that is external in the process.

If we end up doing this, then we are going to be able to create a temporary table to work with and then store our view in there for now. And we can really use this to make sure that we are not selecting from the table in the subquery and try to modify this table when we do not want to.
Along with this idea, we are able to force MySQL to do a few things here, including use the algorithm that we want. The right one to work with here is going to be the temptable one. This is done with the code of ALGORITHM = TEMPTABLE when we are in the definition of the view. From there, we are going to choose to either drop or alter the table based on whether we would like to modify or delete it. But keep in mind when we do this one, we are not going to get a warning at all.
The error that is going to show up when we try to do this will not appear until later when you actually use the view. The view definition is going to be frozen based on the instructions that are there. if the instructions were prepared with the command of PREPARE and it goes back and refers

to the view, then the contents of this particular view are going to be the same any time that the execution happens. This is going to be true even if you find that the definition of view is going to be changed once the statement is prepared, but this does have to be done before we execute that statement or it is not going to work. A good example of how we can do this is below:

```
CREATE VIEW v AS SELECT 1;
PREPARE s FROM 'SELECT * FROM v';
ALTER VIEW v AS SELECT 2;
EXECUTE s;
```

The result returned by the EXECUTE statement is 1, not 2. If you see an instruction that is stored in what is a routine is able to access the view, then the content of the view is going to end up being exactly the same as what we found the first time we executed the instructions. For example, we can see that this will mean that if the statement is going to be done with the help of a loop, the further iterations are going to be in the same view content, even if you see that you will need to change up the view of the definition later on when you are doing the loop.

Regarding updatable views: the overall goal for a view is that if any view is theoretically updatable, it should be updatable and practical. This includes views that have a UNION in their definition. Currently, not all views that are theoretically updated are those in practice (maybe modified). The initial implementation of the view was intentionally written in this way to become usable; updated views in MySQL will be made fast as we are able to. When we have a lot of updated views on the database, it is possible for us to modify them and make changes, but we have to make sure that we know there are still some limitations that will exist on this.

If we are working with some of the subqueries that are present in our WHERE clause, then we know that we are working with ones that are updatable. But if we find that we are working with the subqueries that are found more in the SELECT list, this doesn't mean that we can't update those. Keep in mind here that we are not able to use the UPDATE command in order to work with more than one of these main tables at a time. We also can't go through and use the DELETE command in order to modify a view that has been previously defined as a union.

Along this same idea, if we have granted a user the basic privileges already in order to create a view in the database, then this means that the user is not going to have enough authority along the way in order to do the CREATE, SHOW, VIEW on that object unless you have given them that right along the way as well. This could lead to some problems when you try to copy the database. When you do not provide the user with the right authority to get it done, it is going to fail.

There is a workaround that we are able to use with this to get it to behave the way that we would like. For example, the administrator to manually grant these privileges if they would like to the users who have the authority to do CREATE VIEW.

In this though, we have to remember that there are going to be a few restrictions that we need to be careful about. The maximum tables that we are able to name in a single join will only be 61. This is going to also come up with the number of tables that can be named when we work with the view of definition.

Chapter 11: Data Security - What Could Go Wrong?

When it comes to the databases that you are using, you want to make sure that you are working with a format that is going to be as safe and secure as possible. Most of the databases that are out there are going to contain valuable information for a big company. They will hold onto the data that a company needs in order to get ahead, to help them keep track of their customers and more.

For example, it is not that uncommon for a company to go through and decide to work with a database to hold onto information about customers, and what they purchased at their store. This means that the company would have a lot of valuable information, including information on the individual's name, their address, their credit card information, and more. For a hacker or someone who would like to steal these identities, that is some really valuable information.

This is why, if you plan to have your own database along the way, you need to make sure that you actually take care of the data that you are working with, rather than taking advantage and assuming that it is all going to be safe. This is a wealth of information in your database, and certainly, a lot of other people outside of you would like to be able to get ahold of this information and use it for their own needs as well. If you are not careful with that information, then it is likely that they will, and this can cause you a loss of reputation and money, and really harm your customers

Now, there are going to be a few different types of security attacks that a hacker is able to do against your system, and you need to make sure that you take care of these along the way, and do your best to keep the network safe and secure as well. We are going to spend some time in this guidebook looking at some of the basics that come with this process, and explore how you can work to keep the database as safe and secure as possible.

SQL injection (also known as "Violation of the integrity of the structure of the SQL-query") is one of the vulnerabilities that we need to really take a look at when it comes to the security of our database is the SQL injections. These are so dangerous because they will allow the hacker to open up a back door into your network and system, and allow unlimited access: for example, delete tables, modify the database, and even gain access to the internal corporate network. An SQL injection is a pure software bug and has nothing to do with the hosting provider. So, you were looking for safe JSP hosting, PHP hosting, or any other, you should know that only developers, not the hosting provider, are responsible for the prevention of SQL injections.

Why do SQL Injections Happen?

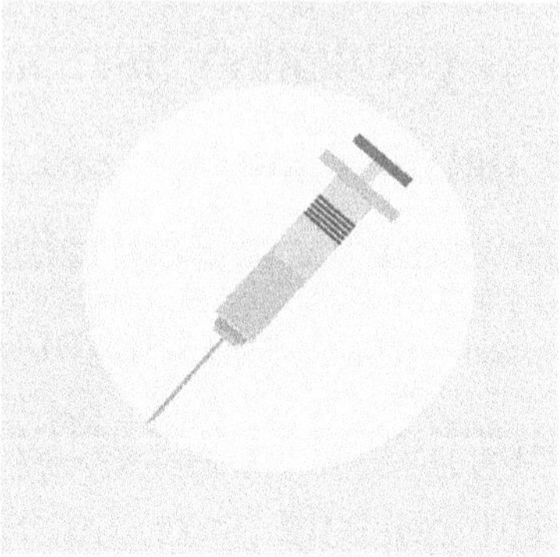

SQL injections are a very common problem, but ironically, they are also easy to prevent. SQL injections are so widespread, since there are so many places where the vulnerability can be present, and if the injection is successful, the hacker can get a good reward (for example, full access to the database data).

The risk of SQL injection occurs whenever a programmer creates a dynamic query to the database containing user input. This means that there are two ways to prevent SQL injection:

- Do not use dynamic database queries.
- Do not use user data in queries.

Everything seems to be simple, but these are theories; in practice, it is impossible to refuse dynamic queries, as well as to exclude user data input. But this does not mean that it is impossible to avoid injections. There are some tricks and technical features of programming languages that will help prevent SQL injections.

How to Prevent an SQL Injection

Although the decision is highly dependent on the particular programming language, the general principles for preventing SQL injection are similar. Here are some examples of how this can be done:

1.) Don't Bring Out the SQL Queries All the Time

There are times when the dynamic query is going to be necessary. But for most cases, you will find that we are able to replace these with some stored procedures, parameterized queries, and even prepared statements. This can actually clean up some of the code that we are working with and will make it look a little bit nicer overall.

For example, rather than working with the dynamic SQL like you may feel needs to be done, you can use the PreparedStatement() in Java with some bound parameters to get it done. When working with the .NET platform, you are able to work with some of the parameterized queries, like SqlCommand or the OleDB Command() and then add in some of your own bound parameters to make it work.

Along with some of the prepared statements that we just talked about, it is also possible to work with stored procedures. Unlike the prepared procedures, these stored ones are going to be the type that you keep handy and stored up in the databases. But in both of these situations, the query from SQL is going to first help us to determine which parameters we should work within it.

2.) Validation of entered data in queries

Validating data entry is less efficient than parameterized queries and stored procedures, but if it is not possible to use parameterized queries and stored procedures, then it is better to validate the entered data - this is better than nothing. The exact syntax for user input validation is highly dependent on the database; read the docks on your specific database.

3.) Do not rely on Magic Quotes

Enabling the magic_quotes_gpc parameter can help us to sometimes prevent injections of SQL> The Magic Quotes is not the last defense and should not be treated as such, especially since they could be turned off without you knowing, or do not have the ability to turn it on. That is why it is necessary to use code that will escape quotation marks. Here's a piece of code suggested:

• Regular and timely installation of patches. Even when your code does not have vulnerabilities, there is a database server, server operating system, or developer utilities that may have vulnerabilities. That is why always install patches immediately after they appear, especially if it is a fix for SQL injections.

• Remove all functionality that you are not using.

The database server is a complex creation and has much more functionality than you require. And as far as security is concerned, here the principle "the more the better" does not work. For example, the extended system procedure xp_cmdshell in MS SQL gives access to the operating system, and this is just a dream for a hacker. That is why this function needs to be turned off, like any others, which makes it easy to abuse the functionality.

4.) Using automated tools for finding SQL injections

Even if the developers followed all the above rules to avoid dynamic queries with the substitution of unverified user data, you still need to confirm this with tests and checks. There are automated testing tools for detecting SQL injections, and there is no excuse for those who do not use these tools to verify procedures and queries.

One of the simple tools (and one of the more or less reliable) for detecting SQL injection is an extension for Firefox called SQL Inject Me. After installing this extension, the tool is available by right-clicking in the context menu, or from the menu Tools → Options.

You can choose which test to run, and with what parameters. At the end of the test, you will see a report on the test results.

As you can see, there are many solutions (and above all, all simple ones) that you can take to clear the code of potential vulnerabilities to SQL injections. Do not neglect these simple things, as you endanger not only your security but all the sites hosted on your host provider.

Conclusion

SQL Commands

SQL commands are divided into the following groups:

Data Definition Language Commands - DDL (Data Definition Language). These **SQL** commands can be used to create, modify, and delete various database objects.

Data Management Language Commands - DCL (Data Control Language). Using these **SQL** commands, you can control user access to the database and use specific data (tables, views, etc.).

Commands of the transaction management language are TCL (Transaction Control Language). These **SQL** commands allow you to determine the outcome of a transaction.

Data Manipulation Language Commands - DML (Data Manipulation Language). These **SQL** commands allow the user to move data to and from the database.

This guide, as you know now, is devoted to the study of Structured Query Language (SQL) and is complemented by a large number of examples that clearly demonstrate the capabilities of SQL. SQL is an ANSI standard, but there are a large number of versions of this query language. Whichever you choose, I wish you fun and success in your endeavor!

SQL

A 7-Day Crash Course to Quickly Learn Structured Query Language Programming, Database Management, and Server Administration for Absolute Beginners

Introduction

Congratulations on purchasing *SQL Programming,* and thank you for doing so.

The following chapters will discuss all of the different things that you need to know in order to get started with the SQL language and to ensure that this is going to be something that you can use to really manage your database and get it to work for your needs. In this guidebook, we have spent some time splitting up the information and the tasks that you are able to do with SQL up into a week's worth of lessons, helping you to get some of the benefits that you need out of all this coding.

To start with, we will take a look at some of the basics that come with the SQL language. This includes some information on what SQL is all about, how the relational database is going to compare to the older, more traditional styles of databases out there, and some of the biggest components that we need to know when it comes to the SQL language. This will help us to get a good start when it is time to work with this language and will get us on the right track to success with these relational databases.

Then it is time for us to move on to some of the things that we need to know when it is time to handle the development of our database form the ground up. We will look at some of the components that show up in a database, some of the lifecycle of the system development, and how to build, create, and delete the tables that are a big part of your database. We will finish off with a look at how we need to value and maintain some of the integrity of the data that is found in our database, as well.

On the next day, that is going to focus more on some of the different things that you need to do as the administrator of the database. These include things like setting up a maintenance plan for your database, so it stays safe and secures all of the time, how to handle the transaction logs, the best ways to do backup and recovery on the data, and so much more. Spending some time here is one of the best ways to ensure that your data stays safe all of the time, and will not start to get lost or corrupted.

Next on the list is taking a look at some of the simple queries that we are able to do with this language, as well. This means that it is time to dive into what a query is all about, how to handle some of the functions in your coding with SQL, how to work with expressions, and where the predicates and operators can add in some power to this as well.

The SQL server is another important part of this whole process, and we are going to spend a good deal of time learning what this server is and getting it all set up for some of our needs as well. We are going to learn how to add in the Oracle database, work with the SQL developer, and so much more. This ensures that all of the parts are going to come together for this database to work.

Then we are able to move on to the users and the roles. As someone who is in charge of running the database and setting things up, you also have to spend some time setting up the permissions and more of everyone who is allowed on your system. This chapter is going to be important because it can help us to log into the server that we have, assign the right roles to the right people in the database, and even shows us some of the commands that we need when it is time to handle these users and roles as well.

On the final day of this course, we are going to take a closer look at some of the tables and how they work in these databases, and how we can work with SQL in order to change some of the data that is found in these as well. There are times when you will want to create, add, delete, or change the data that is found in the different parts of the database, and this is exactly what we are going to spend some of our time discussing and working on in this chapter! This can really help to make the database into what we would like, and even though it may seem complicated, the SQL language is going to take some of the work and will ensure that it works the way that we would like.

There are a lot of times when we will want to work with a database to help our business to grow and to keep all of the data and information that we have that concerns our business in order. And the SQL language is going to ensure that we are able to make all of this happen for our needs. When you are ready to learn more about SQL and how this language can make the management and all of the other parts of running our database easier, make sure to read through this guidebook to help you get started.

There are plenty of books on this subject on the market, thanks again for choosing this one! We took every effort that we could to help us provide you with as much useful information as we could. We hope that you enjoy!

Day 1: Introducing SQL

Many companies are going to spend their time working with a database of some kind. We live in a world where technology and data are around us all of the time, and being able to use that data can make the difference in what results we are going to get overall in no time at all. It can help us to learn more about our customers, know how to reduce the waste that we are finding, and can make it easier for us to beat out the competition and provides us with a good way to make smart business decisions overall.

There are a lot of benefits when it comes to working with all of the data that is out there. But just gathering up the data is not going to be enough to help us get all of this work done. We also need to learn more about what this data means, how we are able to use it and to see some of the complex information that is there. When our database gets really big and has thousands, if not millions of points in it, we need to make sure that we have a good system in place that is going to help us to work with this language, and get the results that we are looking for all at once.

This is where the SQL language is going to come into play. There are other coding languages that are able to handle some of our needs when it comes to coding and looking through databases, but the SQL option is often one of the best ones that we are able to choose. We will find that this is a language that we can work with when we want to create the tables for our databases, put things together in our databases, and so much more. Let's examine some of the things that we are able to do when it comes to using these databases, and SQL for our own needs.

If you haven't worked with any kind of programming in the past, you will find that SQL is going to be a great option to help you get some of this work done in the process. The coding is simple, and even some of the longer codes that we need to focus on later will be straightforward and easy for us to learn how to work with.

Often you can look through some of the codes that are there and learn what they are saying, even before we actually go through and talk about them as much as we should. This makes it easier for us to gain some confidence in the coding that we want to do along the way, as well. With this in mind, let's dive into some of the work that we are able to do with the help of the SQL language, and see just how great this language can be for some of our needs as well.

A Look at SQL

The first thing that we need to take a look at here is what the SQL, or Structured Query Language, is going to be all about. This is going to be one of the standardized programming languages that will be used to help us manage some relational databases and carry out other operations on the data that is found in these. Initially, this was created in the 1970s, and it was used often to help database administrators but could also help developers when they were ready to write out scripts for data integration. It can also be used by those who are data analysts who want to be able to set up and then run some analytical queries as well.

There are a lot of ways that we are able to work with this language, including helping us to modify the table and index structures of a database, adding, updating, and deleting rows of data that is found in our database, and helping us to retrieve some of the information that we need out of the database to help with processing the transactions or to help with analyzing the data.

As we go through this language, we will find that the various things that we want to do with SQL, including queries and other operations, are going to turn into commands that are written out like statements. There are a lot of different options that we are able to use when it comes to these along the way, but some of the most common options are going to include SELECT, ADD, INSERT, DELETE, UPDATE, ALTER, TRUNCATE, CREATE.

SQL has become kind of the de facto standard programming language when it comes to relational databases after it showed up in the early 1980s. also known as the databases of SQL, these relational kinds of systems are going to comprise of a set of tables that will contain a lot of data that is in the form of rows and columns. Each of these columns in the table is responsible for corresponding back to a category of data, such as the name of a customer and their address, while each of the rows will hold onto the value of the data for that kind of column that you need.

Today, while there are other languages out there that are able to handle some of the work that we want to do in our databases and are able to make sure that we can gather up the information that we would like, it is important to note how well we are able to work with some of the SQL commands in order to get things done in no time. This is often the go-to language that we are able to use when it comes to SQL and getting our work accomplished in a database, and it is important to learn how to make this work for our needs as well.

What are Relational Databases

One thing to notice here is that when we talk about the SQL language, we are going to focus our attention on what is known as a relational database. This is going to be a set of tables that is formally described and from which we are able to access and even reassemble data in many different ways, without us having to actually go through and do any organization or changes to the tables that are found in the database.

The standard users, as well as the API that is going to be used in this, of one of these kinds of databases, is going to be the SQL that we talked about before. It will not take long before you are able to see how these statements are going to be used for both all of the information that is going to come off the database and some of the queries that are seen as interactive and then will help us to gather some of the reports about all of that data that we would like to work with.

The relational database is something that was originally invented in 1970. The idea that came with this one is that we needed to shift from storing data in a structure of the past, which was more navigational in structure, all the way over to helping us organize data in the manner that we do today, which includes organizing all of that data into a table with rows and columns that we need here. Each of the tables that we will work with, which is sometimes going to be known as a relation, in a relational database, it will contain least one of these categories of data inside of the attributes that helps keep it together.

To take this further, we are able to see each of the rows, which we can call by the name of a tuple or a record as well, is going to contain a completely unique instance of any kind of data that we are working with at the time. This is going to be known as the key to the database. You will find that these keys are going to go with the categories and will be defined based on the information. Each table is going to come with its own primary key that is pretty unique, to help us to identify the information that is found in that table. The relationship that we would like to see between the tables is something that we are able to set with the help of some foreign keys, such as one of the fields that are found in the table and hopefully we will be able to get it to link back to our primary key, and sometimes it is going to link us back over to one of the other tables that are found in our database as well.

To see a good example of this, we may find that one of these order databases for business would need to contain a database that helps us to keep track of our own customers. This one would include some information on the customer inside, including the address, the phone number, and name. Then we would have another table that is able to describe other information like the order, the customer, the data, the product, and the sales price of that item as well. A user of the relational database is going to be able to give us the view of a database so that we are able to find the information that we need for any purpose.

For example, if you are one of the branch office managers, you may decide that you would like to take a look at one of the reports that is found in the database, the one that will let us know how much customers are able to purchase a certain product within a date range. But it is possible to be in that same company but works in the financial part of the company, and will want to take the same tables in the same database, could get a report of all the accounts that still need to be paid.

We will find that when we work with creating one of these relational databases, we are able to go through and define all of the possible values domain with the help of the data column, along with some of the other constraints that we want to be able to apply over to that value. For example, it is possible to come up with one domain that is going to show us our future customers and then would hold ten names of these customers. But then we can constrain these to one of our tables, which would only allow us to go through and specify three of these names. Two constraints are going to be there in order to help us relate to the integrity of the data, along with the primary and the foreign keys as well.

While we are here, we need to spend a moment looking at a few key terms that we are able to work with along the path to making this kind of database work for our needs. These are going to include:

1. Entity integrity: This is the one that will make sure our primary keys in the table will be unique, and that we will not have the value of this get set to null at any time.
2. Referential integrity: This is going to require from us that every value in a foreign key column is going to be found in

our primary key from the table that it originated in from the first place.

Before we end on this topic, we need to spend some time looking at some of the examples of a relational database that we are able to work with. These kinds of databases are going to enable a user to manage some of the predefined relationships of the data through more than one database. Some of the popular examples of this kind of database would include things like the Oracle Database, Microsoft SQL Server, and more.

While there are many companies who are holding fast to some of the older types of databases that are out there, it is already being seen that these databases are not the right option for many at all. These databases are hard to work with, do not add in a lot of flexibility, and can make it hard to keep up with some of the work and technology that we are experiencing in our modern world. This technology is following us into all industries of the world, and it is so important to be able to find a database that will keep up and provide us with the results that we want for the success of our business.

This is where the relational database is going to come into play. We will find that when we are able to work with this kind of database, things are just going to get easier. We will be able to understand what is going on in the database. We will be able to explore what is in there, and really be able to pull up the information that we need. And as long as we set up the tables in the manner that we should, and focus on keeping the information safe and secure and upholding some of the integrity of the database along the way, we will find that it is so much easier to work with these relational databases more than any other kind.

Another added bonus to all of this is that the relational database is going to work with that SQL language that we are focusing on in this guidebook. And what could be better than focusing on this language and getting some of the results that we would like out of that in the process as well? SQL does the work that we want to accomplish with our database easier than ever before, and since SQL and relational databases work so well together, we are going to find that this is an added bonus to help us make our lives and our work easier.

New Databases vs. Old Databases

Most of the software products that we are going to work with today are going to help us to meet the compliances for both the relational database and some of the regular databases that are out there. this means that they are going to be able to manage both of these types of databases based on what you would like to accomplish. in today's market, you will find that a relational database is usually what people are talking about when they bring up the term database. But you will find that there are going to be some big differences when it comes to the way that data is stored between both of these systems.

One of the biggest differences that you will notice between the newer relational databases and the ones that were used in the past is how the relational database is going to be able to store all of its data in a more tabular form. This means that it is going to be arranged more in a table with rows and columns. But the database is going to store the data more as files. Some of the other differences that you may see when it comes to these databases will include:

1. You will find that a process known as database normalization is going to be present when we are working with the relational databases, but it is not going to be found in some of the more traditional forms of databases.

2. A relational database is going to support what is known as a distributed database. This is not something that is found in a more traditional database out there.

3. A relational database will find that the values of data will be stored in the tables, and then each of these tables will hold onto a primary key to help us pull it out and use it when needed. A traditional database will find that the data is going to be stored in either a navigational or a hierarchical kind of form.

4. Since we are going to store the data in tables when we work with a relational database, then the relationship between these values of data is going to be stored as well. Since the more traditional database is going to store the data more as files, then there is not going to be a relationship that happens between the tables or the values.

5. When we are inside of a relational database, the integrity constraints are going to be defined for the purpose of what is ACID. But a traditional database is not going to use this kind of security, or much security at all, to help us be protected against some data manipulation.

6. While this relational database is going to be there to help us work with a large amount of data and to let more than one user on at a time, a traditional database is instead

designed to handle small amounts of data, and usually, only one or two users can get on it at a time.

One of the final and big distinctions that we are going to see here is that the storage of the data on a relational database is going to be more accessible. This means that the values are something that we are able to update in the system. And then, the data that is found inside of the RDBMS is going to be logically and physically independent at the time.

The Benefits of a Relational Database

There are some advantages that you will notice when it comes to these relational databases, and this is why a lot of programmers and businesses are going to rely on these kinds of databases to get their work done. One of the main perks of working with these relational databases is that they are going to make it more convenient for the users to go through and categorize and store the data that they want in an easy manner. They are then able to query the information later and filter it to extract some of the specific information for the reports that they would like.

The relational databases are going to be really easy for us to extend, and they are not going to be reliant on any specific information for the reports that you would like. After the creation of the original database, we will find that a new data category can be added without having to modify all of the applications that are already there in the process.

This is just one of the advantages that you are able to be able to see when you get started with these relational databases, though.

Some of the other options that are available to you will include:

1. Accuracy: Data is going to be stored just one time in this kind of database, which is going to help eliminate an issue that shows up in other choices called data deduplication.

2. Flexibility: Some of the queries that may be considered more complex will end up being easier for users to carry out with this option.

3. Collaboration: It is possible for more than one user to get onto this database at the same time if they would like.
4. Trust: The models that are going to work with the relational database are going to be more mature and can be understood better than others, and this gains a lot of trust with the users.

5. Security: The data that fall within this kind of database can be limited so that only particular users are able to access them if this is what is best for your company.

SQL and the Relational Model

While we are here, we need to spend some time taking a look at the relational model. This is will be some of the conceptual basis of the relational database that we have been talking about so far in this guidebook. It was proposed by E.F Codd in 1969, and it is going to be a method of structuring our data with the help of relations. Remember that these are going to be some of the grid-like mathematical parts that are going to include the columns and rows of our system. Codd proposed this model for IBM at the time, but he did not know how vital and influential this work would become when it came to working on these relational databases later on.

It will not take long to find out that this relational model is going to borrow pretty heavily form things like mathematics, and it is going to work with a lot of the terms that are found in math like domains, ranges, and unions. You will find though that the conditions and the various features that it is going to describe are going to be easier to define when we use some of basic English that we are used to as well.

When we work with this relational model, we will find that all of the data has to be stored in relations, which are also known as tables, and then each of these relations will need to have a number of columns and rows in place. Each of the relations needs to have a body and a header as well. To start with, the header is just going to be a list of all of the columns that we will see in that table, and then the body is going to be all of the rows.

The second part that we are going to see with the relational model is going to be the usage of the keys. These are going to be specially designed columns within the relation, and they will be used to help us order data or relate data to some of the other tables within that database. One of the keys that is the most important here is the primary key, which is going to be used to help uniquely identify each row of the data that we have. to make querying for the data easier, most of the databases that are relational are going to spend some time and physically order the data in relation to the primary key as well.

In addition to helping us define how the data should be structured as we talked about above, the relational model is also going to set up some of the rules that we need to use to make sure that the data is held to a high level of integrity, which will be known as the integrity constraints. It is also going to define how the data should be changed up and manipulated. The model is going to help us to define the special features and the normalization to make sure that the data is stored in the manner that it should be.

Another thing that we have to consider here is how the SQL is going to fit in. basically, this language is able to provide us with some of the commands that we need to ensure that we can pull up, create, delete, and do other things within the relational database. It is a simple language that really only needs a few parts to be accomplished, but you will find that it is really going to come into play and will help us to get so much more done within our code in no time at all, and can make working with this database a breeze in the process.

The Major Components of SQL

The final thing that we need to take a look at here is some of the key components that are going to be found in our SQL. This one is going to be made up of about four primary components, and three of these are going to come with some acronyms for us to learn as well. Some of these are going to include the following:

1. A database engine. This is going to be part of our SQL that will help us to create and then drive the relational database that we are working with.

2. SSAS: This one is going to stand for the SQL Server Analysis Services, and it is going to be part of the data analysis component of all of this. If you are organizing a database in order to help you go through the data and learn more about it in the process, then this is the part that you need to spend some of your time on as well.
    a. This one is going to help us to create some OLAP cubes, which are going to be programming objects that are more sophisticated and can help us to organize the data that we have inside of this database. It is also useful for helping us to complete a process that is known as data mining, which means that we are going to pull out some of the relevant data from our database in response to the questions that we sent out.
3. SSRS: This one is going to stand for the SQL Server Reporting Service. It is going to be a component of this server that is going to provide us with some of the reporting that we need. It will be able to accomplish all of this, no matter what kind of operating system the database chooses to work with.
4. SSIS: This one is going to stand for the SQL Server Integration Services. This is going to be the part that will be responsible for doing the ETL or the Extract, Transform, and Load process. Basically, this is going to be a process that we are able to use in order to clean up and then format the raw data that we get from other sources so that it fits into and will work well with the database that we want to focus on.

There are a lot of times when we will want to work with the SQL system in order to get some of the great results that we are looking for. If you ever want to work with a database and are hoping to see some great results when it comes to this as well, then working with the SQL is going to make sure that you can accomplish all of this at any time that you would like. We will spend some more time exploring what we are able to do with the SQL language, and how important these databases are going to be for our needs, but we can find that this is a great starting place for us to know some of what is going to happen later on, and how we are able to use that for our needs as well.

Day 2: Database Development

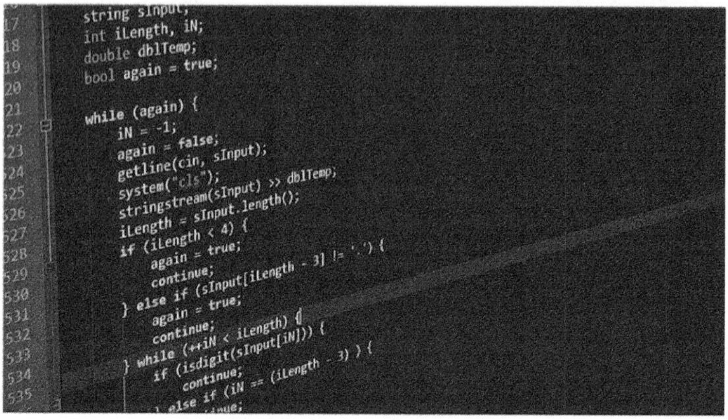

Now that we have had some time to take a look at what SQL is all about, and why we are going to see so much when it comes to working with the relational database, it is time for us to dive into some of the steps that we need to follow in order to start developing our own database as well. There are a lot of parts that need to come together to make this work for us, and we are going to explore those a bit more in this chapter, so let's get started.

The Components of a Database

The first thing that we need to spend our time taking a look at is the components that are going to be found in our database. The relational database is certainly going to be among the most common of these databases, and it is likely that you are going to spend a good deal of your time looking through this and figuring out how to use them. That is why we are going to start out our journey with a closer look at some of the components of this kind of table over some of the others.

First, we will see that there are some tables found in our database. The table is going to basically be the same thing as a record, which is going to be one of the fundamental components of the data. It is going to be comprised of a set of fields that are going to be the same in every record that you have, such as the name, address, and the product that the customer purchased.

This kind of database is also going to dictate how the tables are going to work. For example, this database is going to control how we are able to present this data onscreen and how we are able to organize the output that we have, based on what kind of query we use and more.

Then there will be the rows. You will find that the tables that come in this kind of database are going to look similar to what we see with a spreadsheet in Excel when we diagram them for a visual reference. The row on each of these tables will represent a sequential value where the value in row 1A, to start with, is going to relate to the values that will show up in all of the other fields that we use in row 1.

In addition to working with the rows, we are also going to see some use of the columns. These are going to be more of the control features, and they will show us a field of data that is going to occur in a consistent manner with each of the tables in our database. For example, you could have a column that has a header for address, name, email, and telephone. These are going to be the fields of data that we would like to have shown up for all of the records.

Primary keys are going to be the next thing that we need to work with as well. These are going to be kind of like the identification tags for all of the rows of data that you would like to work with.

Each record is going to come with its own primary key in this kind of database, and it needs to be unique. The primary key could be something like a number that we have assigned over to the customer or be a unique kind of identifier, such as their SS number. These keys are important because they are going to be used as the queries within this database, but will not be used for some of the external databases at all.

And finally, we are going to end with the foreign keys. These are going to allow us to do some manipulation and searches of the data between the primary database table and some of the other databases that are related at the time. This can help to keep things more organized and allows us to find more of the information that we are looking for throughout more than one table at a time.

The Lifecycle of System Development

Now it is time for us to look at another topic that is going to be really important to what we can do with some of these databases, and this is more about the lifecycle that we will need to follow when it comes to developing our own system along the way. There is definitely going to be a cycle that we need to go through time and again in order to make sure that we are going to set up the database that we need, and get it to work, without having to worry about whether it is going to work the way that we want, and without having to waste a lot of time in the process.

You will find that there are a number of steps that we are able to take when it is time to work with this process, and if we are careful and go through each of them in the right manner, then our codes and our databases are going to work the way that we would like. Some of the steps that we need to follow when it is time to work on a system development project will include:

Planning. The first step here is going to be all about planning. In this step, we are going to spend some time discovering, identifying, and defining the scope that we would like to see with the project and then we are going to decide the course of action that we want to work with, hopefully to help us address the issues that we would like to be able to solve in this system solution.

This is a very important phase, and we need to spend some time with it because it is going to help set the tone for how successful we can be in this project overall. This is why, during this phase, we need to focus on doing a thorough amount of research to help us figure out the resources, budget, personnel, technical aspects, and more of the project that we want to handle.

Once we have had some time to take a look at the planning stage, it is time for us to work on the analysis. The purpose of working through this phase is to help us to better understand the business as well as the processing needs of our project at this time. In this stage, we are going to see that the development team is going to consider some of the functional requirements of the system to assess how the solution we are coming up with is going to help meet the expectations that are there for the end-user, right from the beginning.

We are able to figure out the requirements of our end-users, thanks to some of the research that we did before, and we are able to document these right away. Then we have to go through a feasibility study to help us to determine if the project is going to be feasible from a financial, organizational, social, or even a more technological standpoint along the way.

Now we are ready to go onto the third phase, which is going to be all about the design. After we have gone through and done a pretty comprehensive kind of analysis phase, it is time to work on the design phase. This one is going to take a look at the elements, components, security levels, modules, and more that we need to define for the system and then evaluate how we would like to see this finished system work for our needs, and even how it is going to look like in the end. This is going to need to be done in a lot of details to ensure that the system is going to include all of the necessary features to meet the operational and functional aspects of all projects.

Development is next on the list. We will find that an approved design phase from above is going to be important when we will work with the development of this system. When we reach this phase, we will find that our development team is going to be hard at work writing out the code and making sure that the system is going to get up and running. This one is often going to be the more robust of all the other ones because it is going to include all of the labor-intensive efforts and can help us to get the database done.

During this phase, we have to make sure that we test and work on the database a bit, as well. This ensures that we are positive that the data is going to stay in the database and that it is going to work the way that we would like in the process as well. We also need to go through and double-check that everything is safe and secure and that we, as well as the customers, are going to be able to rely on the database that we are creating in the process.

And finally, we need to spend some time working on the maintenance of our system. We can't just put a database up and hope that it is good forever on its own without any help from others or from some maintenance along the way. You have to take the time to check on the database all of the time, ensuring that we are going to see some of the results that we want and that no one will be able to get into the data and steal what they would like.

How to Build a Database

Now it is time for us to go through and do some of the fun stuff. We are going to spend some time looking at the simple steps that we are able to take in order to create one of our own databases in this process. It is actually easier to work on than you would think and can make a big difference in how safe and secure your own database is going to be in the process. Some of the steps that we need in order to create a database will include (we are using the SQL Server Management Studio from Microsoft to do this):

1. When we are in Object Explorer, we want to make sure that we are able to connect to the SQL Server Database Engine. Make sure to expand the said instance here.

2. Right-click on the part for Databases, and then click that you would like to make a New Database

3. When we are on that tab, we need t make sure that we are giving the database a good descriptive name that we will be able to remember.

4. To finish off this process of creating a database, we need to accept all of the values that are there by default. Then we can click on OK.

5. To change up the name of the owner, we can click on the three dots that are upon the top, and then select who can be the owner of this.

6. To help us go through and change up some of the default values of our primary data and transaction log files, we need to find our way to the grid for the Database Files,

click on the right cell, and then add in the new value that we would like to use.

7. If you would like to go through and change up the collation of the database, we need to select the Options page, and then select the collation from that list.

8. We can also go through and change up things so that we are working with the recovery model. To make this happen, we need to end up on the Options page and select what is known as the recovered model from that list.

9. We can then move on and change up some of the database options if we would like. To do this, we need to click on the Options page, and then we can click to modify the options for the database in any manner that we would like.

10. To add in a new filegroup, if we would like, we can click on the Filegroups page. Then click Add, and then enter in the values that we would like to have for this.

11. We also have the option to go through and extend out a property so that it works with the database as well. To do this, we need to follow a few steps, but the first one is to select the Extended Properties page.
    a. When we see the Name column, we need to go through and enter the name for the property that we would like to extend.

    b. From there, we will need to take a look at the Value column. We can enter in the extended property text. For example, we could enter in one or more statements that we would like to use to describe the database that we are using.

12. And finally, we can create our database when all of this is done. We can click on OK to get this done.

There is one other method that we are able to work in order to help us create a database. If you are more into working with code and speeding up the process a little bit more, then this is the right one for you to work with. For this to happen, we are going to work with using the Transact-SQL. To make this happen, we need to work with the following steps:

1. First, we have to connect over to the database engine.
2. From the Standard bar that is there, we need to click on the tab for New Query.
3. We can then copy and past the following code that we will have into the query window that is there. when that is done, you can click on Execute to get it all finished:

```
USE master ;
GO
CREATE DATABASE Sales
ON
( NAME = Sales_dat,
  FILENAME = 'C:\Program Files\Microsoft SQL
Server\MSSQL13.MSSQLSERVER\MSSQL\DATA\saledat.mdf',
  SIZE = 10,
  MAXSIZE = 50,
  FILEGROWTH = 5 )
LOG ON
( NAME = Sales_log,
```

```
  FILENAME = 'C:\Program Files\Microsoft SQL
Server\MSSQL13.MSSQLSERVER\MSSQL\DATA\salelog.ldf',
  SIZE = 5MB,
  MAXSIZE = 25MB,
  FILEGROWTH = 5MB ) ;
GO
```

How to Create a Table

Now that we have been able to go through and create a database of our own, it is time for us to go through and actually create one of the tables that we are talking about here. You will find that once the database is done and ready to go, it is pretty easy to use a simple command in SQL in order to create one of the tables. You can technically add in as many of these tables to the database as you would need to help keep your information nice and safe in the process. The syntax that you are able to use when it is time to work with creating the tables that you need in your new database will include:

```
CREATE TABLE table_name (
  column1 datatype,
  column2 datatype,
  column3 datatype,
  ....
);
```

With this one, you will find that the parameters that we have around the columns are going to help us to specify the names of the columns that we have in this kind of table. Then we will also have the parameter for the data type that we want to work with, and this one is going to be important because it tells us the data type that we would like the column to hold. You can choose what kind of data you would like to place here, but it would be something like a date, an integer, or varchar, for example.

How to Delete Tables

We have now taken some time to see how we are able to create one of the tables that we need in our database. This is going to be useful when we need to sort through some of the data that we are using in SQL and want to make sure that it is all found in one place. Creating these tables is pretty easy, and you are able to use as many of these as you would like along the way.

With this in mind, we need to also take a quick look at how we are able to delete some of these tables. Over time, you may find that one of the tables that you are working with is going to not work the way that you would like, or maybe the information is outdated, and you would just like to clean it up and make it look a bit nicer without that table. This is definitely something that you are able to do with the right codes in place. The code that you will be able to use to make it easier to delete any of the tables that you would like in your database will include:

DELETE FROM *table_name* WHERE *condition*;

One thing to remember with this is that we need to be careful at any time that we want to be able to delete a record out of a table. We have to notice the WHERE clause as well as the DELETE statement. The WHERE clause is there to let the compiler know which of the records in specific you would like to see deleted. But if you do not add in this clause, you will find that all of the records of the table will be deleted. If that was your original goal, that is not a big deal, but it can make you lose a lot of information if you are not careful about what you are doing.

Checking the Integrity of a Database

Before we end with this chapter, we need to make sure that we are checking the integrity of our SQL database. This will ensure that the information is safe and secure and that all of the data that is coming in is going to be secure and will work the way that you would like.

There are a few reasons why you would like to make sure that you check out the integrity of this SQL database. Some of these are going to include:

1. If you find that one of the servers is running into some issues or has bugs in the environment and this is starting to go over to more than one of the servers of your SQL.

2. There is the potential for some inconsistencies between the server primary and log files and the database as well.

3. When you need to run some diagnostics to make sure that we are going to be able to check all of the integrity points of all the objects that are found in a specific database.

4. When we want to make sure that we are able to remove any of the corruption of our data that could potentially cause all sorts of issues inside of the database that we are working with.

5. Frequently when we end up with lots of statements in SQL that are failing, when we are not getting the results that we

need that are correct, and when the instances are not working.

There are a number of methods that we are able to work with in order to maintain some of the integrity that we need with our database, but you will find that it takes some time, and you need to make sure that you are maintaining the right focus on the things that are needed. Always pay the most attention to the high priority kinds of databases, and then work your way down. This makes sure that the information that is the most important is going to end up getting the most attention in the process.

Day 3: Database Administration

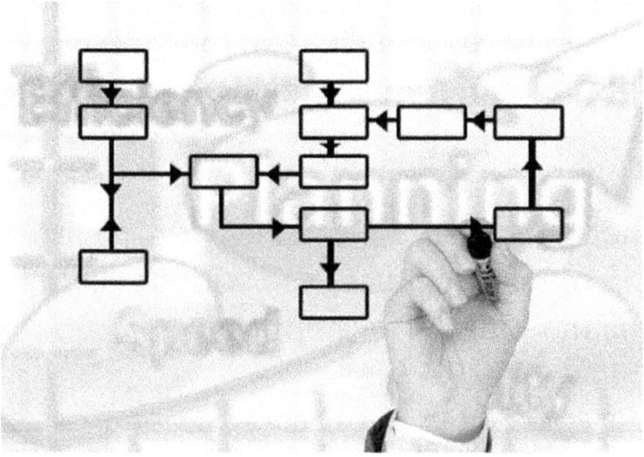

Now we need to take some time to look at some of the administration work that has to be done with any database that you would like to spend your time on. Those who are in charge of the database have to make sure that they are maintaining the database, that the information is correct and updated at the right times, and that only the right people are able to access the database and the information that is found on them. That is why we are going to spend a bit of time in this chapter looking more at some of the tasks of database administration and what we are able to do these work for our needs as well. Let's get started!

How to Set Up Your SQL Server Maintenance Plan

Making sure that you have an appropriate maintenance plan in place for some of the work that you would like to handle on the database is important. This will ensure that all of the information is going to stay safe and secure when it is time to work on your database, and will also help to add in some trust and more to some of the users who want to rely on that database as well. There are a few different steps and methods that we are able to use when it is time to set up our server maintenance plan. We are going to take a look at each one, but keep in mind that all of them work well, you just need to make sure that you are choosing the one that is right for you. And then make sure to stick with it for the long-term and keep up with it.

The first method that we are able to use for this is to help us create this kind of maintenance plan with the help of the maintenance plan wizard. The steps that we need to follow in order to get this done will include:

1. When you are inside of Object Explorer, we need to click on the little plus sign that is there to expand the server where you would like to have this plan.

2. Click on that sign so that you can expand out the management folder

3. Right-click on the fold for Maintenance Plan and then select on the part that says Maintenance Plan Wizard.

4. You can then go through the steps that are there in order to create your own plan for maintaining your database.

And then there is another option that we can use if you prefer, it will follow a pattern that is similar to what we see with the option that we had above. With this one, we are going to work with what is known as the design surface to get things done. This will include the following steps

1. When we are in the Object Explorer, we are able to click on the plus sign to help expand out the server where we would like to see this kind of plan.

2. You can then click on the plus sign that is there and get the Management folder to expand out.

3. While there, right-click so that you are on the Maintenance Plans folder. You can then navigate to the New Maintenance Plan.

4. Create the plan that you would like to follow, going through the prompts that come up.

The next option that we are going to spend some time on is using the Transact-SQL option. If you are fond of working with some coding to get all of this setup and to make sure that it is going to work the way that you would like, then this is going to be one of the best ways to get it done. To help you create your own maintenance plan with this option, we need to work with the following option:

1. When we are in the Object Explorer tab, we need to connect ourselves so that we are in an instance of the Database Engine.

2. On the Standard bar that we should see on this screen, click so that you are creating a New Query.

3. Copy and paste the ode that we have below and when it is done and set up nicely in the query window, make sure to click on Execute:

```
USE msdb;
GO
-- Adds a new job, executed by the SQL Server Agent service, called
"HistoryCleanupTask_1".
EXEC dbo.sp_add_job
  @job_name = N'HistoryCleanupTask_1',
  @enabled = 1,
  @description = N'Clean up old task history' ;
GO
-- Adds a job step for reorganizing all of the indexes in the
HumanResources.Employee table to the HistoryCleanupTask_1 job.
EXEC dbo.sp_add_jobstep
   @job_name = N'HistoryCleanupTask_1',
   @step_name = N'Reorganize all indexes on HumanResources.Employee table',
   @subsystem = N'TSQL',
   @command = N'USE AdventureWorks2012
GO
ALTER INDEX AK_Employee_LoginID ON HumanResources.Employee
REORGANIZE WITH ( LOB_COMPACTION = ON )
GO
USE AdventureWorks2012
GO
ALTER INDEX AK_Employee_NationalIDNumber ON
HumanResources.Employee REORGANIZE WITH ( LOB_COMPACTION = ON )
GO
USE AdventureWorks2012
```

```
GO
ALTER INDEX AK_Employee_rowguid ON HumanResources.Employee
REORGANIZE WITH ( LOB_COMPACTION = ON )
GO
USE AdventureWorks2012
GO
ALTER INDEX IX_Employee_OrganizationLevel_OrganizationNode ON
HumanResources.Employee REORGANIZE WITH ( LOB_COMPACTION = ON )
GO
USE AdventureWorks2012
GO
ALTER INDEX IX_Employee_OrganizationNode ON
HumanResources.Employee REORGANIZE WITH ( LOB_COMPACTION = ON )
GO
USE AdventureWorks2012
GO
ALTER INDEX PK_Employee_BusinessEntityID ON
HumanResources.Employee REORGANIZE WITH ( LOB_COMPACTION = ON )
GO
',
  @retry_attempts = 5,
  @retry_interval = 5 ;
GO
-- Creates a schedule named RunOnce that executes every day when the time on
the server is 23:00.
EXEC dbo.sp_add_schedule
  @schedule_name = N'RunOnce',
  @freq_type = 4,
  @freq_interval = 1,
  @active_start_time = 233000 ;
GO
-- Attaches the RunOnce schedule to the job HistoryCleanupTask_1.
EXEC sp_attach_schedule
  @job_name = N'HistoryCleanupTask_1',
  @schedule_name = N'RunOnce' ;
GO
```

This code is going to look a bit long, but it is going to be necessary to ensure that we are able to get the accurate results that we need, and for helping us to really make sure that the maintenance plan is set up and ready to go when we need it.

Backup and Recovery for Best Results

If you have a database, you need to go through the steps to make sure that you are backing up all of the data on a regular basis. There are things that can happen, even on a system that is working, and you really do not want to lose all of the information that is on the database. And if there is an outage, a mistake, a virus that gets on the computer or something else that could harm your database, you could find that you will lose it all, and have to start from scratch, if something like this goes on.

No matter how big or small your database is, you need to make sure that you work with some kind of backup plan. And it is often a good option to do this a few times. You should, along with your maintenance plan, have something in place that is going to help you to back up your information on a regular basis. The more often that you do this, the better.

There are a few options that we are able to use when it is time to back up our information on the database. There are some nice cloud-based options to work with. But working with some hardware is a good option as well because it ensures that you are not going to run into problems if something happens with that cloud-based service. If you would like to work with both of these, that can be a good option as well just to be extra safe.

Then, if the worst-case scenario does happen, you will be able to just go to the latest back up that you have, and hopefully it hasn't been too long since you last did it, and get the information back. It is hopeful that you have been using the right security measures so that this never has to happen. But just in case, having this organized is going to make a difference in how much of a headache the whole situation can be.

The Transaction Log

Next, we need to take a look at the transaction log. All of the SQL databases that you work with will come with a transaction log. This will hold onto all of the transactions and the modifications that happen to the database when each of the transactions between you and the customer happens. This is going to be a very important part of the database that you work with, and it is not something that you should skim over at all. If you find that at some point, you have a failure in the system, you would need to work with this log in order to bring this database back to where you need it.

One thing that we need to keep in mind is that we should not move or delete this log unless we fully know some of the ramifications that could happen when we do this. You can always use this kind of transaction log when you need to help recover your database to help make sure that all of the parts are going to head back where they belong.

There are a few different operations that we are able to support when we work with one of these transaction logs. Some of the most common options and the ones that you will be able to rely on quite a bit with your database will include:

1. Individual transaction recovery when you need that information back.
2. Recovery of all the transactions that are incomplete when the server is started up again. This could include some of those that were in the cart, and the customer was deciding on at that time.

3. Rolling in a restored page, filegroup, file, or database, so it goes forward to the point of failure in many cases.

4. Supports the replication of the transactions that we have.

5. Supports high quality and strategies for disaster recovery. This can include some options like log shipping, database mirroring, and Always On availability groups if you would need them.

There are also a few different characteristics that we are going to see in this kind of transaction log. This is going to be something that can be implemented either on its own as a separate file, or you can have it come in as a set of files in the database. The log cache is going to be managed in a separated manner from the bugger cache that we see with the data pages, which is going to provide us with some code that is robust, fast, and simple.

The format that is going to log the records and pages is not going to have some of the same constraints as other parts of the code. This means that the log records will not have to follow the same kind of format that we see with the data pages unless we would like them to.

Next, we will find that we are able to implement the transaction log on more than one file. The files can be defined in a manner to expand out automatically when we go through and set the value of FILEGROWTH for the log. This is going to reduce the potential that we have when it comes to running out of space in our log while reducing the overhead that we have to deal with. The mechanism that we have to work with to reuse the space inside of this log file is going to be quick, and it is not going to have a big effect on the throughput of that particular transaction either.

Database Restores

Now, we all hope that we are able to start up with a new database, and it is all going to work nice and easy the way that we would like. But sometimes, we may find that it is hard to go through and get the database to work, and we will have to take a few steps to help us to back up the database that we have. before we are able to restore our database, though, with the full, or even the bulk-logged recovery model, you may need to spend some time backing up the active transaction log.

When you want to restore a database from another instance, you would have to consider a few things, such as figuring out how to manage your metadata when it is time to make a database available on another instance of a server. If you would like to go through and restore some of the encrypted types of databases, you have to make sure that you access the certificate or an asymmetric key that was originally used to encrypt the database. Without this, it is impossible to restore the database in the manner that we need. You need to retain the certificate used to help encrypt the database for as long as you would need to when it is time to save the backup.

It is even possible to go through and restore one of the older versions of a database in this server. When you do this, though, you will find that it is going to upgrade your SQL Server to the newest version. In this case, it would be the 2019 version. This is going to preclude the database from being used with one of the older versions of the database engine. This is going to relate more to the metadata upgrade, and it is not going to affect you when it comes to the compatibility level of the database. This means that it will keep the same kind of compatibility level when the upgrade is done.

Often you will find that the database is going to be available for you to use right away. However, if a Server 2005 database has the full-text indexes, the upgrade process will either import, reset, ore rebuild the indexes based on the choices that you made. If you then go through and set the option of the upgrade to Rebuild or Import, then these indexes will take some time and not be available during the upgrade. Depending on how much of the data you are trying to index, this could take a few hours to import and even longer to rebuild, so keep that in mind. It will get done, but it will take a bit of time to get that far.

When you set an upgrade option on one of these servers to import, and you are not working with an available full-text catalog, then the associated full-text indexes are going to be the one that we rebuild. This process does, however, take some time to finish, but it is going to be important to ensure that our database is going to work the way that we would like.

Recovery Models, You Can Use

And finally, we need to take a look at some of the different recovery models that we are able to choose from. The option that you work with is going to depend on what makes the most sense for your needs and what you would like to see happen with some of the work that you are doing on your database.

With the first option, we are going to work with the simple recovery model. The first thing that we need to remember about this is that there will not be any log backups. This one is automatically going to reclaim some of the log space so that the requirements that you have for this are going to stay small. This helps to keep some of the need that we have for managing the transaction log space that we have as well.

Operations that are going to require that their transaction lock backups are not going to be something that the simple recovery model is going to be able to handle. And there are a few other features that we are going to miss out on when we work with this kind of backup option. Some of these are going to include:

1. Log shipping
2. The mirroring of the database or Always On.
3. Media recovery without some kind of loss in the data.
4. Point-in-time restores.

We also have to take a look at some of the exposure that we have to lose our work. In this simple method, the changes since the latest backup are not going to be unprotected. This means that if there is some kind of disaster that shows up, you will need to go through and redo these changes along the way. This one is only able to recover to the end of the backup and nothing else. If you are working with a really large dataset or some sensitive information in this one, then you should go with one of the other options that are available.

The second option that we are going to work with is going to be the full backup. This one is going to require that we have some kind of log backup with it. No work is going to be lost due to damaged data files or files that are lost. It is also able to recover to a point in time that is arbitrary, such as the past error of the user or the past application that you would like to use.

In the full backup, your potential to lose the information is going to be pretty small. If the tail of our log does happen to get damaged in this, the changes since the most recent log backup have to be done over again, but since this is not going to happen all that much, you will not need to worry about this at all. One thing to note here is that if you are working with two or more full-recovery model databases that have to be logically consistent, then you need to be able to implement some of the special procedures to help make sure that you are able o recover on these databases.

And the third option that we are able to work with when it comes to recovering your data is the bulk-logged option. This one is also going to require a backup for the logs. It is going to be a kind of adjunct to the full recovery model that is going to allow us to handle copy operations of a bulk amount of information. This one is also good because it is going to reduce some of the usages of the log space using a minimum logging amount for these operations.

When you are working with the bulk-logged backup, you will find that the potential loss is not going to be that much. If you notice that the log is corrupted or some of the large-scale operations have taken place since the latest of these backups, sometimes the changes since that time need to be redone as well. Otherwise, you will not need to worry about the work being lost. You are also able to recover to the end of the backup that you do. You will find that the idea of a point in time recovery will not be supported in this.

Taking care of the database that you are working on is going to be so important if you want to make sure that it is going to behave in the manner that you want. Backing up the information, whether you do it with some of the methods above or not, is going to ensure that you don't lose things when the worst-case scenario does happen along the way.

Day 4: Working with Simple Queries in SQL

Now it is time for us to take a look at some of the great things that we are able to do when it is time to handle queries and more in our database. When your database starts to get really large, it is likely that you will want to spend some time searching for the information that you want. Without the help of a few commands to help you to get all of this done, you are going to end up with a bit of a problem along the way, as well. We are going to spend some time here taking a look at some of the ways that you can search through your database and some of the other commands that we need to know in order to help us to get things done in SQL in the database.

What is a Query?

A query of the database is going to be able to help us to take out information out of the database that we have, and then will be able to go through and format it into a form that is easier for us to read through and understand. A query needs to be written out in the syntax that a database requires. Each database is going t be a bit different, but you will find that many of them are going to work with the SQL that we are talking about here.

These SQL queries, with the help of a Data Manipulation Language, is going to come in with four different blocks. The first two are not going to be optional, so we need to make sure that they are there. These are going to tell the compiler what we are hoping to bring out and where it is going to be found. And often, this is going to include the SELECT command to help us get it all done. At the most basic form, we will find that the SQL query is going to look like the following:

SELECT X from Y;

In this one, the SELECT keyword is going to help us identify what information we would like to display out of the database, and then the FROM keyword is going to help us to identify where the data is going to come from and how these data sources are going to associate with each other.

There are some optional points that we are able to see with this one, as well. We can work with the WHERE command if we would like to set up some criteria that limit the search a little bit. Then there is the ORDER BY and the GROUP BY statements that are going to help us to associate the values that we need and go through and display them in the sequence that is needed the most.

Bringing in the Functions

The next thing that we will need to spend some time on is the functions that show up in our database. These functions are important because they are going to help us perform various actions on the database that we are working with. For the most part, we are going to spend our time working with the four main types of database functions because these are the ones that will help us to get things done. In particular, we are going to look at the functions that are able to help us change, create, delete, or retrieve the data that we need along the way.

With this in mind, the four functions of the database that we want to spend our time on are going to include:

1. Create an object (CRTOBJ): This one is going to help us to define a routine that will add a record over to the file that we have. It is also going to help us to do some processing to check that the record is not already something that exists before we update that record in the database.

2. Change object (CHGOBJ): This one is going to help us to define a routine to update the record that is already in the file. It is going to include all of the necessary processing to check that the record already exists before we try to update the record of the database.

3. Delete object (DLTOBJ): This one is going to help us to define a routine that will delete a record out of a file of the database. It is going to be where we will process this through and check whether that is a record that is still on the file before we delete it along the way.

4. Retrieve object (RTVOBJ): This one is going to help us to define a routine to retrieve one or more objects or records

from the file in the database. The processing can be specified for each record that is read when we modify the action diagram that comes with the function as well.

This is just the start of what we are able to do with some of these functions. But we can already see where they are going to come into good use and be worth our time to learn a little bit more about as well. These functions are great for doing a lot of the different things that we need in our files so that they work well in some of the work that we are doing with our database.

Using Expressions

Another thing that we are able to explore when it comes to the database is the expression. An expression in SQL is going to be a string that is able to make up either all or part of a statement in SQL. For example, if we are using the FindFirst method on a Recordset object, we are going to find that this is an expression that will consist of the selection criteria that are found in the WHERE command.

These expressions can help us to get a lot of the work done when we are handling some of our data online. You will find that these can help us to evaluate some of the functions that we were talking about before and even perform some of the simple math as we would like. And all of the operations that use the SQL expressions in the Microsoft Access database engine are going to be defined with the help of the VBA expression service.

Some of the Common Commands in SQL

Now it is time for us to take a look at some of the most common commands that we are able to use when it is time to work with the SQL language. There are a lot of commands to work with, and it is often going to depend on what you would like to gather up or do with the database ahead of time. Remember that this is a type of coding language that has been designed in order to help us manage, in any manner that we would like, some of the data that has been stored in the relational databases.

This means that this kind of language is going to operate through some simple, declarative statements. This just shows us that the data is going to always be secure and accurate, and it will help the program to maintain some of the integrity of the database, no matter what size it is in the first place, or how big it will get in the future.

1. ALTER TABLE: This one is going to help us to add in some of the columns that we would like to have in the database.

2. AND: This one is going to help us to combine together two conditions to meet our needs. We have to make sure that the conditions, both of them, are true in order to get that row to be included in the results that are sent back to us.

3. AS: This one is going to be a keyword that helps sus to rename a column or a table with the help of an alias.

4. CREATE TABLE: This one is going to help us to create the new table that we want inside of a database. This helps us to specify the table name, as we wish to call it, and the

name of each of the columns that show up in the table as well.

5. DELETE: This one is going to be a statement that we would use in order to remove one or more rows out of the table that we are working with.

6. GROUP BY: This one is going to be a clause that we can use in SQL to help us out with some aggregate functions. It is often going to be used along with the SELECT statement so that we are able to arrange the data that is identical into groups to look for later on.

7. INSERT: This is a statement that is going to be used when we would like to add a new row to our table.

8. IS NULL / IS NOT NULL: These are going to be the operators that are used along with the WHERE clause to help us test out whether there are some empty values found in the database.

9. ORDER BY: This is going to be a clause that will indicate to the database that you would like to sort out the results set by a particular column. You can choose whether you would like to do this numerically or alphabetically.

10. SELECT: This one is going to be a statement that is used in order to fetch any of the information that you would like from the database. Every query that you would like to use, just like we talked about before, is going, to begin with, this command.

11. SUM: This is going to be an example of a function that you can use. This one, in particular, is going to take the name of a column as the argument and then will return the sum of all of the values that you find in that column.

12. UPDATE: This is a statement that is going to allow you to edit some of the rows that are found in the table.

13. WHERE: This is going to be another example of a clause that will indicate how you would like to filter out the result set to help us only include the rows where the condition that you set is going to be seen as true.

14. WITH: This is going to be a clause that will help us to store the result of a query, usually in a table that is temporary and comes with an alias. You are also able to define multiple temporary tables using a comma and with one instance of the WITH keyword if you would like. We will find that this clause is often going to be known as a common table expression and can help with subquery factoring as well.

The Operators and Predicates

We can also take a look at some of the different operators and predicates that we are able to add to some of the searches that we want to do when working with the SQL language. First, we are going to look at some of the operators that we are able to use. These should be familiar if you have worked with some other coding languages in the past, but we are still going to take a moment to look at them. Some of the standard relational operators that you are able to work within your coding will include:

1. Equals
2. Greater than or equal to
3. Less than or equal to
4. Less than
5. Greater than
6. Not equal to.

Notice that when you are working with a combined relation, for example, less than or equal to or greater than or equal to, we need to make sure that we always put the equal sign as the last sign in this kind of relation. This will ensure that the compiler knows what we are doing and will bring up the results that we are looking for here.

Then it is time for us to take a look at what is known as the predicates in this kind of language. These predicates are going to be a type of expression in SQL that is able to evaluate a search condition as either TRUE or FALSE and sometimes as UNKNOWN depending on the code that we are trying to write out.

The TRUE means that we see that the expression is correct based on our conditions, and then the FALSE is going to mean that the expression is not right. Then there is the possibility for UNONWN, which means that the expression is not going to be true or false in this situation. All of the values that are used in SQL as a predicate need to be compatible data types for us to compare them to one another. Some of the predicates that we are able to use in this kind of language will include:

1. All of the comparisons that we want, including greater than less than, and the other options that we did above with the operators.
2. NULL
3. IN / NOT IN
4. EXISTS / NOT EXISTS
5. LIKE BETWEEN

Day 5: The SQL Server

Today, we are going to spend some time taking a look at some of the steps that we are able to use when it is time to handle the SQL server and get it to work for our own needs. There are a number of things that we need to do to make this chapter as effective as possible, and we are going to jump right in and look at how we can make this happen below!

How to Install the Oracle Database

The first part of this process that we are going to take a look at is how we are able to install and work with the Oracle database. There are a number of options that we are able to work with. We need to first make sure that we are on the website for Oracle so that you can get the installer. After you have the installation files, which should be in the format of a zip file, then you will need to do an extraction to get them to be on the folder that you want on your computer.

From here, we need to double-click so that you can get the setup.exe file that you have to start up the installation process. Most of the following steps that we are going to work with will go through the process automatically. But we are going to divide them up into 9 steps so that you can better see how they work and what you are able to do with them.

1. The installer is going to start by asking you to provide the email address that you want. This allows you to get the latest in updates and security issues sent right to you.

Clicking on the next button though will allow you to skip this part.

2. The installer is then going to ask you whether or not you would like to create and configure a new database if you want to install the software for the database only, or go through and upgrade a database that you already have. Because you are installing the Oracle database for the first time, we are going to pick out option one and then click on Next.

3. The installer will also allow you to choose the system class. Because you are installing this on your computer, rather than on a server, you will choose to go with the desktop-class and click on the Next button.

4. This fourth step is going to allow you to specify which Windows user account you would like to install and then configure for the Oracle Home to give you more security. The best option here is to usually go with the option for "Use Windows Built-in Account."

5. In this step, you are going to choose a few things. The first one is to choose which folder you would like to install this new database. The second is to choose the global name that you want for the database. And then, finally, we need to choose the pluggable database name we want to go with.

6. Once we have those things down, the installer is going to go through and do its own prerequisite check.

7. Now the installer is going to show you a summary of the information that you have, including information on the

database and the global information. Mae sure to review the information to see if it is how you would like it. You can then click on the Install button if it all looks good.

8. The installer in this step is going to start installing this database. It may take a few minutes. The speeds will vary based on how fast your computer can go with this.

9. Once the installation has had some time to complete, the installer is going to show you that this is done. You can click on the button to close up the window at this point.

Installing the SQL Developer

The next thing that we are able to work with is installing and starting up your SQL developer. This is not going to require the installer, so that will make it a bit easier to work with. But to get started on this developer, you will need to work with some kind of unzip tool of your choice. We have to make sure that we are not installing this developer onto an existing ORACLE_HOME. You will not be able to uninstall it later on when we are doing with the Oracle Universal Installer.

If you are going with one of the pre-release versions of the SQL Developer, and if you would like to continue going with one of these versions after you are done installing the official release kit, you will need to go through and unzip the official release kit in a separate folder to the one you used for the pre-release version.

The Oracle Database may be installed on your computer, and if this is true, then you will be able to find a version of this program also included. You would then be able to access it through the menu system that is on Oracle, which can make things a bit easier to work with. This particular version of the SQL developer is going to be separate from the other one that we have been talking about so far, so you will need to consider which version you would rather work with.

For the Windows system, though, there are going to be two kits that you are able to work with. One is going to be for the systems that work with the Sun Java SDK that is version 1.5 0_06 or later .and then there is a kit that works for the later versions as well. You need to double-check which version is going to be the best for your needs.

Before you go through the steps to install this developer, we need to look at some of the versions that we want to work with and more. The steps that we need to work with when it is time to install this developer is going to be depending on whether you are using the Windows system with the Sun Java SDK 1.5 0_06 or later installed or not. For both of these, though, you will find that going through and getting the file and following the steps that are needed to unzip it will be the best way to ensure that you get things to work the way that you would like.

Creating a System Connection

At some point, you will connect to the database with the help of the SQL developer that we talked about above. The database connection is going to be one of the objects that will specify the necessary information that will help you to connect the database that you would like to someone who is able to use that database. You need to make sure that there are at least one of these connections, whether it is imported, created, or existing, in order to work with this developer.

To help us create a database connection, there are a few different steps that we will need to follow to see it happen. Some of the best steps to follow will include:

1. When we are in Connections navigator in SQL, we need to be able to right-click on the Connections node and then select the New Connection. This dialog box is going to appear on your computer screen, and you should see the tab for Oracle displaying here.

2. Then there is some information that we need to add to this part. First, in the Connection Name field, we need to enter the name that we would like to have for this connection. Then in the Username field, we need to be able to enter the name of the user for whom we are creating this connection to the database. Then the Password field and the Connection Type need to be filled in.
    a. There are a few different connection types that we are able to work with, including Basic, TNS, LDAP, Advanced, and Local/Bequeath.
    b. When you have chosen the connection type that you want to work with, the fields are going to change up so that they are ready for the right connection type.

3. We need to take a look at how these are going to change. If we are using the Basic type of connection, we are going to see a few changes including:
    a. In the Role field, we will be able to select out either SYSDBA or Default based on the role that has been assigned to the user.
    b. In the field for the Hostname, we will be able to enter the name of the host where we will find this database.
    c. Then we move on to the Port field. This is where we are going to enter the port of our database.
    d. Then we are in the SID field. This is where we are going to enter the SID for the database. This is when the database connection for a non-CDB user.
    e. In the Service name field, we can enter the product name for all the components of the plug-in list. This could include some things like the domain name when the database connection ends up being for the PDB user.

4. In addition, we have the option to go through and click on the Test. This helps us to test that all of the data that we already went through and provided will be able to allow the user you would like onto the database and can form the connection you are hoping for.

5. When you are done testing this, and it is all set up, you can click on Connect in order to connect with the help of that new database connection, or you can click on Save to help save the database creation that you would like.

Running a Statement

Now that we have all of the database set up and ready to get going, it is time for us to do some of the work that we need on this system. We are going to look at a few options, such as running a statement inserting rows and storing things on the database. But we need to start out with some of the steps of running a statement on this system.

To start with this one, we need to open up a new SQL Worksheet. Then we are able to click on the arrow that is to the right of the button to open up the worksheet so that you are able to see what connections are present there. Make sure you select the connection that you would like to use right from the beginning. This is going to open up a Worksheet under the right kind of connection. If the connection isn't in the current session that you are, then you will receive a prompt to get the password to set up this connection.

Once you have that Worksheet open, you are able to use some of the standard techniques that you are used to seeing with SQL in order to either enter or edit one of these statements. As you work on entering the statements, you will notice that this SQL Developer that we set up is automatically going to apply some colors to the various elements. For example, the keywords that you use are going to show up in blue. This is going to make all of the statements a bit easier to read and understand, and will help us to find some of the errors that show up in our coding.

Any time that you enter in a statement in SQL, you will notice that the Developer is going to automatically display a list that drops down to help us enter some of these statements. This is a feature that can help provide us with some of the help that we need when entering some of the SQL keywords, table names column names, and so on.

If you spend some time experimenting with this kind of feature that is going to help you to complete your code, you may find that the Developer is not going to display the names of the columns automatically until the name of the table used by the sentence is entered. Because of this, if you want to use the functionality of code completion, you'll want to go through the table name and then work on the column names.

For the most part, though, you will find that this Developer is automatically going to display the drop-down list after you start adding in some of the statements that you would like to work with. Sometimes though, it is true that you will need to go through and manually prompt the Developer to show this list off. To do this, you can press on the Ctrl Key and the spacebar, and it will work well for you.

In addition, it is possible to work with this Developer to help automatically take some of your statements and comment or uncomment them. To make this happen, you'd have to move the line insertion point. Then, at the same time, we push the Ctrl key and the front slash. But if you would like to execute just one of the SQL statements, you would want to press on the F9 button or click the Execute Statement button that is in the toolbar for this process.

If you do the steps above and you get a statement that provides you with some data in return, then the data is going to show up in the Results tab. This will help us to get some of the information that we want out of the process and can make life a bit easier when handling some of the things that we want with our coding overall.

There are many times when you will need to work with some of these statements with your database, and the SQL Developer is going to make this process as easy to work with as possible. These statements can help to add things into the database, take them out, and so much more. Learning how to use them, and working with some of the steps that we have in this guidebook, can make it easier than ever to really make sure that you get the statements in this language to work the way that you would like.

Inserting Rows

There are also going to be some situations when we are looking at one of our tables in the database, and we will want to work with inserting some rows into the table as well. To make this happen, we are able to work with the statements of INSERT and SELECT. There are two methods that we are able to use to make this work, including:

1. We would want to work with the statement for INSERT because it can help us to list out the values we want right from one of our subqueries.
2. We would then want to work with the statement for SELECT because it can help us work with the clause of INTO here to tell the compiler where we want the information to go.

We are able to start this one out with the help of the INSERT statement. This one is going to add in one or more new rows to our table. We would be able to just use the INSERT command along with information on where we would like all of this to be added to. The INSERT statement or command is going to help us insert the data values that can be at least one, and sometimes it is possible to use them as more of these rows that are in our specific table. Then we have the column list as the name of all the columns, with a comma going in between all of them, that can then be used to help us to list out the columns so that we know where the data supply is coming from. If this is something that we take the time to add in, then the columns that show up in the table that we are in will receive the data.

The INSERT statement is not going to be able to specify all of the values that are out there. In particular, they will not be able to help us out with the following options for the columns because the SQL Server Database Engine can create its own values on these columns:

1. The columns that have an IDENTITY property are going to generate the values automatically for the column.
2. Columns that are going to use the function of NEWID as their default will be able to bring up a value for GUID that is pretty unique here.
3. Then we are able to work with some columns that we are able to get through computation. These are going to be some of the columns that are more virtual and can be defined more as one of the expressions. We are able to get these expressions with a few calculations from at least one of the other columns in the table, although this is usually going to need more work than that to make it happen. A good code that can show us how to make this happen will include:

```
CREATE TABLE TestTable
 (ColA INT PRIMARY KEY,
  ColB INT NOT NULL,
  ColC AS (ColA + ColB) * 2);
```

We can take another look at how we are able to work with this as well. We are going to take a look at how we are able to place any lines in the already columned table that will be able to generate automatically the value that you need, or it will have a default value. The INSERT statement is going to help us to insert the rows that we need, the ones that have the values for some of the columns but will not do this for all of them. This is something new compared with some of the other people because, in the last one, no columns will be listed, and you will have to find the values that are the default and insert them. The coding that we are able to use for this one will include the following:

```
USE AdventureWorks2008R2;
GO
IF OBJECT_ID ('dbo.T1', 'U') IS NOT NULL
   DROP TABLE dbo.T1;
GO
CREATE TABLE dbo.T1
(
   column_1 AS 'Computed column ' + column_2,
   column_2 varchar(30)
      CONSTRAINT default_name DEFAULT ('my column default'),
   column_3 rowversion,
   column_4 varchar(40) NULL
);
GO
INSERT INTO dbo.T1 (column_4)
   VALUES ('Explicit value');
INSERT INTO dbo.T1 (column_2, column_4)
   VALUES ('Explicit value', 'Explicit value');
INSERT INTO dbo.T1 (column_2)
   VALUES ('Explicit value');
INSERT INTO T1 DEFAULT VALUES;
GO
SELECT column_1, column_2, column_3, column_4
FROM dbo.T1;
GO
```

How to Store Things in the Database

While we are here, we need to take some time to look at how we will be able to take our database and use it to store some of the information that we need. This can take some time to accomplish, and it will be important for us to make sure that the data we take time working on will be able to handle being in the database without being lost at all.

We have already taken a look at how we are able to create the database that we are working with; it is time for us to look at how we are able to create one of our own scripts on the server-side that will store the form data to your MySQL. We are going to take a look at how to do this on the cloud with the help of PHP, but you will find that we are able to work with to help us get it onto that MySQL. The code that we are able to use to make all of this happen will include:

```
<?php
// Connecting to the MySQL server
$host="mysql.yourdomain.com";
$user_name="username";
$pwd="kj67GbF54";
$database_name="visitors"; //assuming you created this
$db=mysql_connect($host, $user_name, $pwd);
if (mysql_error() > "") print mysql_error() . "<br>";
mysql_select_db($database_name, $db);
if (mysql_error() > "") print mysql_error() . "<br>";
// Storing form values into PHP variables
$fname = $_POST["fname"]; // Since method="post" in the
form
$lname = $_POST["lname"];
$gender = $_POST["gender"];
$age = $_POST["age"];
$city = $_POST["city"];
$submitdate = date("Ymd");
// Inserting these values into the MySQL table
```

```
// we created above
$query = "insert into form_data (first_name, last_name, gender, age, city, submit_date) values ('" . $fname . "', '" . $lname . "', '" . $gender . "', " . $age . ", '" . $city . "', '" . $submitdate . "')";
$result = mysql_query($query);
// mysql_query() is a PHP function for executing
// MySQL queries
echo "<h1>Thank you for submitting your details!</h1>";
?>
```

When we are trying to store some of our values in one of these kinds of tables, we need to make sure that we are doing a few things. We need to include the alphanumeric values, the data, and then the text values in the quotes. This is going to be done with three single quotes, and how we are going to see that in the code above. They are actually going to be a single quote that is followed by a double quote. The single quote is going to be important because it is going to be the final string in SQL that you can work with.

We are able to use this kind of code and more in order to see the results that you want. You will find that this helps us to take all of the data that we have and will make it easier to store inside of all the databases that you are working with, helping you to set it up for later.

How to Run SQL from a File

Another thing that we are going to take a look at is how to run Transact-SQL from the script files that we are working with. We are going to learn how to create this kind of file, how to run it, and how to save the output to the right text file that we want to work with.

First, we need to work with the command of sqlcmd to help us run this kind of file where we need it. This is going to be a text file that is able to hold onto a combination of the Transact-SQL statements, the commands that you need for the sqlcmd, and then some of the variables that are needed in the scripting variables as well.

So, to get this started, we need to go through and create our own script file to make this happen. We are able to do this with the help of the Notepad. The steps that we are able to use for it will include:

1. Click on the Start button on your computer. Point over to All Programs. In there, we are going to click on the Accessories and then click on the Notepad as well.
2. When the Notepad is open in Windows, we are going to want to copy and then past the code below:

```
USE AdventureWorks2012;
GO
SELECT p.FirstName + ' ' + p.LastName AS 'Employee Name',
a.AddressLine1, a.AddressLine2 , a.City, a.PostalCode
FROM Person.Person AS p
  INNER JOIN HumanResources.Employee AS e
      ON p.BusinessEntityID = e.BusinessEntityID
   INNER JOIN Person.BusinessEntityAddress bea
      ON bea.BusinessEntityID = e.BusinessEntityID
   INNER JOIN Person.Address AS a
      ON a.AddressID = bea.AddressID;
GO
```

When this code is added to Notepad, we will want to save it into our C drive as the myScript.sql so that we are able to find it later. At this time, we will be able to run the script file. To do this, open up the window for the command prompt. Then we can type out, in that command prompt, "sqlcmd -S myServer\instanceName -I C:\myScript.sql " Press Enter to continue.

When you are done with this one, you are going to end up with a list of the employee names of Adventure Works, along with their addresses. This should come up in the command prompt window if you went through and did the rest of the coding properly.

To finish this one off, we want to make sure that we are able to save the output that we have over to a text file. This will ensure that we are able to get through with this and see the option that we would like to work with later and bring it out without having to do all of the codings again. The steps that we need to do in order to save the output over to a text file, and this will include:

1. Open up the command prompt window that you have.
2. When you are in that window, and it is all set up, we will want to type in sqlcmd -S myServer\instanceName – C"\yscript.sql -o C:\EmpAdds.txt.
3. Press Enter when you are done.

With this one, you will find that the command prompt is not going to return any kind of output to you. Instead, the output is going to be sent over to the file that we listed above. You can double-check that this is what happened by going into the file for EmpAdds.txt and seeing if the output that we did above was actually saved for you or not.

Deleting the System Connection

And finally, we are going to take a look at how to delete the system and the views that we are able to work with. We are able to delete or drop some of the views that come with our SQL Server. Before you do this, though, we have a few limitations and restrictions that we are able to remember here. When you drop a view, the definition that you get with the view, along with the other information about the view will be deleted out of the catalog for the system. All of the permissions that you see with the view are going to be deleted as well. In addition, any of the view that is on the table that will be dropped with the DROP TABLE command need to be dropped with the explicit use of the DROP VIEW.

Now we are able to take a look at how we are able to delete these things out of the database as we go along. To delete a view from the database, we will need to take a look at some of the steps below:

1. We first need to get into the part known as Object Explorer. From here, we are able to expand out the database that contains the view that you are hoping to delete. From that part then, we need to expand out the folder for Views.
2. At this point, we can right-click on the view that we would like to delete before clicking on the button there for Delete.
3. In the dialog box that shows up for Delete Object, we can just click on OK in order to make it happen.

Another option that we are able to work with is the Transact-SQL. To make this one, we need to take a look at a few of the options that we are able to work with includes:

1. In the Object Explorer and then we are able to connect it to the instance that shows up for the Database Engine.

2. Then we can move to the Standard bar and click on a New Query.

3. Then we are able to copy and paste the code that we are able to work with the following code in order to help us to get things done. And then we will click on the Execute it. The example that we are going to do here is going to delete the specified view only if the view is already in existence. The code that we need here is going to include:

```
USE AdventureWorks2012 ;
GO
IF OBJECT_ID ('HumanResources.EmployeeHireDate', 'V') IS
NOT NULL
DROP VIEW HumanResources.EmployeeHireDate;
GO
```

When we go through and delete some of the parts that we need out of the database, we need to be careful. We are not able to go back through and add them back in if we would like. So we need to use caution and make sure that we are only deleting the things that we need during this time.

Day 6: Users and Roles

One of the things that we will need to focus on when we are handling some of our databases and what we are able to do with all of this is to look at who is allowed to gain access to the database, what each person on the database is allowed to do, and so on. If you have a large database that your customers are able to get onto, it is likely that you want to go through and set up some limitations, for example, so that they are not able to make major changes to what is on the database overall. This chapter is going to take some time to look at the users and the roles of your database, and how you are able to get these set up for some of your own needs as well.

Logins to the Server

The first thing that we will take a look at is how we are able to log into one of our servers with SQL. You are able to do this with the help of the command prompt on your computer, or by use of any of the graphical management tools that you have. When you do go through and log into an SQL server instance using the administration tools, though, you are going to be prompted to answer a few things like adding in the server name, the login for the SQL Server, and a password.

You can also go through and log into this with the help of Windows Authentication. With this option, you will not need to provide this information each time that you get onto the server because you are able to use the information from your Windows account to do this automatically. If your server is running in the authentication for mixed-mode, and you log in with the SQL Server Authentication, then you have to work with the password and log in as we talked about before. It is usually suggested that you work with Windows Authentication if possible.

Sometimes when you go through this process, you will need to spend some time verifying the connection protocol that you have. When you do connect over to the Database Engine, you will need to go through and work with some query in order to help check out the current connection and to ensure that you are going to get the authentication method. If you use this query well, you will be able to tell if the connection you are using is encrypted or not.

```
SELECT net_transport, auth_scheme, encrypt_option
FROM sys.dm_exec_connections
WHERE session_id = @@SPID;
```

And that is all that you need to do to make sure that you are able to log into your own SQL database. If you spend time looking over the Windows Authentication, the process is even easier because you can be logged in automatically if you are already using your Windows account, but the other options are going to be important to all of this as well and will work out if you choose to go with them as well.

Assigning Roles in the Database

We need to make sure that we take some time to assign roles in the database. There are some people who should just get the most basic access to the database, and then some who are going to be in control of running the database and making changes. And there are often a lot of different things that show up in between when it comes to the roles and the access points of the people who can be on that database.

You are able to spend some time grouping privileges in the database roles with the help of Oracle. Instead of an object owner going through and individually granting privileges to one or more of the users, especially when they have a similar description of the job that they do, the object owner is able to create a role and then grant that over when needed.

For example, maybe you are an administrator for a database for a big retailer. Each day, some new store clerks are going to be hired. The application of your database at the time is going to allow them the option of doing a dozen different requirements, and these can include:

1. INSERT into the table for sales.
2. UPDATE the table for inventory when it is needed.
3. DELETE from the table of orders as well.

There are going to be a few roles that are already created and set up when it is in the database, which is going to make it easier to manage some of the tasks that are out there. You can choose to add in some more if you would like along the way, but these are the basics that will make it easier if you are just looking for something to get started with along the way. Some of the roles that Oracle is going to supply to you when the database is first installed will include:

1. Connect: This is going to include all of the privileges that are needed to ensure that someone is able to connect with that database.
2. Resource: This one is going to include a lot of the roles that a developer is able to use to help create and manage an application, such as altering and creating many types of objects, including tables, sequences, and views.

3. Recovery_catalog_owner: This is going to allow the grantee to come through and administer the Oracle Recovery Manager catalog.

4. Scheduler_Admin: This one is going to allow the grantee the option to manage the Oracle job scheduler.

5. DBA: This one is going to help provide a user with many of the major privileges that are required to help administer the database. These can manage the users, the security, the space, the parameters of the system, and even some of the backups that should happen as well.

As the administrator of your own database, you need to consider what kinds of access you would like to assign to the different people who are going to get onto your system. The decisions that you make will often depend on the information that is going to be found on the database, and even some of the different people who you think will be there as well. This will make it easier to have more control over the database and who is able to access it, make changes, and more.

Commands to Help with Users and Roles

With some of this in mind, we are going to spend a moment to look at a few more of the commands that we have not had the time to look over yet in this guidebook. These commands are going to help you with some of the different user roles and more that you have, and some of the other administrative tasks that you would want to focus your attention on here as well. Some of the other options that we need to spend our time here will include:

1. LIKE: This is going to be the special operator that we are able to use along with the WHERE clause. It is a good one to help us find the specific patterns that are going to show up in our column.

2. AVG: This is the command that we are going to use when we want to make sure that we are able to get the average function for any of our columns that are numeric at the time.

3. ROUND: This is going to be a type of function that is able to take the name of the column as an integer as the arguments. It is going to round the values in the column to the number of decimal places that is specified by the integer.

4. SUM: Then, we can move on to the SUM function. This one is going to be able to take its argument from the name of the column and then will allow us to return the sum of all of the values that we are able to find in that column.

5. MAX: This one is going to be the function that is able to take the name of a column and use that as its argument. It is then able to return the largest value to this column, as well.

6. MIN: This is the final function that we are going to take a look at, and it is going to help us take the name of a column as the main argument that we want to work with and then will return the smallest value that is in that column at the time.

Day 7: Tables and Data Modification

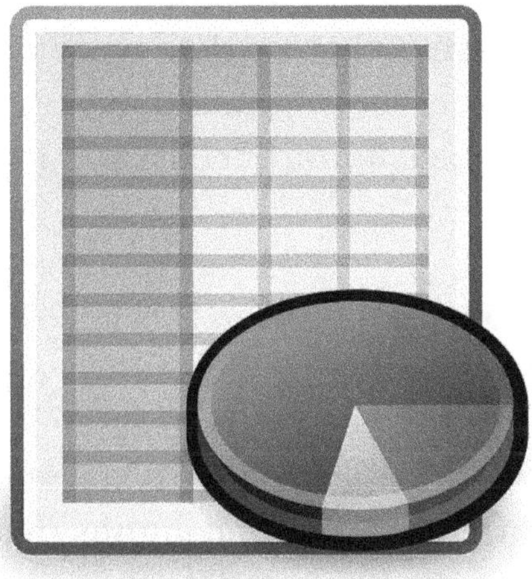

One of the things that you will spend a lot of time working on when it comes to your database and the SQL language is working with a lot of tables, and making some modifications to the information that is found in those tables as well. This is why we are going to devote our last day of this course to looking more into these tables and how we are able to use them, add data to them, and make some modifications to ensure that it will work the way that we want throughout the database.

What is a Table in SQL?

The first place to start here is a look at what the SQL tables are going to be all about. The data that we need in our database is going to be stored inside of one of these tables and then added to our database. A single database can be large, and could potentially hold onto hundreds of these tables. Each table is going to have its own unique role when it comes to the schema of the database.

While the schema and the architecture of the database are going to be concepts that are higher up than what we are going to explore in this chapter, you will find that they are going to help us to create the right tables for our needs, and get some good results in the process.

When you create your own table in this language, you will find that they are going to be comprised of rows and columns. The columns in the table are going to be responsible for storing a variety of data types, like files, dates, texts, and numbers. There are even a lot of different types of columns that we are able to add to the table, and the types of data that we are going to use will often vary depending on how the developer created the SQL table.

Then we are able to work with a table row as well. This one is going to be a horizontal record of values that are all going to fit into each of the columns of the table. When both of these are able to come together, you will find that it can provide you with the information that you need to ensure that you will see the best results as well.

Before we move on, though, we need to take a look at how we are able to create one of these tables through the use of a query. The coding that we will need for this one is below:

```
USE mydatabase;

CREATE TABLE orders
```

```
(id INT IDENTITY(1,1) PRIMARY KEY,
customer VARCHAR(50),
day_of_order DATETIME,
product VARCHAR(50),
quantity INT);
```

The first line that we see here is going to show us where we are going to get the scope of our query ad will direct the SQL to run the command against that object that we can create. Then the blank line that we are able to see here is going to be something that is not required, but we add it in to help with some of the readability that is there.

Then we can move on to the line that starts with CREATE. This is a clause that has to be there because it is going to tell SQL that we would like it to create a new table at this point. And with the code above, we are going to name that table orders. You are able to name it anything that you would like.

Each of the columns in the table is going to come with their own guidelines, and the code above that we put inside of the parenthesis is going to tell SQL how to go about setting up these guidelines. The columns of the table are often going to be shown in a list format, and then we are able to separate these with a comma as well. For now, the most important thing that we need to focus on is making sure that we know that with the code above, we are creating a new, empty table in SQL that is going to go by the name of orders, and it has five columns total.

And that is as simple as it can be! We are able to go in and add in a lot of other features to the mix if we would like. But we can also keep it this simple to ensure that we get some of the results that we would like as well. You can make the table bigger or smaller, add in more parts or take them away. And in the next few sections, we will take a look at some more things that we can do with the table as well. But being able to create a simple table is going to be a great way to get started as well.

How to Insert a Data

Next, we need to take a look is to insert some data into that table that we just went through and created. We are going to work with the INSERT command to help us to draw up a query that is going to insert some of the data that we need into that orders table that we did before. The coding that we need to make this happen is going to be below:

USE mydatabase;

INSERT INTO orders
(customer, day_of_order, product quantity)
VALUES('Tizag', '8/1/08', Pen', 4

If we go through and use this in the proper manner, you will find that all of the information that we have above about that customer will show up in the first row of the table that we created above. We can go through this and add in all of the information that we need for all five columns, or more if we are working with another table, in order to make sure that this is going to fill up the database in the manner that we would like.

Doing a Bulk Insert

The next thing that we need to take a look at is how we are able to do a bulk insert of our information. We have spent some time so far looking at how we are able to add in information to just a few of the columns of our table. But if we need to add in a lot of information to the table, that process can be really hard and take too long. That is why we need to work with the process of creating our own bulk insert as well.

This is a simple process to work with, but you will be able to go through and add in as many columns and such as you would like to this kind of table to make it work the way that you would like.

While we are here, we can take a look at some of the arguments that will show up in this kind of coding. The first one is going to be the database name, which is going to be the name that we will have for the specified table or view and where the view is going to reside. If you do not specify this, it is going to be the current database.

Then we can work with the schema name, which is going to be the name of the table or the view schema. This one is going to be optional if the schema for the user performing the bulk-import operation is the schema of the specified table or view. If the schema is not specified and the default schema of the user performing the bulk operation is different from the view or the table that you are specifying, then the server is going to return an error message, and this will all be canceled for you.

Then there is the table name. This one is going to be the name of the table or view to import all of the data into. Only views in which all the columns use the same base table can be used on this one. We can then move on to the data file. This is going to be the full path of the file of data that is going to contain data to import into the view or the table that you would like. A BULK INSERT is able to import the data from either Azure Blob storage or a disk, which can include a floppy disk, network, and even a hard dis.

The data file that you are working with needs to have a valid path specified on the server which this is going to run. If this ends up being a remote file that you are using, then you will need to spend some time specifying the Universal Naming Convention to get it to work.

Deleting Data

There will be some times when you are doing the work in your database, and you decide that you need to delete a specific part, or sometimes even the whole database that is there. In order to make this happen, you would need to work with the SQL DELETE statement. This is going to be the option that we can use in order to delete the existing records that are on a table that you have. The syntax that we are able to work with to make this happen will include;

DELETE FROM table name WHERE condition;

We can add more to this if we would like, but this is a basic option to get us started and will ensure that we are going to be able to get the results that we would like overall. One thing to remember with this one, though, is that we need to use caution when deleting the records on the table. We have to notice the WHERE clause in this statement. This is going to be the part that will specify which records we would like to have deleted in the table. If you do not add in this clause, then you will delete the whole table. If that is what you would like to do in the first place, then that is fine, but if you just want to delete a few records, make sure that WHERE clause is put inside.

What is the process of Truncate?

Another option that we are able to work with is the TRUNCATE command. This one is a bit different than some of the others but can still provide us with some neat work that we are able to do in our database. To start with, this process is going to help us remove all of the rows from a table, or even from special parts of the table, without having to log the individual row deletions as we go through.

TRUNCATE TABLE, like we are going to discuss in this section, is going to be similar to the statement of DELETE, without the WHERE clause like we did above, but it is faster and will not use up as many systems and transaction log resources. If you know that you need to delete the whole table or a lot of the information that is inside of it, then this is most likely the right one for you to choose to use here.

We can take a look at the syntax that is necessary to get this one started below:

```
-- Syntax for SQL Server and Azure SQL Database

TRUNCATE TABLE
   { database_name.schema_name.table_name |
schema_name.table_name | table_name }
   [ WITH ( PARTITIONS ( { <partition_number_expression> |
<range> }
   [ , ...n ] ) ) ]
[ ; ]

<range> ::=
<partition_number_expression> TO
<partition_number_expression>
```

There are going to be a few arguments that you are able to work with on this one. First, the database_name is going to be the name that you choose to give the database. Then we have the schema_name, which is going to be the name of the schema that you have the table in to start with. Then there is table_name, that is going to be the name of the table that you would like to truncate, or to remove all the rows from. We have to make sure that the table name is literal here for it to work. You cannot use an OBJECT_ID() function or any kind of variable to do this.

We are going to work with the part that is known as the <partition_number_expression) as well. There are multiple ways that we are able to specify this one, and some of them will include the following:

1. We are able to go through and provide it with the number of partitions that we would like to work with. We can write it out something like the following WITH (PARTITIONS (2))
2. We can go through and provide it with the partition numbers for several of the individual partitions that we want to handle, and then separate it out with some commas. So this one would like something like this WITH (PARTITIONS (1, 5))
3. We can even go through and provide both the ranges and the individual's partitions. A good example of how this one would work would be something like the following WITH (PARTITIONS (2, 4, 6 TO 8))

There are a few times when we will want to work with the TRUNCATE TABLE option rather than the DELETE statement that we talked about above. First, we will find that the latter is going to use up less log space, which can be ideal for a lot of businesses. The DELETE statement is going to take its tie, removing one row at a time and then will record this entry into the transaction log when it is done. The TRUNCATE TABLE is going to remove the data when it deallocates the pages of the data used in order to store the table records and data, and only the page of that is going to show up in the transaction log, saving a lot of tie and hassle.

There are also going to be fewer locks that are going to be used. When we execute out the DELETE statement, we will use a row lock. This means that each row contained in the table will need to be locked so that we are able to delete it properly. When working with the TRUNCATE TABLE, it is always going to lock the table and the page, but it will not go through and lock up each individual row in the process.

Without any exceptions, there will not be any pages that are left in the table. After we have been able to work with the statement for DELETE, our table is going to end up with a few pages that are empty. In this case, the empty pages that we do end up with are going to be shown in a heap, and we have to add in at least an exclusive table lock to help deallocate them, or it will not work. You will find that the operation for the delete function is not going to work here, and the table is going to hold onto a lot of empty pages along the way. For the indexes, the delete operation can leave some of these empty pages behind, even though these are going to be deallocated quickly with some of the cleanup processes that are happening in the background.

When you work with the TRUNCATE TABLE, though you will find that it is able to remove all of the rows from the table, the structure of our table and its columns, constraints, indexes, and so on are going to remain in place. To make sure that we are able to remove the data definition along with some of its data, we are able to work with the DROP TABLE statement as well.

How to Merge Your Data

It is also possible for us to go through and merge some of the data that we have in our tables. This can help if we are working with cases of duplicate data in the table, or if we would like to be able to combine two tables into one to either update it or to make a brand new one.

Before you do some of the mergings, though, we need to make sure that we are really paying attention to some of the work that we are doing here. If we do not merge the tables properly, then we may end up ruining the data and losing some of the information that we really need in these situations, as well. We want to make sure that we are combining the right parts of the table together to make the new one and that we are not losing information in the process.

How to Combine and Join Tables

There are some situations when you are working with your data when you will want to merge it into one or merge at least a few columns into one. We are going to look at how we are able to run inserts, updates, and remove operations from the effects of the join with the origin table on the target column. For example, we can use this to help us to synchronize two tables when we delete, update, or insert rows into one table based on some of the differences that may show up in the other table along the way.

The conditional behavior that shows up when we use the MERGE statement is going to work best when we have two tables that are going to come up with a mixture of characteristics that do match with each other. To help us with this, if we try to insert in a new row when it doesn't exist in in the first place, or we would like to update a row when it isn't going to match up in our code, it is going to show up the way we want. But when we just want to update one of the tables in the database and have it use the information that is found in the rows of an additional table, you would be able to prove the performance and the scalability of this with some of the basic commands in this process including INSERT, DELETE< and UPDATE statements.

The code that we are able to use for this is pretty long, but it is going to help us to handle a lot of what we need to do when it comes to the coding we would like to accomplish. It is going to help us to set up the temporary name that we need with all of this, using the WITH <common_table_expression> part. This is going to also make sure that we are staying within the scope of our specific MERGE statement that we spent our time with.

Another thing that we need to take a look at with this one is the TOP expression. This one is going to specify the percentage or number of rows that are going to be affected by this. It can either show up as a percentage or a number depending on the tables that you are trying to combine. This clause is something that is going to apply after the whole source table, and the target table that you are using is able to join, and then we know that the rows are not going to have any kind of insert, update, or delete action on them.

This kind of clause is also going to reduce how many joined rows go to a certain value. The insert, delete and update actions or commands are going to be distributed among the actions that we are able to define when we bring in the WHEN clauses. For example, if we specify something like TOP (10), it is going to affect ten rows. Of these, 7 may be the ones that we update, 3 are inserted, and 1 deleted and soon.

Because the statement for MERGE is going to work on a full table scan the two tables we're going to work with, sometimes we will see the I/O performance affected when we use this clause to change a large table by creating multiple batches. When this happens, make sure that all of the successive batches that we use target the new rows.

Doing an Outer Join

While we are in this chapter, we need to spend some time taking a look at what an outer joint is all about. This is going to be a specific construction of a query that is going to be set up to make for more arrays than usual. The process of building up the specific queries that we need in SQL to get to a database is going to be really technical, and the outer join is going to help us to work with some of the details that we need for all of this to come together.

A programmer who is trying to write out a query is able to work with either a right or a left outer join in order to include table results that only come with a given kind of component, rather than having to see more components present. A left outer join is going to help us include all of the rows that we need in the table, regardless of whether that position column has some results in it or not. Then the inner join is going to require that both of the components have to be present to work.

Because these joins are going to provide for some ore diversity, they are going to be found in a lot of the searches that are less rigid and will not require some strict adherence to the concept of having consistent data from multiple components of the search that we are doing.

Conclusion

Thank you for making it through to the end of *SQL Programming*. Let's hope it was able to provide you with all the tools you need to achieve your go als.

The next step is to get to work with creating some of your own databases and being able to use the SQL language to help you get all of the work done in no time. This is a great language to work with, and as we were able to go through a few of the codes that you are able to use in this database, you can quickly see why it is such a great one to work with. SQL gets right to the point and ensures that we are able to work with our database in any manner that we would like.

There are many businesses that will want to create, modify, and work with one of these databases for some of their own needs. It allows them to keep track of their customers, to make sure that their orders are placed in the right, to show off some of the products that they want to sell, and more. There are a lot of reasons to work with a database, but it will not take long to figure out that they can grow large, and you need some method to help keep the management of that database in line along the way.

This guidebook is meant to help you to get all of that done and more. We took a look at many of the commands, codes, and other parts that you need to really make sure that your database is going to behave the way that you want. Even if you haven't been able to do much work with the databases in the past, you will find that with the tips and tricks and codes that we handle in this guidebook, you will be able to really get some of the work done that you would like on that database, and your management skills of that information will go through the roof.

We split this information up into seven days so that you can learn the information and get it down in no time. Don't let the fear of a large database scare you. Tackle it right on with the help of the SQL language, and all that this is able to offer to you along the way. Taking this process day by day will make it easier to understand what is going on with all of the parts of the database and can set you up for some of the success that you are looking for.

Many companies are going to rely on a database to help them see some of the results that they would like in no time. It helps them to keep their business organized and can ensure that all of the information that they need is going to be able to stay in order and be secure. When you're ready to learn how to work with SQL on your database to make database management easier than ever before, check out this guide to get you started.